T0157808

OVERCOMING
DEPRESSION
WITHOUT DRUGS

OVERCOMING
DEPRESSION
WITHOUT DRUGS

MAHLER'S POLKA
with Introductory Funeral March

Dr. John A. Snyder
with Dr. Nancy Steffen-Fluhr

authorHOUSE®

AuthorHouse™
1663 Liberty Drive
Bloomington, IN 47403
www.authorhouse.com
Phone: 1-800-839-8640

© 2012 by John A. Snyder, Ed.D. All rights reserved.
Authored by John A. Snyder Ed.D.
Contributions by Nancy Steffen-Fluhr Ph.D.

No part of this book may be reproduced, stored in a retrieval system, or transmitted by any means
without the written permission of the author.

First published by AuthorHouse   02/11/2012

ISBN: 978-1-4685-4962-1 (sc)
ISBN: 978-1-4685-4961-4 (hc)
ISBN: 978-1-4685-4960-7 (ebk)

Library of Congress Control Number: 2012902101

Printed in the United States of America

Any people depicted in stock imagery provided by Thinkstock are models, and such images are being
used for illustrative purposes only.
Certain stock imagery © Thinkstock.

This book is printed on acid-free paper.

Because of the dynamic nature of the Internet, any web addresses or links contained in this book may
have changed since publication and may no longer be valid. The views expressed in this work are
solely those of the author and do not necessarily reflect the views of the publisher, and the publisher
hereby disclaims any responsibility for them.

For Carolyn

With special thanks to Kathleen Mills Woodring for her technical assistance.

WARNING

As Dr. Peter Breggin and others in the medical profession have been careful to research and document, many psychiatric drugs can be dangerous to take, and they also can be dangerous to stop taking. They can produce withdrawal symptoms that are emotionally and physically distressing and sometimes can be life threatening. Tapering off psychiatric drugs should usually be done gradually and should always be done with an experienced psychiatrist. This book is in no way intended as a substitute for individualized medical care in the use of antidepressant medications.

ACKNOWLEDGEMENTS

FIRST OF ALL, I want to acknowledge Dr. Nancy Steffen-Fluhr as having been far more than my editor. She has been a true collaborator in the process of shaping and developing these insights from my professional experience and, indeed, she has made this a work that represents her own admirable writing style. I presented Nancy with the daunting task of combining two quite distinctive parts of this book. The first part describes how any true understanding of depression has been obliterated by a concerted campaign to define normal expressions of human distress as pathological symptoms caused by bad brain chemistry. The second part involves a shift in tone that is both didactic and experiential. The reader is invited to stop, listen to feelings, and become involved in the life of a powerful but often-misunderstood man: composer Gustav Mahler. Mahler experienced great tragedy without every becoming seriously depressed because he remained in touch with even the darkest of his feelings, a capacity that serves as a model for us all. Nancy made this complex dance of ideas flow beautifully and at the same time patiently supported my desire that this would be an unpretentious book that would be enjoyable to read.

Of the hundreds of works cited as background for this study, there are several authors who have been especially influential in prompting me to write.

Christopher Lane, in *Shyness: How Normal Behavior Became a Sickness*, makes clear what many of us had been experiencing in our involvement with patients. He provides details of the back-room takeover by a few psychiatrists that redefined emotional issues as medical problems, specifically, problems in the brain to be treated by drugs. Those of us who, in our intense involvement with troubled people, were discovering more and more effective ways to be helpful, sensed something was beginning to undermine our entire therapeutic approach, but we did not take the threat seriously enough.

For the past twenty years, I have read Peter Breggin's countless publications, books that raise powerful concerns about psychiatric drugs. Breggin's work has been a strong source of support for my own observations that antidepressants are being overprescribed and are having dreadful consequences for people. I have witnessed the attacks by the pharmaceutical industry on Breggin, an exceptionally dedicated man, and my dismay has moved me to reaffirm the commitment that he and I share not to abandon emotionally troubled people to pharmacology.

Writing about the importance of feelings and emotions from the perspective of a neuroscientist, Antonio Damasio has given powerful support to my own beliefs as a psychotherapist. Damasio is one of the few sane voices in a wilderness of craziness, implicitly disputing the wildly-accepted premise of the psychopharmacology establishment that some emotions are "bad" and can be chemically erased without consequence. In *Looking for Spinoza: Joy, Sorrow, and the Feeling Brain*,

Damasio uses his life-long interest in Spinoza in a way that is similar to my use of Gustav Mahler in this book: to challenge assumptions. In Damasio's case, the goal is to show the fallacy of Descartes' dualism of mind and body; in my case, it is to show the fallacy of feeling avoidance.

Henry-Louis de LaGrange has spent over fifty years collecting every last bit of information about Gustav Mahler and publishing these findings in a massive four-volume biography. I had the first volume in my hands in the late 1970's. I secured the fourth volume as soon as it was published in English in 2008. With de LaGrange's help, I feel as if I have lived next door to Mahler for years! In this book (subtitled "Mahler's Polka") I share some of what I have learned with you.

Finally, and especially, I acknowledge the thousands of men and women who, over the past forty years, have trusted me with their feelings. Often with excruciating anxiety, crying uncontrollably, they have allowed themselves to feel feelings they had blocked for years, feelings so easily devalued in our efforts to stay in control. They have taught me that spending so much of their precious life energy to keep feelings at bay was the very cause of their depression. They allowed me to be a privileged observer of this process, affirming that going into the dark places, as scary and painful as it may be, can result in marvelous emotional freedom and relief from immobilizing depression. If you gain insight from this book that enables you to live without depression, these men and women are the ones who deserve the credit.

TABLE OF CONTENTS

LIST OF MUSIC

Selection One: Gustav Mahler, Symphony One, Third Movement. NBC Symphony Orchestra, Bruno Walter Conducting, 1939. (11:33)

Selection Two: Gustav Mahler, Symphony Two, First Movement. Royal Concertgebouw Orchestra, Otto Klemperer Conducting, 1951. (17:41)

Selection Three: Gustav Mahler, Symphony Two, Third Movement. Vienna Philharmonic Orchestra, Bruno Walter, Conducting, 1948. (10:36)

Selection Four: Gustav Mahler, Symphony Two, Fourth Movement. Royal Concertgebouw Orchestra, Otto Klemperer Conducting, 1951. (4:02)

Selection Five: Gustav Mahler, Symphony Four, First Movement. New York Philharmonic Orchestra, Bruno Walter Conducting 1945. (16:45)

Selection Six: Gustav Mahler, Symphony Ten (unfinished), First Movement. Wiener Staatsoper Orchestra, Bruno Walter Conducting, 1952. (28:45)

Selection Seven: Gustav Mahler, Kindertotenlieder, Lieder Five. Berlin Philharmonic Orchestra, Rudolf Kempe Conducting, Dietrich Fischer-Dieskau, Baritone, 1955. (6:45)

Selection Eight: Gustav Mahler, Symphony Five, Fourth Movement. New York Philharmonic Orchestra, Bruno Walter Conducting, 1947. (7:35)

Listen to the selections as you encounter each music passage as you read. Download the mp3 files at: http://www.overcomingdepressionwithoutdrugs.com/music

LIST OF ILLUSTRATIONS

FORWARD

BY WILLIAM IMBRIE PACKARD, M.D.

OVERCOMING DEPRESSION WITHOUT DRUGS could save your life and the lives of your patients! Dr. Snyder offers a radical departure from the current trend in how depression is understood and treated. He offers alternatives for understanding human emotion and for treating people in psychic distress. He forcefully challenges what is currently being taught in medical schools and conveyed to the public about feeling states. His insights are invaluable for any person interested in the most human of experiences—how we understand, process and ultimately integrate feeling into our daily lives. I especially recommend this book to any professional who works with people suffering from depression. By the time you finish reading Snyder's heartfelt and passionate arguments, you will feel empowered to guide your patients to feel the feelings they often are working so hard to escape.

In *Overcoming Depression,"* Dr. Snyder begins by challenging the prevailing biopsychiatric views of depression put forth by the psychiatric community. He is especially troubled by what he calls "the pathologizing of normal human variance" through the ever-expanding definition of what constitutes clinical depression. Snyder elegantly documents a fifty-year trend during which psychiatric "leaders" and "scholars" have reduced complex human processes to simple disease states. Most disturbing is the section of this book that documents the equivalent of a medical/industrial complex. In collaboration with the academic psychiatric community, the pharmaceutical industry has made hundreds of billions of dollars from antidepressants. The net of what their medical collaborators define as "clinical depression" has been enlarged to include normal states of feeling.

As Dr. Snyder demonstrates, psychotropic medications are being over prescribed. At the same time, institutions are training new generations of nurses, doctors, and psychologists in a disease model in which sadness, grief, anxiety, and other normal feeling states are treated as pathological and similar to severe depressions. All of us should be concerned about this trend, not just health professionals. We need to be much better informed about what only a few have been brave enough to say. This is the only way that we can make informed decisions.

Snyder has integrated beautifully the history of antidepressants, their dangers and misuses. He chronicles convincingly the way the public is being sold the idea that all feelings of sadness or anxiety are bad and should be medicated. He is appropriately alarmed by this development. People are being taught that it is better not to feel. Our humanness is being taken away from us; we are being taught that feeling too much is dangerous to our well-being. Snyder is equally forceful in reminding us of a little known truth about antidepressants. SSI's and SNRI's, the most prescribed of the antidepressants, suppress sexual desire, cause impotence, and flatten normal range of feeling permanently. I have had many patients say to me, "I don't feel depressed anymore, but I don't feel much of anything. I miss the normal intensity of feeling I used to have."

The most fascinating and profound part of this book is John Snyder's ideas on what makes us human and what we need to do to be fully sentient beings. He passionately believes that to experience our feelings is the essence of being human and at the heart of existence. He embraces the Buddhist view that "life is full of uncontrollable ups and downs (of feeling and experience) joined together in a continuous flow." He encourages us to acknowledge when we feel helpless and to allow ourselves to feel vulnerable.

Using the music and life of Gustav Mahler, Snyder is able to illustrate in an intimate and magical way how one man dealt with adversity and enormous psychic pain without resorting to repression. Mahler knew that he must take the time to experience the full intensity of his feelings and have the faith that he would survive. (If Mahler had been given Prozac or Lithium would we be listening to the gorgeous sadness of his *Kindertotenlieder*? I doubt it.) In addition to making this crucial point, the multimedia structure of *Overcoming Depression* offers the unique treat of allowing us to actually listen to Mahler's music as we read about the life events that challenged his personal beliefs to his core. John Snyder uses Mahler and his music to integrate the many facets of this rich book into one complete whole.

After reading *Overcoming Depression,* I feel rejuvenated in my approach to my own life and to the care of my patients. In my role as psychiatrist and psychotherapist, I am no longer afraid to ask the question, "What are you trying *not* to feel?" Some years ago I treated a fellow psychiatrist for depression. He was a deeply wounded man struggling to feel whole and good. He was my first patient to emphatically reject SSRI's. He said that he felt "tortured by not being able to feel normal intensity of emotions" caused by the medication. He recognized the danger that antidepressants posed to his psyche and, like Mahler, chose to live through the feelings of grief and helplessness that he had experienced as a child. The experience saved his psychic life. Reading this book may save yours.

Dr. William Packard is a psychiatrist in private practice, specializing in the treatment of young adults. Earlier in his career, he was Director of Psychiatry in two hospitals, where he taught family practice residents and medical students.

FORWARD

BY JUDITH D. FISHER, M.D.

I HAVE KNOWN JOHN SNYDER over half my life. Late October 1982, my father had died. I hated my job, and my love relationship needed CPR. Once I realized I was succumbing to overwhelming anxiety, fear, and grief, I made an appointment with John. You see, I am a psychiatrist, and I naively thought my professional training would inherently make me immune to all these feelings or, at the very least insure my ability to handle any "neurotic stuff" that came along. No one could convince me otherwise, at least not until late October 1982.

I sometimes wonder if John remembers how I ruined the beautiful gray suit he was wearing that day I came to his office. I spent the entire session crying, sobbing, and speaking the unintelligible language of pain onto his shoulder. My tears and makeup stained his shirt, his lapels and his tie. Even though no words passed between us, I got exactly what I needed. I've always felt John knew what to prescribe from the start, for he has perfected the art of listening for the noise inside others by remaining perfectly still inside himself.

Over time, John has become more than a therapist to me. He is my friend. We have had lots of conversations about the way psychiatry has changed. We have confessed our frustrations about, and our resistance to, the practice of "cosmetic psychiatry," that is to say, "better living through chemistry." As a community psychiatrist, I serve populations that society throws away: the homeless, the drug dependent, and others who are, ala Frantz Fanon, "the wretched of the earth". Since 1992, these folk have been diagnosed with depression, bipolar disorder, ADHD and PTSD in alarming numbers at even more alarming rates. They have been prescribed every antidepressant, anxiolytic, mood stabilizer, and antipsychotic medication on the market. Even worse, they have embraced these psychoactive drugs and *become* their diagnoses while remaining just as fearful of experiencing their emotions as they were before. In spite of the medications and the DSM-IV labels, their lives remain functionally unchanged, if not worse.

In response to this appalling situation, John began this book, a labor of love in every sense of the word. His profound, healing insights, formerly available only to the fortunate few who know him personally, are now available to everyone. The book's lively and straightforward style makes even subtle concepts easy to grasp. Using composer Gustav Mahler as an illustrative case study might seem a reach in a text designed for the general public, but it's not. Like Leonard Bernstein in his "Young People's Concerts," John makes Mahler come alive. We see him, and, through him, ourselves, in a startling new ways. This is not a simplistic "How To Do" book. There is no "pop psychology techno fix." Instead, John traces the emotional threads that are woven through Mahler's life-in-music, creating a tapestry that helps us better understand our own "life symphony" and how to orchestrate it.

When new patients enter the Addiction Treatment Center where I work, I try to simplify the process of treatment for them by asking one crucial question:" What have you been trying not to feel in all these years of drug addiction?" Some look at me askance as if I were from blue space. Others connect the dots and after a few days come back with the beginnings of a new understanding of their behavior. They don't know it, but the dot connectors have Dr John Snyder to thank for this new start. I just passed the concept on.

When John asked if I would write the foreword for his book I was thrilled and humbled at the same time. His asking me told me that he respected the things I have to say and that he trusted me to say them to you. I have tried to do that by sharing these words, and a bit of myself. For the really good stuff, read this book. Your life song lies within.

Psychiatrist Judith D. Fisher received her degree from the Howard University College of Medicine in Washington, DC, and did her psychiatric residency at Howard University Hospital and Hahnemann Hospital, where she was trained as a community psychiatrist. Currently, she practices in New York, where she is the psychiatrist for the Bronx Addiction Treatment Center and a psychiatric consultant for the Visiting Nurse of New York's AIDS Family Support Team.

PREFACE

ANYONE LIVING IN THE WORLD TODAY has a right to feel a little bit crazy given all of the craziness around us. What drives me especially crazy right now is the crazy decision of the mental health profession to attribute virtually all forms of emotional distress to "brain dysfunction," obliterating more than a century of clinical knowledge about the complexities of human experience. There has been a wholesale selling out: suffering men, women, and children have been persuaded to believe that there is a quick drug fix for their supposedly troubled brains that will solve any and all emotional difficulties.

I have devoted my professional life to helping people in emotional distress. I know as surely as I know day from night what is helpful and what is not helpful in guiding them through dark feelings into the bright light and joy of being alive. It is clear to me that prescribing pills leaves troubled people in a Hades of grayness. The alternative is equally clear: troubled people need to be supported and encouraged to embrace *all* of their feelings, especially those feelings they most abhor and are inclined to deny.

Unfortunately, the availability of skilled professionals to aid in this process has radically diminished over the years. Indeed, most people have no access to psychotherapy at all. The mental health professionals at the top of the ladder, to whom desperate people with means are invariably referred—the psychiatrists—get little or no training in understanding feelings, either their own feelings or their patients'. They know only about psychotropic drugs. Crazier still, psychiatrists themselves are often bypassed in the treatment process. These days, any physician can prescribe psychiatric medication, regardless of whether or not he has the time and expertise to assess the nature of his patient's emotional distress or the appropriateness of the drug he is dispensing.

So I have felt compelled to write—not just to describe this horrible turn of events, but also to put something before you that has been hidden in plain sight. It is strikingly simple. We need to feel whatever we feel, all of it, however painful or sad or scary. Otherwise, we invariably become depressed, pushing down all feelings in order not to feel the feelings to which we object. Embracing abhorrent feelings is a scary and painful process—often involving crying like a child—so we need to have someone there to encourage us and support us . . . and to celebrate with us as we become healthier and stronger and more fully alive. Avoiding abhorrent feelings by taking antidepressants, or by keeping so agitatedly busy we don't have time to feel, will kill us emotionally. Thirty million people in the United States are doing just that. One in every ten Americans now takes antidepressants—a statistic that suggests we are well on our way to becoming a nation of Zombies. A statistic that makes me crazy.

That being said, this book is not primarily an exposé of the pharmaceutical industry. It is a book about the nature of emotional life, joy and sadness. I want to challenge you to rethink everything you've been told about "negative feelings." I want you to consider the possibility that there are no negative feelings, that emotional ebb and flow—the ups and the downs—is intrinsic to being alive, "the continuous musical line of our minds." *Overcoming Depression* is a fugue on that theme, weaving together the art of listening to music with the art of listening to feelings.

I talk about music in this book because it is through music that I have been able to trudge through the swamplands of my own soul. Music takes us all to the feeling places inside ourselves. Listening to music and listening to feelings are analogous processes. In this book, I'll show you how to do both.

The simple principals you will find in this book have provided a profound and lasting healing for my clients over the years. The mental health professionals I supervise—psychiatrists, psychologists, clinical social workers, and others, have enthusiastically embraced those same principals. Both my clients and my colleagues have for quite some time urged me to make this helpful healing approach more available to others. Which is how I came to write *Overcoming Depression*. I think you will find it interesting, regardless of your circumstances. If you are in emotional distress and considering taking antidepressants, it may just save your life.

INTRODUCTION

FOR THE LAST THIRTY YEARS, we have been told, over and over again, that depression is a disease caused by a chemical imbalance in the brain (low serotonin)—that the symptoms of this disease are negative emotions (sadness, anxiety) and that antidepressant medications can treat this disease effectively and safely. ("Depression hurts; Cymbalta helps.") None of this is true. There is no credible scientific support for the chemical imbalance theory (low serotonin = low mood). Antidepressants are little more effective than placebos (sugar pills) in relieving depression, an ill-defined condition to begin with. Moreover, antidepressants have frequent, serious side effects—including, paradoxically, suicidal depression—and they create long-term addiction, trapping users in a permanent pharmacological nightmare.

Over 30 million people in the US alone—one in every ten Americans—take prescription antidepressants. (1) This mass addiction is the result of a sweeping medicalization of emotion that took place in 1980's, with the active support of the pharmaceutical industry. Biopsychiatrists reorganized the emotional spectrum into a binary system of good feelings and bad feelings, attributing the latter to Bad Brain Chemistry. Sadness became a disease. Joy became a symptom of bi-polar disorder. What got lost in the process was a simple but crucial insight: feelings are facts. We don't choose our feelings. They choose us. And when we try to choose what we want to feel—or

1

what we *don't* want to feel—we damn up the flow within us, i.e., if we block feelings that for any number of reasons we don't want to feel, we end up not being able to feel anything at all. In short, depression is not a disease. It is a behavior, something we do to ourselves. And, as you will see, we can learn not to do it.

The pharmaceutical industry's marketing campaign has been so effective in selling the dangers of Bad Brain Chemistry to doctors and patients alike that, for many of you, everything I have just said may sound incredible; so I will spend some time demonstrating why Bad Brain Chemistry is bad science. That is not the real point of this book, however. Learning to overcome depression is important. (Depression does hurt!) But it is not enough just to know that. What we really need to learn is how to live more intensely, more passionately, more joyfully—a joy that comes from being whole, connected to all the feelings within us (including anxiety and sadness) and, through our feelings, connected to each other and to the cosmos.

Emotional ebb and flow is intrinsic to being alive. Even thinking requires feeling, as neuroscientist Antonio Damasio reminds us. Emotion is "the continuous musical line of our minds, the unstoppable humming of the most universal of melodies that only dies down when we go to sleep." (2) In this book, I do an extended riff on Damasio's line, weaving together the art of listening to music with the art of listening to feelings. That's where the strange subtitle comes in. "A Funeral March with Introductory Polka" is the name that composer Gustav Mahler (1860-1911) gave to his first piece of music, written when he was barely six years old. The stark juxtaposition of sorrow and joy in the title epitomizes the extraordinary emotional range in Mahler's music as a whole. Throughout this book, especially in the second half, I explore the relationship between music and emotion through Mahler, painting a revisionist portrait of a man who is often misunderstood as neurotic and depressed. Although his life was short and filled with tragedy, Mahler was never truly depressed, in fact. His ability to go with the flow of his feelings gave him extraordinary strength and resilience. In the concluding chapters, I explain how all of us can access that same emotional strength in our own lives.

Here is what to expect, chapter by chapter:

In the first chapter, I trace the history of depression as a concept and diagnostic category. I begin with the ancient Greeks and their view of depression as constitutional, having to do with too much black bile—an old idea that is mirrored in the new idea of "too little serotonin." Even in the ancient past, however, there were those who took a different view, observing that mood swings were part of being human—and that dramatic mood swings were essential to artists and seers. Ancient treatments for depression were sometimes surprisingly caring, allowing troubled people to separate momentarily from relational conflicts and have support to wail and moan. These patients got better. The more common approach, however, was to get rid of "bad" feelings, or to get rid of the people having them. We take a brief tour of the horrible places in which suffering men and women were confined, and then turn to horrors of another sort: prefrontal lobotomies, insulin and electroshock treatments, and the new antidepressants, all treatments designed to disable the offending brain, or the person whose feelings disturb us.

I trace my personal journey through this more recent past observing how depression was defined and treated when I was in training as a psychotherapist under Harry Stack Sullivan. In the past fifty years, Sullivan has been dismissed, along with hundreds of the best thinkers in psychology and psychiatry—Freud, Jung, Adolph Meyer, Theodor Reik, R.D. Lang, Szasz and many more. These men and women understood the complexities of human emotions and human relationships and realized that depression and anxiety were often symptoms of unresolved conflict. Their work was marginalized in a take-over by a few psychiatrists who, impatient with the complexities of human relationships, wanted a simple answer—a definition of depression that would support one kind of treatment: drugs. Chapter Two (*"Bad" Feelings Become a Disease*) traces this deadly take-over, focusing on the period 1974-1987 during which Columbia University psychiatry professor Dr. Robert Spitzer led a task force that produced a new revision of the *Diagnostic and Statistical Manual* (the manual used to define mental illness), the DSM-III. Spitzer's goal was to bring all diagnostic categories into compliance with this biopsychiatric model, an effort strongly supported by the pharmaceutical industry. (If Spitzer could create a disease, they could create a cure.)

Chapter Three continues the story with a more detailed look at antidepressants, what they do and what they don't do. The marketing of these drugs has been so successful that they are now the most widely used of all medications, far outnumbering medications for heart disease, diabetes, high cholesterol, and infections. (3) The way in which antidepressants are prescribed is fundamentally different from other drugs, however, and subject to far fewer controls. For example, imagine that I start to experience a set of physical symptoms: frequent urination, unusual thirst, blurred vision, cuts that are slow to heal. I present these symptoms to my general practitioner, who, suspecting diabetes, orders a glycated hemoglobin test. The results—an A1C level of 8 percent—confirm that I have the disease. My GP refers me to an endocrinologist who runs additional blood tests and prescribes insulin. "Depression" is not a clearly defined disease like diabetes, however. Patients report symptoms—sadness, for example—often in language very similar to the drug company ads they have heard on TV. The *Diagnostic and Statistical Manual of Mental Disorders* categorizes these symptoms, but there is no gold standard equivalent to the glycated hemoglobin test, no biopsy that can be performed on the psyche. Moreover, in an era when the practice of medicine has become hyper-specialized, non-specialists (including nurse practitioners) write many of the prescriptions for antidepressants. If I become very emotional and teary-eyed during a visit to my foot doctor, chances are he will write me a script for Paxil even before he goes to work on my sore toe. My podiatrist is a nice man, and he doesn't want me to feel "bad" or commit suicide, two things that antidepressants are supposed to prevent.

But they don't. Recent studies at the University of Pennsylvania show that antidepressants are no more effective than sugar pills in treating mild depression. (4) If the patient's symptoms improve at all, it is only after weeks of trial and error with many different drugs. Since other studies indicate that most symptoms of depression improve spontaneously in ten or twelve weeks anyway, taking antidepressants and "feeling better" may be coincidental rather than causative. Moreover, there is no objective, scientific method for measuring improvement. Psycho-pharmacologists rely entirely on the patient's own reports. This is especially problematic because, at this point, the patient is under the influence of drugs that anesthetize and flatten emotion. As the work of Antonio Damasio demonstrates, thinking and feeling are so intertwined in our brains, indeed in our whole bodies, that disabling part of the brain not only dulls feeling; it dulls thinking as well. For this reason and several others, psychiatrist Dr. Peter Breggin concludes that a person on antidepressant medication is an especially poor judge of his own condition. Dr. Marcia Angell concurs: "Deciding simply on the basis of whether individual patients seem to respond is a notoriously unreliable and dangerous method." (5)

Antidepressants may be ineffective, but they are not innocuous. Unlike the sugar pill, which gives hope and does no harm, antidepressant medications can irreparably damage the people they purport to help. Although the voice on the TV ad may sound soothing as it ticks off the drug side effects, the sheer number and severity is daunting: *difficulty concentrating, memory impairment, confusion, hallucination, anxiety, trouble sleeping, mania, difficult breathing, trembling or shaking, disturbing dreams, agitation, seizure, coma, respiratory arrest, death*. Children and teenagers are especially susceptible to the worse side effects of antidepressants including uncontrollable rage or despair that, more often than we have been told, leads to suicide or murder—a possibility that has prompted the FDA to require drug manufacturers to place a black box warning on their products. (6) Ironically, in both children and adults, the use of antidepressants is a major *cause* of depression, especially when people try to wean themselves from the drugs. For example, suppose that I am disturbed that I cried in my foot doctor's office (in the hypothetical example above) and that I start taking the antidepressant he prescribed. After awhile, I am not feeling sad or anxious any more, but I am not feeling much of anything else, either—no appetite, no loving feelings, no sex drive. I am not myself. When I stop taking the drug, however, I am plunged into a very dark place, overwhelmed by lethargy. None of the pleasurable activities that used to give me pleasure interest me anymore. Emotionally, I am dead inside. In short, what began as a normal transitory feeling of sadness has now become a major depressive episode from which I may or may not recover. Chances are, I will start taking antidepressants again, unaware that I have initiated a vicious cycle from which there is no exit.

This is what happens when we take antidepressants—and when we use other methods to prevent ourselves from feeling what we feel. There is powerful cultural support for this kind of emotional editing. Over the past 60 years, anxiety, sadness and other so-called negative emotions have been relentlessly medicalized and pathologized by many psychiatrists (and some psychologists) working in tandem with the pharmaceutical industry. The illusion that emotions come in two flavors; negative and positive, is virtually universal, as is the belief that negative feelings are symptoms of an illness that needs to be cured. Most of my clients—including some who have been initially institutionalized as dysfunctional—end up in my office not because they have some mysterious Bad Brain Chemistry but because they are spending most of their life energy objecting to their own emotions. Often the simple question—"What is it you are trying not to feel?"—will open the floodgates. The psychiatrists whom I supervise are often amazed when they discover that such a simple approach can literally bring a client back to life.

"Janet" is a perfect example. She came into my office with all the classical symptoms of depression: fatigue and loss of energy, difficulty sleeping, diminished ability to concentrate. She was down in the dumps most of the day, every day. She experienced very little pleasure, even in the things that used to give her great pleasure. There was a good reason for her low mood, of course: Abe, her beloved husband of 36 years, had died recently; and yet as I listened to her, I sensed that something else was going on. Bit by bit, over many weeks, Janet told me her story . . . . The trauma of her first son's premature birth; how she had grieved because she could not have more children of her own; her painful struggles with Abe before he finally agreed to adopt; the conflicts and estrangement that periodically developed between her two sons. As she spoke about her feelings, Janet's symptoms of depression began to disappear. But not entirely. An inordinate sense of guilt seemed to be weighing her down, depressing her mood.

"What are you feeling so guilty about, Janet?" I asked.

After much silence and distress, she responded.

"It's me. It's me I feel so badly about. Abe was so good, but I made him so miserable. It's about sex . . . The more excited he was, the more I would freeze. I got scared. I feel so ashamed and so guilty about that now. He had to put up with my sickness."

"Your "sickness"? Where does that come from?"

And so it began—the story within the story. We talked about Janet's childhood and adolescence. As a little girl she overheard violent rows between her parents, mostly about sex—her mother's anger as she fought off sexual advances, her father's rage at being denied. Her father's sexual interest in Janet's own youthful body made her even more uncomfortable than his anger. He insisted the bathroom door could not be locked, and he would come in at will when she was bathing or on the toilet and look at her. She felt ashamed. When she complained to her mother, she was accused of making up stories to cause trouble. As a teenager, when she came home from her first date with her lipstick smeared, her mother struck her across the face, called her a whore, and sent her to the basement. It was clear from these incidents how difficult it would have been for Janet to have experienced her adolescent sexuality in a healthy way. She confirmed that her first complete sexual experience was with Abe, and not accomplished easily.

As she began to understand and integrate these early life experiences, Janet gradually overcame her view of herself as sick. The symptoms of depression disappeared, replaced by a delightful sense of humor. A charming lady with dramatic red hair, she came alive, her intense brown eyes sharp and clearly focused . . . elegant, achingly articulate, psychologically nuanced, layered and complex.

Is that the end of the story? No. Over the years, Janet would become depressed again occasionally and would call for an appointment. By this time, however, she knew what I would ask: *What is the feeling you are trying so hard not to feel?*

Sometimes it is enough simply to support people in expressing emotions they already recognize in themselves, reassuring them that they are not crazy but merely human. We can do this for each other outside of clinical settings as well. For example, in the hypothetical situation described above, imagine that I had recently lost a close friend to lung cancer. Entering my podiatrist's office, I saw a picture on the wall of a beach in Mexico near where my friend spent her last days. Thinking of her and my loss of her, I began to cry. There was nothing negative, much less pathological, about my sadness. It was perfectly appropriate to my life circumstances. Instead of trying to stop me from "breaking down," my podiatrist could have put aside his own Big-Boys-Don't-Cry inhibitions and given me a supportive hug. And thrown away his prescription pad.

It is not always that simple, of course; but many of the truths about depression *are* simple, hidden in plain sight. Intuitively, we already know there is a problem with our pill popping. If the accepted therapy for garden-variety depression was electroconvulsive therapy (ECT . . . "shock treatments"), most of us would say, "I'm not *that* depressed!" and run away. However, we take so many pills these days—dozens of OTC nostrums, herbal supplements, and vitamins—that one more pill doesn't seem to matter much.

These first three chapters draw from and add support to a spate of recent books that challenge the widespread use of antidepressants, including Peter Breggin's *The Anti-Depressant Fact Book* (2001), Timothy Scott's *America Fooled: The Truth About Antidepressants, Antipsychotics and How We've Been Deceived* (2006), Christopher Lane's *Shyness: How Normal Behavior Became a Sickness* (2007), Peter Conrad's *The Medicalization of Society* (2007), Breggin's revised edition of *Brain-Disabling Treatments in Psychiatry* (2008) and *Medication Madness* (2008), and Robert Whitaker's *Anatomy of an Epidemic* (2010) among others. *Overcoming Depression Drugs* differs from these volumes in several important respects, however. Throughout the book, I approach the problem of depression and antidepressants, not as a sociologist or journalist, but as a therapist who has helped thousands of people overcome depression and recover excitement in their lives. In particular, I draw on my early experiences working with men who had been warehoused in the back wards of St. Elizabeth's Hospital, formerly the Government Hospital for the Insane—ostensibly crazy men who gave me gifts of insight that profoundly changed my clinical practice, and changed my life. My goal in this book is not simply to critique the pharmaceutical industry but to offer practical alternatives to its products—sharing the gifts I have been given with a wider audience.

Chapter Four (*Objecting to Feelings: Agitated Depression*) draws from my practice, introducing a poorly understood mode of depression that manifests itself, not as sadness and lethargy, but as energetic activity (*mania* in its extreme clinical form). In a culture that values producing and coping and devalues receptivity and introspection, agitated depression is often seen as a healthy orientation to life. In fact, it is the flip side of melancholia. One way to stop ourselves from hearing the music of sadness and anxiety is to turn down the volume on all our feelings. That is what we do when we depress ourselves, and that is what antidepressants do to us, often without our knowing. In agitated depression, we try to achieve the same goal—not to feel what we feel—by keeping ourselves so busy we don't feel anything at all. In effect, we turn up the noise. At the end of Chapter Four, I introduce a concept that I return to later in the book: how we sometimes conspire behind our own backs to entitle ourselves to regress and become vulnerable children again, momentarily overcome with feelings we were never allowed to feel. These episodes of regression—often seen as pathological—are really opportunities for healthier integration. They give us a chance to go back and collect missing pieces of ourselves that we have left behind in our hurry to answer our email and get everything done on our To Do lists. I also introduce a figure that has been lurking in the wings throughout the first part of the book: my illustrative case study, Gustav Mahler.

Mahler takes center stage in Chapter Five (*Listening to Feelings, Listening to Mahler*) as we move from the pharmaceutical dance of death (antidepressant use) to the dance of feelings that lies at the heart of this book. At first glance, Mahler seems an odd choice for an emotional role model. With his pinched face, strange spasmodic gait, and apparently morbid interest in death, he looks like a poster boy for the creativity and madness movement. The image of Mahler as neurotic was aggressively promoted by his wife Alma, whose 1989 memoir, *My Life, My Loves,* portrays her husband as *fin de siecle* Woody Allen, compulsively controlling, beset by eccentricities. Alma's view seems to be confirmed by Mahler's own decision in 1910 to consult Sigmund Freud who concluded, without much originality, that the composer had a "mother fixation."(7) The psychiatric consensus today is that, at the very least, Mahler spent much too much time alone in his imagination. He has been diagnosed (post mortem) as suffering from Obsessive Compulsive Disorder (based largely on the perfectionism he demanded as a conductor) and as Cyclothymic or Manic Depressive (8) (Based largely on the emotional range and juxtapositions in his music). Were Mahler alive today, Alma would undoubtedly pack him off to the nearest psychopharmacologist who would fix him up with a lithium cocktail and a chlorpromazine chaser. Leveled out in this manner, Mahler would be a much more tractable husband, although it is unlikely that any of us would be listening to his music.

As my tone here suggests, the Mahler who appears in this book is not the Neurasthenic Genius who appears in Wikipedia and popular film. Alma aside, the people who knew Mahler best describe him as a man who, though small of stature, was robust and athletic—full of joy and infectious laughter. (9) Immensely practical and driving, he carved out a brilliantly successful career in one of the toughest businesses in the world (highbrow showbiz). Beginning in 1880, he rapidly achieved an international reputation as an opera conductor, despite being subjected to brutal anti-Semitic attacks and unjust firings.

Mahler always regarded conducting as his "day job," however. His real life's work was composing symphonies, and it is for those symphonies that we remember him today—music at once rooted in 19th century Romanticism and yet startling in its modernity. Mahler intended his symphonies to be universal "statements" about life, death, love, religion, God, nature, and the human condition. At the very least, they are statements about Mahler himself and provide us with extraordinarily direct access to his inner emotional life—access that is enriched by the ongoing self-analysis he conducted in his diaries and letters.

Mahler's ability to go with the flow of his feelings reveals itself everywhere in his music—a mixture of brilliant, irregularly changing harmonies, extraordinary juxtapositions of mood, strutting march music yoked back-to-back with Viennese love music, "overwhelming passion untempered by the civilizing effect of artistic control and manipulation." (10) Mahler's artistic achievement is all the more moving when placed in the essentially tragic context of his life. In addition to enduring chronic physical pain, he suffered an almost unending sequence of immense emotional losses: seven of his 13 siblings died in infancy. His beloved younger brother Ernst died at age 12 literally in Mahler's arms. His brother Otto killed himself. Mahler survived these early wounds; just as later he survived the death of his little daughter and a diagnosis of fatal heart disease. He even survived Alma Schindler, if not physically then certainly spiritually. Her sexual betrayal and threats of abandonment sent him into the abyss, but he emerged "reborn." Alma got Walter Gropius; we got *Das Lied von der Erde*. In short, the Mahler in *Overcoming Depression* is a survivor—not an example of mental illness but an example of emotional health. He had every reason to be depressed, but he wasn't. And we *know* he wasn't every time we listen to his music and are moved by it. *Depression* and *passion* are antonyms. To recognize that truth—that depression is the absence/blockage of feelings not the presence of "bad" feelings—is to begin to understand the source of Mahler's inner strength, a strength we can acquire for ourselves. For Mahler, music in the key of pain and music in the key of joy were both an inseparable part of the music of life, the enduring song of the earth. He did not choose to live his life at middle C; he wanted the whole keyboard.

There is a famous Taoist story about a terrible flood that destroys much of the Middle Kingdom. Only one man survives. The Three Sages journey to meet him. "How is it that you alone did not drown, good sir?" they ask him. "What is your secret?" "It is simple," he replies. "I went down with the water. I came up with the water. I survived." Intuitively, Mahler knew this secret, even as a child—knew how to go with the flow around him and within him and not to block it, even when it threatened to overwhelm him. Some of his most powerful music came to him as he sat in his alpine composing hut listening to the lake outside his window. He listened to the "continuous musical line" of his own psyche with the same passionate attention.

Fig. 1 Gustav Mahler, 1902.

Music Selection One: *Listen to the beginning of this third movement of Mahler's first symphony. You will hear a familiar folk dance (in the French "Frere Jacques"), but set to a slow funeral march cadence. This agonizing march is then interrupted by the second theme, a spirited dance. I believe we have a perfect example of what the six-year-old Mahler had in mind when he entitled his composition "Polka with Introductory Funeral March." Robert Greenberg says that no other composer's music better describes the inner landscape and struggles of its creator, but it was the juxtaposition of these extremes of feeling that got Mahler into so much trouble with his critics. Mahler said of this first symphony that it must include the whole world. What surely he meant was that it must include the whole world of human feelings – all the highs, all the lows, and everything in between. Accept the scratchiness in this vintage recording because I believe, of all the recordings, it most faithfully captures the depth of feeling Mahler intended. It was made over three quarters of a century ago by Bruno Walter, a young protégé and friend of Mahler's.*

Bruno Walter, NBC Symphony Orchestra, 1939.
http://www.overcomingdepressionwithoutdrugs.com/music

Because the content of his emotional life is so accessible, so well known, and so profoundly misunderstood, Mahler is an ideal figure through which to introduce this fresh perspective on depression. There is a more personal reason that Mahler and depression are together in this book, however: because they are together in *me*. As a young man, I learned to be a skilled debater, able to talk at people, able to hold the floor. Over the years, I had to learn a balance of those skills, in order to become a man who can listen to others because he listens to himself. Gustav Mahler was my life coach in that journey, my *guru* (a Sanskrit word in which the roots of *darkness* and *light* are conjoined). Listening to Mahler was an intuitive search for balance, an apprenticeship of the spirit.

I grew up in a world of music. My father loved the great composers—Bach, Mozart, Beethoven—and insisted on playing classical music on the radio stations he owned, despite the fact none of his local listeners tuned in. Sophisticated in his tastes, he appreciated Mahler early on, long before Mahler's work became generally accepted. I began to listen to Mahler in my early teens, at a time when most of my friends were swinging to Glenn Miller and the Andrews sisters. Maybe I was trying to please my father (that's what my sister thought!) but only at first. The more I listened, the more deeply attracted I was to Mahler's music—

<u>**Music Selection Two:**</u> *Music has deep connections to my emotional life, and that is especially true of this Second Symphony. Listening to this first movement, listen to Mahler: "My need to express myself musically—symphonic ally—begins at the point where the dark feelings hold sway." The movement opens with the violins and violas entering abruptly, tenuously, and recedes to a soft quivering as the bases mount a menacing attack. This is a prelude to the whole movement that alternates between a love of nature and life itself, and a threatening nullification of all aspirations. Thus Mahler confronts us with the basic questions: What is life all about? What is the significance of our strivings? When the music soars and there seems to be hope the funeral march returns and the music arrives at a painful dissonant climax. Then silence. The strings return suggesting a survival from the darkest of feelings, survival from music in the key of pain. The music moves tentatively, then more firmly, only to end with a descent from fortissimo to pianissimo. The movement has an inconclusive and doubt-ridden end, as if a coffin is being lowered into a grave.*

Otto Klemperer, Royal Concertgebouw Orchestra, 1951.
www.overcomingdepressionwithoutdrugs.com/music

especially the Second Sympathy with its dramatic shifts in mood. I knew it was dark, heavy. ("Maybe I'm a masochist," I worried.) But even then, it felt right to me. Long before I knew anything about Mahler's strengths as a man, I sensed that he was taking me to places I needed to go, scary places, healing places. Intuitively, I knew that in listening to Mahler I was somehow listening to myself, immersing myself in a flow of emotions that I normally kept dammed up.

I could never have emotionally survived the death of a beloved daughter, Julie, if I had not learned these lessons from Mahler. What had been before merely an empathetic understanding of Mahler's losses became suddenly an intensely personal experience for me and my partner, Carolyn. Have we gotten over it? Of course not! We remember Julie. Sometimes we laugh. Sometimes we feel incredibly sad. Sometimes we play the CD "Kindertotenlieder" (Mahler's "Songs on the Death of Children") and cry our hearts out. At these times, I think not only of Mahler but also of my aunt Edith who lost her only son in war. She did not get the support she needed to wail and moan and slipped into a state of deep, unremitting depression. After several electroshock treatments, she said to her niece: "I know what they are trying to do. They are trying to get me to forget Dick. I don't want to forget Dick." In the end, her doctors threw up their hands and made sure she would forget: they gave her a prefrontal lobotomy. She survived, but the operation permanently dulled her capacity to feel.

The final chapters of *Overcoming Depression* explore alternatives to this kind of living death, using Mahler's life as an example. I stress again that to dance the dance of life, you have to do *all* the steps, not just the easy ones, and to embrace all the dissonant parts of yourself. If you turn down the volume (by using antidepressants) or turn up the noise (by being too busy to feel) then you won't be able to hear the music. And if you can't hear the music, you can't dance.

Chapter Six (Introversion and the Feeling Life) explores the composer's life and work in order to offer a radically different view of the much-misunderstood term "schizoid personality" (aka "introvert"). I make case for the positive nature of introversion, a source of emotional strength that is often obscured because the extroverts tend to define the norms in our world.

Chapter Seven (*Joy and Angst*) introduces the most difficult steps in the dance of life: going with the flow of our existential vulnerability. I explain why we tend to object to so many of our feeling states, especially feelings of anxiety. Drawing on Ernst Becker (*The Denial of Death*) and other work, I identify three interrelated flavors of anxiety, all of them bitter to us: anxiety associated with elemental fears of abandonment—fears that begin the moment we leave the amniotic oneness of our mother's womb and are thrust into the outer air; elemental fears that come from our knowledge that, from that moment we take our first breath of outer air, we are dying animals, finite and immensely vulnerable; and the fear of regression—of losing our adult defenses and becoming helpless children again, awash in the unmanageable flood of our emotions. Fears of regression are often associated with specific traumatic experiences in our childhood that we block in order to get on with our lives. Using Mahler as an example, I demonstrate that often the only way to really get on with our lives is to go back to the moment of pain/blockage and reconnect with our estranged emotional experience, entitling ourselves to *all* of our feelings, not merely a selected subset.

In Chapter Eight (Regression in the Service of the Ego) I develop this understanding of regression in greater detail by analyzing how Gustav Mahler responded when his wife Alma told him, in the most brutal possible way, that she was having an affair with young Bauhaus architect Walter Gropius. Mahler's subsequent "breakdown" is usually presented as evidence of his crippling neurosis, but I rethink that view, arguing that it was really a creative *reculer pour mieux sauter* (going back in order to leap forward), an agonizing experience but a liberating one. Paradoxically to truly master the dance of life, we sometimes have to be willing to let go of everything and be master of nothing for a while, honoring our need to regress. Freud intuited this principle, albeit without fully developing it, in his concept of *repetition compulsion*. He understood that we may repress powerful feelings at times in our lives when such feelings are unacceptable or even dangerous to our survival. These feelings can then return later with great force and cry out for our attention, triggered often by a relatively minor precipitating event. Entitling ourselves to these scary, painful feelings is a way of going back and retrieving a part of ourselves we have left behind—a way of becoming more integrated, more whole. The other choice is to employ all the life energy we can muster to keep these feelings at bay. *This* is the true meaning of depression.

In Chapter Nine (Death and the Preciousness of Life) I begin to follow Mahler into the final adagio, a temporal space in which there are no feelings that need be avoided, even the most dreaded feelings of all: that the dance of life will someday end, and there will be no more music, no more us. Mahler was much more aware than most of us of the fragility of human existence. He suffered many blows—the death of his daughter, the betrayal of his wife, and dire threats to his health. Terrible as they were, all of these experiences were precious to him, however; because life was precious. Mahler was exceptionally sensitive to the transitory nature of feelings. Bliss cannot be maintained at will, and periods of despair never last except in our refusal to feel them. Mahler could go down into the grave and get lost in the stars in a single afternoon, and write music that takes us to both places at once.

Chapter Ten (*Mahler, Music and the Eternal Feminine*) goes to the heart of Mahler's life experience, and mine, exploring how the ability to accept our vulnerability and the finite nature of our lives liberates us in an even deeper way. There was very little support in Mahler's culture for this kind of profound existential surrender, and there is even less support in ours, where *coping* and *multitasking* have become synonyms for *living*. The default position involves stances that are stereotypically "masculine," striving upward toward some goal, using reason to measure everything that can be measured and control everything that can be controlled.

Mahler's stance was different. In a letter to Alma, he wrote in praise of the "Eternal Feminine," "that which is at rest"—what the Taoists call "stillness." The opposite of this stillness is "striving," akin to the notion of agitated depression that I described earlier, an empty busyness that estranges us from ourselves and from the universe. For Mahler, as for Lao-tzu and the Taoists, everything that exists *flows* . . . like water, like music. The Song of the Earth is a waveform. The Eternal Masculine is everything that tries (in vain) to go against the flow—resisting, objecting, damming up—the Army Corp of Engineers within our psyche that arms us against the flood, lest we be overwhelmed. For Mahler, the whole point of life was to be overwhelmed, to surrender, to take flood into oneself and become one with it. In other words, for Mahler, passivity was powerful.

What does all of this have to do with depression? Plenty! Today, as in the era of Mahler and Jung, the fluid expression of emotion is coded as feminine, especially the expression of fear, hurt, or vulnerability. And *feminine* is coded as *weak*. It sometimes seems that the only open expression of feeling licensed for men is anger, which is not really a feeling at all. (It is an unconscious, defensive reaction to feelings of hurt, fear or helplessness.) In this sense, it is not hyperbole to say that to overcome depression we must all "feminize" ourselves, opening ourselves to the flood in the way that Mahler did—an orientation that is often as difficult for women as it is for men these days.

As we move into uncharted emotional waters, it helps to have a good traveling companion on the voyage, especially when the seas get rough. Music can be that companion, for some of us at least, because music "digs into our depths and expresses hidden movements of love and fear and joy that are inside us," as Martha Nussbaum says, "It speaks to us and about us in mysterious ways, going 'to the bottom of things,' as Mahler put it, exposing hidden vulnerabilities." At once measured and immeasurable, coming out of silence and returning to it, music reminds us that "going with the flow" is more than a quaint Hippie motto, associated with pot and bellbottom jeans. Ultimately, all we have is flow. As Jon Kabat-Zinn says, "Wherever you go, there you are." In the long run, rational control proves illusory. (Try reasoning with cancer, or Katrina). In the long run, *here* is where we always are. The only thing we really *know* is what we feel. If we move away from our feelings, we move toward depression. It is only when we move toward our feelings, honoring authenticity in our relationships with each other and with ourselves, that we become fully alive and able, finally, to dance to the music of the universe in the key of joy.

PART I

OBJECTING TO FEELINGS
(The Funeral March)

CHAPTER ONE

A SHORT HISTORY OF DEPRESSION —FROM HIPPOCRATES TO THE DSM

"The fires of a supreme zest for living and the most gnawing desire for death alternate in my heart, sometimes in the course of a single hour."   —Gustav Mahler (1)

SO WHAT IS DEPRESSION? How should we treat it? More fundamentally, how should we think about it? In the Prelude and Introduction to this book, I have already outlined my own answer to those questions. Now I want to go back and fill in that outline in greater deal. The term itself is ambiguous. *Depression* (or *melancholia*) sometimes seems to designate a medical illness, perhaps genetically determined—a problem serious enough to require prefrontal lobotomies or other drastic intervention. Or depression can be understood as something human, something transitory, and something common to us all.

The first references to depression or melancholia go back to 400 B.C. The ancient Greek physician Hippocrates diagnosed melancholia symptomatically, in much the same way that the *Diagnostic and Statistical Manual for Mental Illness* (DSM) does today—as a *persistent* low mood involving anxiety and extreme sadness. ("If a fright or despondency lasts for a long time, it is a melancholic affliction.") (2) And like modern psycho-pharmacologists, Hippocrates saw this cluster of symptoms as a biologically based disease rooted in bad body chemistry. The Greek word *melancholia* (μελαγχολία), denoting sadness, literally means "black bile." Hippocrates and those that followed him centuries later believed that melancholia was caused by an imbalance in the four basic bodily fluids or humors (black bile, yellow bile, phlegm, and blood). A person whose constitution had a preponderance of black bile had a melancholic disposition. To correct this imbalance, Hippocrates advised a spa-like regimen that included bathing, sweating, walking and massage. These therapies may or may not have been effective, but they did much less harm than modern drug therapies for depression, therapies that are rooted in the same black box approach to diagnosis and treatment that Hippocrates used, inferring the presence of "disease" from the presence of symptoms. (3) The principal difference between then and now is that serotonin has replaced black bile as the operative humor. Psychopharmacologists are no more able to account for the complexities of human emotion than Hippocrates was.

The symptoms of depression are nevertheless quite troubling. The warning signs described by Hippocrates are consistent with the symptoms that therapists record in their patients today: a pervasive low mood characterized by little or no life energy; an inability to experience pleasure; feelings of helplessness, hopelessness, and worthlessness. The novelist William Styron captured these symptoms from the inside, describing depression as a "gray drizzle of horror . . . a storm of murk." (4) Depression is usually accompanied by insomnia, low appetite, and disregard of physical health and well-being. In extreme forms, people collapse into a catatonic state in which they cease to move, speak or respond to external stimuli. As I will argue in greater detail as I go along, it would make more sense to use the old term *melancholia* to label really severe mood disorders that manifest such symptoms and to dispense with the notion that garden variety depression, manifested as sadness or anxiety, is an "illness." Otherwise, *all* the low notes on the human emotional scale will end up being classified as signs of pathology requiring drug therapy.

Some physicians in the ancient world had a clearer sense of depression as a process than most doctors do today. In the seventh and eighth centuries, Arabic doctors used the word *huzun* (meaning pain and sorrow occasioned by a loss) to describe a cluster of psychological states that included persistent low mood, the fear of death, relational problems in one's life, and lost love. Unlike Hippocrates who thought in terms of imbalance, they intuited that something was being "pushed down"—which is, in the most literal sense, what our English word *depression* means (derived from the Latin verb *deprimere* "to press down"). As we will see, the Arabic physicians were on the right track. We don't really "get" depressed; we *depress ourselves*, refusing to feel what we feel.

For early Sufis (Islamic mystics) *huzun* was primarily a spiritual condition, a symptom of one's estrangement from God. Medieval Christians took much the same view, categorizing *acedia* (apathy, joylessness, torpor) as one of the Seven Deadly Sins. (In his *Inferno*, Dante condemned depressives to a black swamp, stuck in the mud for all eternity, a fairly accurate metaphor for the real-life experience of depression.) Christian theologians recommended that people cure themselves of aecidia by becoming busy (what I will describe later as "agitated depression") on the general theory that idle hands are the Devil's playthings.

Busyness is Robert Burton's recommended cure as well. "I write of melancholy, by being busy to avoid melancholy," he quips in his 1621 *Anatomy of Melancholy*, an antic tract that combines literary satire with pseudo-medical opinion. Writing as a humanist, Burton's view of melancholy is more complex than the Christian Fathers', however. He taxonomizes the symptoms he describes, making a crucial distinction between the normal ebb and flow of emotion (fear, sorrow, grief)—which he calls *Disposition*—and an unremitting sadness (*Habite*) that is pathological. In addition to purposeful activity, Burton also recommends introspection as a counter to melancholy, particularly receptivity to music: "It is a sovereign remedy against despair and melancholy." (5)

The emotional extravagance of Burton's language in *Anatomy* flows from an earlier tradition in which melancholy is seen as a kind of "divine madness," associated with artistic creativity. (6) This concept, often said to originate with Plato, is developed explicitly by Aristotle: "Why is it that all those who have become eminent in philosophy or politics or poetry or the arts are clearly of an atrabilious temperament, and some of them to such an extent as to be affected by diseases caused by black bile?" (7) The Aristotelian linkage between melancholy and artistic genius can be seen quite clearly in Albrecht Dürer's well-known 1514 engraving *Melencolia I.* There is a mistaken view that the engraving is a literal illustration of depressive symptoms. However, as David Finkelstein points out, Dürer's work is really an allegory. The angel's eyes are *not* downcast, an invariable feature of melancholic iconography. They gaze *up* and to the right. Her mouth is not downcast either, at least not clearly so. Although we cannot be sure because the edge of her sleeve covers the corner of her lip, she may in fact be smiling! "The pose shows contemplation, as in Rodin's Thinker, not melancholy." (8) In other words, what seems at first to be *depression* is really creative *introversion*. Passive-receptive, the angel waits for inspiration, turning her vision upward and inward. All of which, by a circuitous route, leads us to Gustav Mahler and the Second Symphony.

It is March 1893. Mahler began his Second Symphony five years ago during a stint as musical director of the Budapest opera, but there has been a lot of blood under the bridge since then—his father and mother's deaths, his burdensome duties in loco parentis to his siblings—and the overworked Mahler is stalled, suffering from composer's block. Mahler's absent parents are present in his Hamburg study, embodied in a series of physical objects: his father's favorite chair sits at Mahler's desk; his mother's piano leans against the wall. There are other emotionally-charged objects present as well—in particular, three prints that hang on the walls: an illustration from a poetry collection, "Das knaben Wunderhorn," depicting St. Anthony of Padua preaching to the fishes; a copy of Titian's oil painting "The Concert"; and Dürer's engraving "Melencolia I."

Writing from a Freudian perspective, Mahler biographer Stuart Feder (2004) sees the composer's choice of wall art as psychologically expressive, a kind of "autobiography in decor":

> Melancholia' [sic] is a rich representation of depression, the state of mind in which Mahler's barely suppressed rage and sense of helplessness culminated". (9)

Fig. 2 Albrecht Dürer. *Melencolia I.* **c. 1514**

Feder's analysis misreads both Dürer and Mahler, however. Dürer's engraving is not about darkness; it is about the coming of the light into the darkness—the light toward which the angel's upraised eyes are turned, freeze-framed in the moment just before inspiration arrives.

Fig. 3 Titian. *The Concert*, c.1510

He is flanked by a man and a woman who appear to be
listening to the music. No one is looking at anyone else. The
woman's eyes are turned right, away from the musician; the
man's eyes stare blankly straight ahead. The musician's face
is turned away from his piano, sharply to his left, so that we
see the open orifice of his ear at the center of the composition,
as if it were a vortex. His large white eyes are turned up and
away, looking toward the light, looking inward. Like Dürer's
"Melencolia I," the Titian painting captures an artist in the act
of being inspired—a moment of "divine frenzy."

Surely, this is why Mahler has juxtaposed these two paintings on his wall, not because they express his inner darkness ("rage and helplessness") but because they express his longing to turn toward the light within, his music—a longing that has been temporarily blocked by too much worldly busyness and coping. The third print expresses the same longing in a different key.

Feder remarks that the figure of St. Anthony, his arms raised in blessing, resembles a conductor at the podium. The dumb fish are the conductor's audience, who will remain untouched by the "sermon," a satiric interpretation that Mahler explicitly endorsed. However, this picture, too, captures a moment of divine inspiration. God is speaking through Anthony to the fishes. The sound draws them up from the depths of the ocean into the light. The movement upward is even clearer in another illustration of the same subject that Mahler probably knew, an 1892 painting by Arnold Böcklin in which a mesmerized shark rolls its eyes up toward the gesticulating St. Anthony. The three prints on Mahler's wall are thus not merely fragments of psychobiography; they are magical talismans designed to protect the artist from too much attention to the outer world. (10)

Fig. 4 Arnold Böcklin, St. Anthony, 1892

The illustration of St. Anthony will prove to be a particularly potent charm, a proleptic image of Mahler's own aborning creative breakthrough. In the summer of 1893, Mahler will escape from Hamburg to a mountain retreat at Steinbach in Upper Austria. There, in a whitewashed hut on the banks of Lake Attersee, he will isolate himself from distractions and become one with the fishes, attentive to the flow around him and within him. One of the first fruits of that summer, the song "Saint Anthony Preaches to the Fishes," will eventually become the scherzo movement of his Second Symphony, "The Resurrection." In coming to the Attersee, the wandering Mahler has come home.

One of the defining characteristics of Mahler's music is its extraordinary emotional range, the often jarring juxtaposition of joy and angst, light and darkness. Mahler experienced these dramatic mood shifts directly. During the time he was composing his First Symphony, he wrote to his friend Natalie Bauer-Lechner,

> The fires of a supreme zest for living and the most gnawing desire for death alternate in my heart, sometimes in the course of a single hour . . . I tear violently at the links that bind me to the stale disgusting swamps of my existence, and with the energy of despair I cling to sorrow as my only consolation. Then the sun smiles at me again, gone are the ice from my heart, I again see the blue skies and the swaying flowers, and my contemptuous sneer dissolves in tears of

love. And again I have to love this world, with its trumpery, its lightheadedness, its eternal laughter! (11)

Today, a confession of this sort would be seen as a symptom of bipolar personality disorder requiring medication. In the 1880's, however, Mahler's rhetoric merely marked his sensibility as Romantic. The pseudo-Platonic concept of "divine frenzy," which surfaced in the Renaissance, resurfaced in the late 18th and 19th centuries in the belief that the ability to move *toward* powerful feelings, no matter how dark, was the wellspring of all creativity and the special gift of the artist. Johann Wolfgang von Goethe, an important literary influence on Mahler, was one of many artists who believed that plunging into dreaded feelings was necessary for a sense of wholeness and emotional health. Terror, horror, sorrow, and despair were the essential counterparts of joy and awe—a notion that, much later and in somewhat different form, would move pioneering psychologist Carl Jung to undertake the dark inner journey that he chronicles in *The Red Book.*

Music Selection Three: *This Third Movement of the Second Symphony is based on a song composed earlier by Mahler, "St. Anthony of Padua's Sermon to Fish," in which St. Anthony, finding his church empty on Sunday, goes to the riverside to preach to the fish. Although he imagines that they are paying attention, they simply go about their business as usual. Why such a watery, tipsy movement in the middle of a profound struggle with the ultimate questions of life? Mahler gives us a hint when he said it is like watching a dance from a distance without hearing the music. The restlessness of the music is suggestive of the directionless lives people are living. It is Mahler's depiction of the superficial, inauthentic life of the crowd, the agitated busyness to keep from feeling. It is the unexamined life not worth living. Toward the end there is a high dissonant outcry that Mahler called a "cry of disgust" and "a fearful scream of the soul." The music dies away gradually and ends with a low shudder in the bass, contrabassoon, horns, harp and tam-tam – a thoroughly hollow sound.*

♪ **Bruno Walter, Vienna Philharmonic Orchestra, 1948.**
http://www.overcomingdepressionwithoutdrugs.com/music

Sigmund Freud approached melancholia very differently from Goethe and Jung, and yet the core concepts in his work also support the view that moving toward "dark" feelings is healthy. For Freud, depression was not a character trait or a biochemical illness but an *action*: people depress themselves by trying to push down (repress) traumatic feelings from the past that are triggered by events in the present. Freud referred to this process as a *repetition compulsion*. In traumatic situations, especially in childhood, Freud observed that people may experience feelings so unacceptably painful that they have to push them out of awareness in order to be able to function and stay sane. These painful feelings don't disappear, however; they merely go underground where they grow hungry for the attention they deserve. (Strong feelings, however painful, are *our* feelings, an essential part of our identity.) Later, after the immediate danger is past, we may unconsciously create situations that entitle us to experience our estranged feelings.

This is what happens in post-traumatic stress disorder. A door slams in his suburban house, and the combat veteran jumps out of bed screaming hysterically and shaking violently all over. He is re-experiencing feelings he had in the war zone. He has two choices: fall completely apart, feel all the helplessness, the fear, the horror, become a "blubbering idiot" for as long as it takes; or mobilize every last bit of his life energy ("libido" for Freud) and push all of these feeling down again, a repetitive process that is likely to result in compulsive behavior and recurring nightmares.

The "return of the repressed" is not confined to veterans, however. It implicated in every manifestation of depression. Once again, my client "Janet" illustrates the point.

Janet was back. She had already asked herself the question she knew I would ask—*What is the feeling you are trying so hard not to feel?*—But she had been unable to find the answer. All the important things in her life seemed to be going well.

"There was one thing, but I'm not sure I want to talk about it," she said.

"At work, we have just one bathroom for the eight of us. Sometimes when I am concentrating on a client's problems, I get a bit distracted and forget to flush the toilet. Well, in a staff meeting, in front of everyone, Mary said, looking straight at me, 'someone is not flushing the toilet and this is not acceptable.' I felt horrible." [She began to sob.] *"I shouldn't feel so much about something so silly!"*

But, of course, it wasn't silly. Suppressed and repressed feelings can be triggered full force by precipitating events that are in themselves trivial. When Janet was a child, she couldn't express her feelings of shame to anyone who would understand and support her. The very reality of her experiences was continually being called into question. In order to function, she had to repress her feelings; otherwise she could not have coped with her situation. Years later, the coworker's testy accusation, "You didn't flush!" brought up all the old feelings of embarrassment. It was taking more and more of her life energy to keep this flood of emotion from overwhelming her.

"How can I keep this from happening again?" She asked.

"You can't," I said, *"but it is not a bad thing. If anyone is entitled to feelings of embarrassment, you are. Think of it as an opportunity."*

She laughed: *"Well, I won't have any shortage of those!"*

Freud understood that using life energy to push down unwanted feelings was the major way we depress ourselves. Freudian analysis was designed to help patients gain access to estranged feelings and integrate them into a larger and more secure sense of self. Before Freud's "talking cure," however, depressed people who had enough money simply took The Cure, which meant "taking the waters" in an extended visit to a spa. Historically, spas were located at natural water sources that were believed to have special health-giving properties. Egyptians had used baths for therapeutic purposes as early as 2000 B.C., and Hippocrates specifically recommended bathing, sweating, and massage as therapies for depression. By 1800, spas had become widespread throughout Europe as part of genteel life. Grand hotels with casinos and dancing establishments surrounded the spas. Unlike Freud's talking cure, however, "taking the waters" was designed to move melancholics away from strong emotions, not toward them. Like 21st century rehab, the spa visit ostensibly worked by separating the sufferer from stress, social responsibility, and emotional triggers. In this semi-infantilized environment of pampered care, the spa waters (often highly sulfurous) purged people of toxins and negative feelings alike.

It was to such a spa (in Tobelbad, Austria) that Gustav Mahler's distressed wife Alma retreated in 1910, albeit the cure she ultimately took had little to do with sulfur water. (See Chapter Eight.) Had Alma been an American, she likely would have gone to the Battle Creek Sanitarium in Michigan, the largest of these spas anywhere. Battle Creek was *the* place for people with "nervous disorders," offering a treatment regimen of enforced bed rest, cold baths, enemas, pelvic massage, and "lots and lots of corn flakes, which the Kellogg brothers, who ran Battle Creek, invented."(12) A 19th century neurologist, George M. Beard, coined the term *neurasthenia* for these nervous disorders and held that it was a medical condition caused by a failure of the nervous system to keep up with the demands of modern civilization. Notable neurasthenics of the era included Theodore Roosevelt, Edith Wharton, Mary Baker Eddy, and Samuel Clemens, all whom took the cure at Battle Creek.

Although some people were believed to be especially vulnerable to neurasthenia (upper class women, chronic masturbators, e.g.), the symptoms of neurasthenia were generally regarded as transitory and remediable. Treatment at spas and sanatoriums was largely voluntary, the 19th century version of checking into rehab. Involuntary psychiatric treatment for melancholia was a different story. In Europe, people suffering from severe, chronic symptoms of depression, especially if they were also poor, were dumped into "madhouses," mingled indiscriminately with the physically disabled, brain-damaged, and psychotic. The first of these institutions, "Bedlam" (Bethlehem Royal Hospital of London), established in the 14th century, became synonymous with brutal human warehousing.

By the 18th century, a more human view of severe depression and emotional distress had begun to take root, albeit based on a medical view of "mental illness." In England, the Quakers established the York Retreat modeled on an approach to psychosocial care called *moral treatment* that stressed morale building rather than religious judgment. The standard remedies of the day for major depression involved bloodletting, chemical shocks to the body, forced periods of isolation, and sensory deprivation. York Retreat abandoned these methods and instead encouraged friendships between patients and staff, along with a daily routine of work and leisure.

Memory of the Quaker approach still endured when I began my own practice 150 years later. My first summer internship in the early 60's was at Eastern State Hospital in Williamsburg, Virginia, the first mental hospital in the United States, an institution steeped in history. (Eastern State officials claimed it was the first US hospital of any kind, competing with the claim of Pennsylvania Hospital in Philadelphia.) A summer in Williamsburg was like being in a time warp. The hospital and my abode were in the center of town, and most of the people I passed on my way to and from work were in 17th century dress! I constantly felt as if I had been transported back two hundred years. Eastern State Hospital was proud of its history and had volunteers ready to describe what it was like in prerevolutionary days.

In 18th century at Eastern State, moral treatment of depressed patients primarily meant creating a loving, pleasant, family-like atmosphere. There were daily routines of work and leisure, and patients were encouraged to perform chores to give them a sense of responsibility. Patients were free to explore the grounds and the gardens and tend to the plants if they desired. Supportive, caring relationships were established between staff and patients; even small gifts were not discouraged. On Sundays, groups of patients had their turn at dinner with the superintendent in his home. No one amassed careful statistics on cure rates, partly because cures were not expected. People recovered enough from their depression to return to home or work, but they might experience a relapse and return to the hospital for a spell. Eastern State historians were fond of telling one story in particular, insisting that it was true: One winter a group of depressed patients was being taken across the grounds from one building to another. Their attendants led them on a short cut across a frozen pond, a pond I know well. The ice proved to be too thin, and the whole group fell in. Immediately they all recovered from their depression . . . an early version of "shock therapy" perhaps.

I had a similar encounter with the moral treatment approach years later when I joined the staff of Pennsylvania Hospital. Also proud of its long history, the hospital had a museum where volunteers described how depressed people were treated years ago. The hospital's founder, Benjamin Rush, required that the institution hire intelligent and sensitive attendants to work closely with depressed patients, reading and talking to them and taking them on regular walks. Rush was confident that caring treatment was also effective treatment. Unfortunately, this view was not universal, nor did it endure.

The patients in the moral treatment hospitals were the lucky ones. For most severely depressed people, especially the indigent and foreign born, everything changed in the middle of the 19th century. Small curative sanatoriums based on moral treatment gave way to large, centralized, overcrowded asylums that did little but warehouse their populations. The patients were neglected, and so were earlier therapeutic principles. Cost overrode ideals. The homey, family atmosphere was replaced by drab, stark architectural structures with high walls to shut off patients from society and limit their contact with the outside world. These facilities were generally located in remote rural areas, literally pushing the afflicted out of sight. A 1946 *Life Magazine* article by Albert Maisel on Philadelphia's Byberry State Hospital ("Bedlam 1946") exposed the horrible state of custodial care in US asylums, which he compared to "concentration camps on the Belsen pattern":

> Court and grand-jury records document scores of deaths of patients following beatings by attendants . . . . Yet beatings and murders are hardly the most significant of the indignities we have heaped upon most of the 400,000 guiltless patient-prisoners of over 180 state metal institutions. We

feed thousands a starvation diet, often dragged further below the low-budget standard by the withdrawal of the best food for the staff dining rooms. We jam-pack men, women and sometimes even children into hundred-year-old firetraps in wards so crowded that the floors cannot be seen between the rickety cots, while thousands more sleep on ticks, on blankets, or on the bare floors . . . Hundreds—of my own knowledge and sight—spend twenty-four hours a day in stark and filthy nakedness . . . Thousands spend their days—often for weeks at a stretch—locked in devices euphemistically called "restraints": thick leather handcuffs, great canvas camisoles, "muffs," "mitts," wristlets, locks and straps and restraining sheets. Hundreds are confined in "lodges"—bare bedless, rooms reeking with filth and feces—by day lit only through half-inch holes though steel-plated windows, by night merely black tombs in which the cries of the insane echo unheard from the peeling plaster of the walls. (13)

The professional staff, who were there to help these deeply troubled people—psychiatrists, psychologists, social workers, chaplains—experienced almost unbearable frustration and helplessness, knowing that they could do very little to relieve the suffering. I know. I was there. Using an oversimplified version of Freud's hypothesis that depression was anger turned inward on oneself, we were encouraged to get our depressed patients to express their anger about how badly they had been hurt, abused, abandoned, or unfairly treated. Invariably once the anger was expressed, the patients began to cry uncontrollably. Later, it occurred to some of us that we might be able to bypass the angry stage altogether if we could find a way of supporting the pain that was behind the anger. This commonsense approach had promise. Indeed, it worked—and it still does. But it never received institutional support because it required huge amounts of professional time in a supportive clinical setting like the York Retreat, requirements that were too costly for the insurance companies, especially since a quicker, cheaper alternative seemed to be available.

That alternative had appeared on the horizon a decade or two before I began my career: a magical treatment that promised to cure depression permanently almost overnight. It was called prefrontal lobotomy.

The earliest surgeries on the brain to cure mental illness were performed by Gottlieb Burckhardt in 1888 in Switzerland. (14) Burckhardt believed that disordered minds were merely a reflection of disordered brains, and that specific problems such as depression could be linked to a specific location in the brain. (Sound familiar?) In effect, emotional low notes could be excised from the scale. In 1935, Antonio Egas Moniz, a Portuguese physician, explored Burckhardt's theories by drilling holes in a patient's head and destroying tissue in the frontal lobes, the site of emotional experience. (15) The procedure was perfected and zealously promoted by Walter Freeman and his neurosurgeon friend James Watts at the George Washington University Hospital in Washington, D.C. The first surgeries were done by drilling holes in the scalp, but by 1946, Freeman had begun approaching the frontal lobes through the eye sockets. The tools he used were simple: an ice pick and a hammer! Before the fad was over, 40,000 patients in the United States had undergone prefrontal lobotomies. (16)

What did these surgeries accomplish? In some cases, having a lobotomy meant that a person trapped in an almost lifeless state of depression in the back ward of one of these awful state mental hospitals might be able to leave the institution and lead a marginal social life, albeit with little range of feeling.

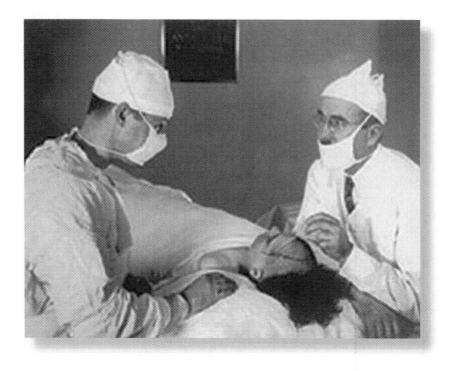

**Fig. 5 Watts (left) and Freeman
performing a lobotomy.**

Sometimes there was a miraculous return to normal functioning: After years in an asylum, French Canadian singer Alys Robi underwent a lobotomy and was able to resume singing professionally. Sometimes not: Swedish painter Sigrid Hjerten died from a lobotomy. The most well-known lobotomy victim was Rosemary Kennedy, the sister of John F. Kennedy.

Although labeled as somewhat "mentally retarded," Rosemary attended school and led an active social life until, in her early 20's; she developed dramatic mood swings that alarmed her family. In 1941, in order to "calm" his daughter, Joseph P. Kennedy agreed to have her lobotomized by Watts and Freeman, an operation that left Rosemary in a semi-vegetative state for the remaining 63 years of her life. (17)

For most lobotomized subjects, the result was less extreme, neither a death nor a resurrection. What Freeman gave them was "a life lived at Middle C." My own aunt Edith is as good an example as any. Her beloved son (my cousin) was valedictorian of his high school class, a star athlete, and an Eagle Scout. When he was killed in combat at 19, my aunt went into a deep, unremitting depression. She had been raised in a German religious tradition (Church of the Brethren) where dancing, for example, was like a cardinal sin. There was no place in her culture for her to scream in pain at her loss. Eventually she underwent a lobotomy. The operation took away her pain but left her emotionally crippled. She was able to live a quiet functional life; however, her ability to experience strong emotion (joy as well as sorrow) was permanently muted. If she were alive today, she would undoubtedly be given antidepressant medications, with much the same result. Like the prefrontal lobotomy, antidepressants not only dull the music in key of pain; they turn down the volume on all the emotional music inside us. They silence our hearts, often forever.

The prefrontal lobotomy was one of several ostensible magic bullet treatments for depression that emerged in the 1930's. In 1936, even before Freeman and his ice pick, the psychiatric community had been excited by the work of Manfred Sakel, a Viennese doctor who moved to New York and introduced American psychiatric hospitals to insulin shock therapy. Sakel claimed success rates of over 80 percent in treating schizophrenic patients, especially those in a highly agitated state—a result of the insulin's "intensification of the tonus of the parasympathetic end of the autonomic nervous system."(18) Most neuropsychiatrists today question this explanation; indeed, it made little sense to Sakel's contemporaries. Nevertheless, insulin shock therapy was used extensively in American mental hospitals in the 1940's and 1950's for patients with severe depression as well as for schizophrenia. By the 1970's, it had disappeared in the United States, although it continued to be used in China and the Soviet Union for many years. It is hardly ever used today.

Since there was never any solid scientific evidence that insulin shock actually worked, why did doctors accept it so uncritically? Some analysts suggest that a few influential doctors were impressed by a few dramatic recoveries, and the fad spread by social contagion. Dr. Harold Bourne questioned insulin shock at the time in his article "The Insulin Myth." (19) This approach enabled many frustrated physicians I knew, a belief that they could help extremely depressed patients and made themselves feel better as doctors.

That is, like Joseph Kennedy, whose discomfort with his inability to control his daughter made him susceptible to Freeman's snake oil, psychiatrists' objection to their own helplessness disarmed their skepticism about insulin shock therapy. The same process will come into play years later when a much more potent magic bullet cure arrives, courtesy of the pharmaceutical industry: psychotropic drug therapy.

In 1937, two Italian neuropsychiatrists, Ugo Ceretti and Lucio Bini, developed the idea of using electricity instead of insulin in convulsive therapy. An observer gave the following description of the first human experiment using ECT:

> They thought, 'Well, we'll try 55 volts, two-tenths of a second. That's not going to do anything terrible to him.' So they did that. [. . .] This fellow —remember, he wasn't even put to sleep —after this major grand mal convulsion, sat right up, looked at these three fellows and said, 'What the fuck are you assholes trying to do?' Well, they were happy as could be, because he hadn't said a rational word in weeks of observation. (20)

Electroshock therapy gradually replaced insulin shock therapy because it was less frightening, more easily controlled, much easier to administer—and, most of all, because it was much cheaper. Through the 1940's and 1950's, ECT became the treatment of choice for serious depression. It is the only form of shock treatment still used by doctors today. For patients suffering from a deep, intractable depression, some psychiatrists see ECT as often the only approach that works.

Nobody knows precisely how and why ECT works, but if we think of depression not as something we *are* or something we *have* but as something we *do*, then ECT could make sense—and so might insulin shock and even the shock of falling into icy pond water. Since depression involves an active blocking of feelings, a potentially life-threatening shock to the body may function as a circuit breaker, disrupting habitual patterns of thinking at the neurological level, breaking the vicious cycle in which objection to some feelings (repression) leads to a global muting of all feeling (depression) and thus allowing dammed up emotion to flow again. (If I'm struggling not to drown in freezing water, I need to be using all my life energy to survive! I can't afford to allocate any of it to the usual work of repression.)

ECT has very serious side effects, however, including long-term memory loss. Dr. Peter Breggin, who has mounted a vocal criticism of ECT for more than 40 years, points out that doctors administering ECT are essentially inflicting a closed-head injury on their patients. Like other forms of head trauma, ECT produces emotional instability, disorientation, confusion and memory dysfunction. Breggin notes, "Long after shock treatment, many patients remain impaired much as if they had been lobotomized. Their personality and emotional life becomes relatively shallow, they are easily irritated, show poor judgment, and lack initiative and self-direction." (21) Obviously, if depression were being more carefully defined as a serious mental illness requiring electroshock as the treatment, physicians would be much more circumspect in handing out the diagnosis of depression to their patients, and there would be far fewer people demanding treatment.

As an intern and resident, I understood firsthand the helplessness that doctors felt when faced with people in serious emotional distress. It was out of this helplessness and frustration that they employed these horrible lobotomies and shock treatments. They yearned for a better solution. In 1956, during my first internship in a mental hospital, it looked like we had finally found it, the elixir that would replace these draconian treatments. They called it Thorazine.

Thorazine (Chlorpromazine) was originally developed in the early 1930's to induce relaxation and indifference in surgical patients. In the late forties it was used as an antihistamine. Then in 1952, a French doctor, Dr. Pierre Deniker, began to administer Thorazine to his psychotic patients. The calming effect was dramatic. The drug was subsequently licensed to Smith Kline & French in the U.S. and by 1954 was being used to treat schizophrenia, mania, and other psychotic disorders. Thorazine rapidly replaced electroconvulsive therapy, pre-frontal lobotomies, and insulin shock therapy as the treatment of choice for depression. Deniker's early description of the effect of Thorazine is worth noting:

Sitting or lying, the patient is motionless in his bed, often pale and with eyelids lowered. He remains silent most of the time. If he is questioned, he answers slowly and deliberately in a monotonous and indifferent voice; he expresses himself in a few words and becomes silent. (22)

These comments accurately describe the hundreds of depressed and delusional men and women I visited in the 1960's who had been prescribed this drug, despite the fact that there was no evidence that Thorazine cured depression or delusions. What it did do was dull the mind and emotions, pushing symptoms into the background. In short, Thorazine was a chemical version of the prefrontal lobotomy. (No ice pick required.). Dr. Peter Sterling, another contemporary psychiatrist, writes:

The blunting of conscious motivation and the inability to solve problems under the influence of Thorazine resembles nothing so much as the effects of frontal lobotomy. Research has suggested that lobotomies and chemicals like chlorpromazine may cause their effects in the same way, by disrupting the activity of the neurochemical dopamine. At any rate, a psychiatrist would be hard put to distinguish a lobotomized patient from one treated with Thorazine. (23)

Like the lobotomy, Thorazine primarily served the interests of the institutional managers, making patients less costly to handle. The economic calculation was clear early on. In *The Tranquilizing of America* (1979), Hughes and Brewin write:

> When used on a large population of institutionalized persons, [it] can help keep the house in order with the minimum program of activities and rehabilitation and the minimum number of attendants, aides, nurses, and doctors. (24)

Another important economic advantage of Thorazine was that it allowed institutions to reduce their workload by releasing chemically lobotomized psychotics into the general population. I believe this mass deinstitutionalization reduced the number of patients in psychiatric hospitals and resulted in *increasing* the number of "street people"

As a young intern and resident in a large state mental institution in the 1960's, I witnessed this cynical process. And I witnessed the increasing reliance on psychiatric pharmacology as well. The drugs dulled the patients' suffering but offered them nothing else, no greater understanding of the complexity of their problems, no insight into their personalities, thoughts, intentions, imaginations, hopes, or dreams. Thorazine transformed troubled (and *troubling*) people into tractable objects to be counted, warehoused, and forgotten.

Two observations from those early years of my career are relevant here. First, there were no children in these mental hospitals. I don't even remember any adolescents, although there may have been one or two. Back then, moodiness was considered normal in children and teenagers. Children were expected to have fits of rage, periods of despondency, even morbid fascination with death. None of this was seen as pathological. Indeed, I had experienced these mood swings myself, as perhaps you have as well. When I was ten, I spent the summer with my grandmother in the mountains of Virginia. For the entire first week, I felt so homesick I wanted to die. Despite my grandmother's loving attention and the beautiful surroundings, I was overwhelmed by dark feelings of estrangement and abandonment. No one suggested that I needed to be medicated, however. Boys and girls get homesick when they're away from home. It was to be expected. In those days before Paxil and Prozac, emotional tumult was synonymous with adolescence: extreme mood swings, uncontrolled crying, irrational anger, and suicidal thoughts when one was rejected by a girlfriend or boyfriend. Caring parents responded to these dramatic mood shifts by setting aside time to talk to their children—and to *listen* to them—providing support and a safe space for the expression of strong feelings. Today, parents are less likely to listen and more likely to act. Magazine articles and ads provide checklists of "dangerous signs" (provided by the drug industry) against which parents are to measure their children's moods. Feelings are no longer just feelings that come and go; they are seen as inevitable precursors of behavior (dark feelings = suicidal actions). The once-normal emotional displays of adolescence are marked as symptoms of mental illness by the DSM. In this context, it is not surprising that too many children under 18 are being prescribed antidepressants.

The horror here is that the *use* of antidepressants can turn normal childhood and adolescent emotional experiences into a form of chronic illness. As Peter Breggin, Robert Whitaker, and others have documented, the addictive nature of antidepressants means that medicated children may have to continue to take drugs, perhaps for the rest of their lives, in order to maintain even a semblance of normal functioning.

The second observation that my colleagues and I made in the 1960's about our depressed patients was that most of them were women. The ratio improved in later years, as women began to support each other in making liberated life choices. At the time, however, it was clear to us that women felt more trapped relationally than did men. The degree to which pre-liberation women needed to repress feelings of helplessness, frustration, and resentment of unfair treatment would astound most young people today for whom gender equality is a shared value, at least in the US. (There are still many places in the world today where gender *inequality* is alive and well, of course.) In the mental hospital, many of these seriously depressed women showed rather rapid improvement soon after admission, particularly in group therapy where they received support and validation for their feelings from other women who had experienced similar marital stress and abuse. However, once they returned to their husbands, they soon regressed, adopting the same pattern of pushing down feelings to avoid the painful conflict that resulted when they tried to confront their abusive mates. These relapses were devastating but understandable. As one of my young colleagues remarked about a much-abused female patient: "I would be depressed as hell, too, if I had to live with that domineering bastard!"

Like others who began their clinical practice in the 1960's, I had been influenced by Adolph Meyer. Meyer obtained an M.D. in neurology in Zurich in 1892, then immediately emigrated to the United States where he eventually became known as "the dean of American psychiatry." His *Commonsense Psychiatry* (1948) became the standard of treatment for the first half of the twentieth century and defined what my colleagues and I accepted as fundamental in our approach to suffering individuals: Take a detailed history of the patient's life; note any physical illnesses and medications; get a family and social history with special attention to the significant others that influenced the client's personality development; document sexual history and any incidents of abuse, work history and hobbies and avocational interests—in short, acquire as much information as possible, anything and everything that might help us understand this person and provide insight into the causes of her distress. Some of us still take it for granted that this is the only proper way to approach a patient with emotional problems. However, by the 1950's, Meyer's *Commonsense Psychiatry* was already being replaced—in fact, obliterated.

Other things were happening as well. The original *Diagnostic and Statistical Manual* (DSM) we had been using since 1952 was being revised. It appeared in l968 as the DSM-II. Reading through the new DSM, my fellow residents and I became concerned about what seemed to be a significant philosophical shift in how our patients were being viewed. The diagnostic descriptor "Schizophrenic reaction" had overnight become a *disease* called "Schizophrenia." Several of us who were enrolled at the Washington School of Psychiatry had been exploring the relational aspects of this "schizophrenic reaction." We were intensely involved with our patients and their families, following the guidance of our teacher and mentor, Dr. Harry Stack Sullivan. Sullivan insisted that we define "functional schizophrenia" as a reaction to profound and constant crazy-making relationships in which the client's Significant Other habitually transmitted feelings that were completely counter to the Other's words and behavior. E.g., the mother of one of my "schizophrenic" patients would tell him, "Of course, I love you" with such obvious hostility that one would cringe. This hostility was confirmed by the records. In private, she had told the attending psychiatrist, "he was an unwanted child, and he ruined my life." She visited every Sunday and brought cookies.

The DSM-II undermined Sullivan's approach, obliterating his insight that a troubled person could be having a schizophrenic *reaction* to relational craziness. The patient's distress became a *disease* inside the person who was now seen as *having schizophrenia*. Not surprisingly, this formulation soon mutated into the essentialist concept that a group of people exist who *are* schizophrenics. Almost overnight, a contextual reaction had become a genetic label. The dehumanization of these deeply troubled people was complete.

Dehumanization made it easy to dismiss the suffering of patients and simply warehouse them. By definition, they were incurable. When Congress passed a law mandating that all patients be seen at least once a year by a psychiatrist, the federal mental hospital where I worked, St. Elizabeth's, went into a panic about how to comply. By that time, I had already chosen to work with a group of profoundly troubled men who had been forgotten in the back wards for decades. Their official diagnosis shifted over the years, as fads came and went; initially, it was "dementia praecox with psychosis," deemed to be an incurable degenerative condition from which nobody recovered. After the DSM-II appeared, they became hopeless "schizophrenics." Either way, it didn't matter much: they were crazy. For long periods of time, they remained in a catatonic state, utterly unmoving, unresponsive. Periodically, they would cycle into a manic mode in which they would talk excitedly but in a disconnected fashion that nobody could follow. (We called it "word salad.") Then back to catatonia. Most of the senior staff viewed them as unreachable.

But I *did* reach them. Applying Sullivan's insight that it is crazy relationships that make crazy people, not some mysterious inherent illness, I reached out to these men on their own terms, trying to understand the logic of their reactions to their circumstances. I learned that they were unusually sensitive individuals who lacked the "proper defenses" to deny, suppress, and repress feelings of hurt, helplessness, and abandonment. Each of them in different ways had grown up in a world of unloved estrangement, and they lived in that world now, locked up in the darkness with only Thorazine to keep them company. Observing (accurately) that nobody cared what they felt, they tuned out completely, the only way they could survive the craziness of the environment in which they found themselves. From the new diagnostic perspective in the DSM-II, these men's experiences had no basis in reality. In fact, they were suffering from authentic problems of the soul, problems that needed to be addressed by empathetic psychologists.

The medicalization of depression and other emotional problems has been so completely successful that most people today cannot imagine that insight-oriented psychotherapy could have the slightest effect on severe "mental illness." The *On Line Medical Dictionary* defines "functional psychosis" as "an obsolete term once used to define schizophrenia . . . before modern science discovered a biological component to some aspects of [this] disorder." In the next chapter, I will show how faulty this "science" has been.

Working from Dr. Harry Stack Sullivan's perspective, and with the cooperation of an enlightened psychiatric supervisor who reduced my patients' Thorazine, over a period of two years I became intensely involved with twelve of the hospital's most severely troubled men, all of whom thought they were Jesus Christ—except when they thought they were shit (literally). All of them had been hospitalized for at least fifteen years, most in locked down wards. Seven of these men eventually left the hospital, got jobs, and formed significant relationships.

Were these men still a little bit "crazy" even after their release from the hospital? Yes, but they were no longer a danger to themselves or to others; and a lot of their residual craziness was simply an expression of their extreme sensitivity. (Had they been musicians like Mahler, their "divine frenzy" would have made for some beautiful music!) One of my men, Ben, had worked in the hospital laundry and got a job in a commercial laundry after he was released. The proprietor, Joe, understood he was hiring a former patient, and I agreed to be in touch if needed. One day Joe called me to say he was concerned about Ben, so I went over to talk. He told me that Ben had arrived the previous morning in an agitated state, scared that "the sky was about to fall." Ben told Joe that he had been enjoying the walk to work—it was beautiful spring day, and the birds were singing. Then, all of a sudden the birds flew to the ground and hid. That's when Ben got very scared because he thought something was happening to the sky. It was clear from Joe's face as he told me the story that he thought Ben was having a psychotic episode. Joe and I sat in silence for a little, and then I said quietly, "I'm not sure about this, but I know Ben is a highly sensitive person who easily picks up on the feelings of other people. It might be that he picks up on the feelings of birds, too. As an amateur ornithologist, I've often observed the behavior of smaller birds, like wood warblers, when they become aware of a hawk entering the area. Most of the time we don't see the hawk until later, but hawks feed on these smaller birds, and they sense its presence immediately and flee to the ground and hide. Could it be that Ben is feeling the fear of these birds?" Joe respected me enough not to laugh, but the look on his face told me that he was thinking that I had become as crazy as the men I was treating.

And in a sense, I had. That was the secret: I had learned to relate to these men, not analytically as "patients" or "Schizophrenics" or "Depressives" but empathetically as fellow human beings, tuning in to the logic of their experiences from their own point of view. And I had learned this secret from the men themselves, a process that I will explore more fully in Chapter Five when I tell the story of the craziest, and wisest, of these Jesus Men, the catatonic "Mr. H."

There is a wry footnote to my tale of enlightened craziness. In my youthful zeal, I had completely missed the obvious symbolism of my choosing exactly 12 of these men to "save." But the crazy men didn't miss it. Sometime in the early months of my interaction with them, one of them said something, in "word salad" group-speak, indicating that he was aware of how comfortable I was in the group, and that he was comfortable, too, because I seemed to identify with what he was experiencing. I thought he was complementing me on my empathetic understanding, but the spontaneous laughter this elicited within the group gave me pause. I didn't get the joke until I was on the way home. "Holy shit!" I screamed, nearly running the car off the road. I had gotten twelve men together to save. "Holy shit" indeed: I *was* one of "them."

And yet, of course, I wasn't, not quite. I was on the outside. Five of "my men," though much improved, were still on the inside. And for them, the handwriting was already on the wall. These exquisitely sensitive, intensely suffering people—and thousands of others like them—were going to be abandoned by the society that had created them. The insight-oriented therapy that I, and others were practicing actually worked, often dramatically; but it took an immense amount of sensitive personal involvement and careful listening to feelings—in short, an immense amount of time. And time is money. As I was ending my residency and going off into private practice, the complete sell-out of the back ward patients had already begun: they were going to be drugged into dead-end quiescence and hidden behind high brick walls as part of a plan to sell drugs to a much larger population of Americans outside the walls. People who thought they were normal were going to discover that they had a dangerous "chemical imbalance of the brain."

Fig. 6 St. Elizabeth's Hospital, c. 1909-1932

CHAPTER TWO

"BAD" FEELINGS BECOME A DISEASE

"If I weren't the way I am, I shouldn't write my symphonies."

-Gustav Mahler (1)

WHAT WE WERE EXPERIENCING at St. Elizabeth's was only the beginning. My approach to the Jesus Men flowed from my training in insight-oriented psychotherapy, grounded in existential philosophy. By 1970, however, a group of psychiatrists—medical doctors specializing in mental disorders—had become increasingly successful in defining all forms of emotional distress, including transitory depression, as a mental *illness* that could be treated only by a physician. This ruled out all psychologists, clinical social workers, nurses and others with special training, regardless of their ability to heal emotional distress. It also ruled out any understanding that emotional distress was rooted in the intricacies of human relationships. Within the American Psychiatric Association itself, the emerging field of biopsychiatry gained dominance. Its basic tenet—that mental "illness" was caused by bad brain chemistry—had obvious appeal, especially for those who had little patience with the complexities of emotional life and wanted to maintain a scientific distance from the Sick People they treated. These psychiatrists found a comfortable place in pharmacology which, over the next decades, offered a dazzling array of new magic bullet cures. Even psychiatrists who had previously been more caring began to change. As Dr. Marcia Angell notes, once they began to refer to themselves as psychopharmacologists, they had less and less interest in exploring the life stories of their patients. (2)

The notion that depression and other forms of emotional distress are caused by "bad brain chemistry" sounds scientific, but it is not. As every student of science learns early on, *congruence does not establish causation*. That two phenomena are observed together does not prove which causes which. From the beginning, biopsychiatrists have fundamentally ignored this most basic of scientific principles. In the early 1970's, my colleagues and I were disturbed when a small group of psychiatrists using neuroimaging blithely concluded that disturbances in the brains of my "schizophrenic" men were what was causing their troubles. The problem with this approach is obvious, I protested: How do you know that it is not the emotional travail these troubled people are experiencing that is causing the disturbances you are observing in their troubled brains? Scientifically, either possibility could be true. To decide where the truth lies, one needs to evaluate all the data available. Biopsychiatrists failed here as well, systematically discarding all observed data about life issues and relational trauma that (using Occam's razor) rather easily explains much of what was happening inside these "schizophrenic" psyches. Priding itself on transcending the unscientific theories of Freud and Jung, biopsychiatry was (and is) fundamentally unscientific in its most basic assumptions about causality.

One might as well join the Flat Earth Society and ignore the observed data that the earth is round.

The biopsychiatric/psychopharmacological approach to emotional stress thrived not because it was so effective or scientific but because, it had an obvious socio-economic appeal: it was quick and therefore cheap. Psychoanalysis/psychotherapy was neither. As US healthcare costs increased, managed-care companies stopped covering the "talking cure," citing the length of treatment and the open-ended nature of the treatment plan, shared only by analyst and patient, which makes this approach impossible to evaluate. Drug companies agreed, not surprisingly. In 1955 alone, Smith, Kline and French made 75 million dollars on Thorazine, (3) and that was only an *appetizer*. The big feeding frenzy was about to begin.

Peter Breggin reports that the American Psychiatric Association made a pact with the drug companies in the early 1970's when the association was in financial crisis. The Board of Directors voted to start taking huge amounts of money from the drug companies in order to stave off bankruptcy. (4) In a recent article in *The New York Review of Books*, Dr. Marcia Angell says that today about a fifth of APA funding comes from the drug companies. (5) The crucial shift in thinking began in 1974 when Columbia University psychiatry professor Robert Spitzer was chosen to chair the task force charged with producing a new version of the *Diagnostic and Statistical Manual*, the DSM-III. This gave Spitzer a golden opportunity to bring all diagnostic categories into compliance with his own biopsychiatric model. In his 2007 book *Shyness:*

How Normal Behavior Became a Disease, Northwestern University professor Christopher Lane gives us a disturbing account of the backroom process that developed the DSM III. (6) Many of us who were practicing insight-oriented psychotherapy suspected that there was a lot was going on behind our backs. Lane confirms those suspicions. Using unpublished documents from the American Psychiatric Association archives, including previously classified memos from drug company executives, and candid interviews with Robert Spitzer, Lane gives us a fly-on-the wall view of what really happened and why. He demonstrates how Spitzer and his team systematically eliminated any reference to the possibility that mental and emotional problems might reflect broad underlying conflicts or maladaptive reactions to relationships or life problems, thus enshrining biopsychiatric psychopharmacology in the diagnostic code.

Spitzer had a somewhat checkered personal history with psychotherapy that may have biased his approach to revising the DSM. His mother had shipped him off to a psychoanalyst when he was only 9 or 10 after he had slapped her. He started full-blown psychoanalysis at 15, an experience that influenced him to become a psychiatrist . . . but not an orthodox Freudian. Spitzer was intrigued by the pseudo-scientific "orgasmotherapy" theories of Wilhelm Reich, centered around a belief in a cosmic life force called "orgone radiation." (Increasingly isolated and eccentric, near the end of his life Reich believed he was fighting a war with aliens from his Orgone Energy Observatory in rural Maine.) Spitzer dutifully trained as a Reichian analyst and attempted to do research following Reich's model but became disillusioned, despite Reich's personal assurance that the problems he was encountering were being caused by fallout from the atomic bomb. Even more importantly perhaps, Spitzer was uncomfortable with the personal interaction between therapist and client that Reich insisted on, including physical contact. (7) (After the DSM-III, the only physical gestures required of a psychiatrist would be delivering the prescription and a firm handshake.)

Rejecting Reich, Spitzer turned violently away from the entire psychoanalytic tradition that had spawned him, throwing out the baby with the bath water, one might argue. He gravitated instead to the work of Victorian psychiatrist Emil Kraepelin who spent his life systematically identifying and charting all mental diseases that he believed had biological cause. As Lane reports, in a typical example from his *Lectures on Clinical Psychiatry*, Kraepelin documents a case of melancholia in a 59-year old farmer, a married father of four, who had been admitted to a psychiatric hospital.

> His expression is dejected . . . He usually stares in front of him, but he glances up when he is spoken to. On being questioned about his illness, he breaks into lamentations, saying that he did not tell the whole truth on his admission, but concealed the fact that he had fallen into sin in his youth and practiced uncleanness with himself: everything he did was wrong. (8)

For Kraepelin, the proof that the farmer was exhibiting the "morbid disease of melancholia" with "physical foundations" is that his symptoms had lasted for months with increasing severity.

> It is true that the patient himself refers to the sins of his youth as the cause of the apprehension, but it is clear that, even if they were ever really committed, they did not particularly disturb him *before his illness*; his conscience has only awakened now. (9)

Because he can discount the man's *own* psychological explanation for his symptoms of depression—i.e., that he is being punished by the devil for having masturbated—Kraepelin jumps to the conclusion that there is no psychological/emotional basis for the man's distress and that, therefore, his melancholia is a biologically-based illness.

Freud started out in the same place as Kraepelin but soon began to see the limitations of this biological approach. The more he understood the complexity of the human psyche, the more he realized that relational factors, along with unconscious mental content, determined the symptoms that Kraepelin was cataloguing. In my own education and professional training, Kraepelin was treated as an interesting early figure in psychiatry, but his examples of "mental diseases" were dismissed as seriously flawed because they never addressed, much less defined, what was *normal* or *abnormal* in the symptoms he listed. In rehabilitating Kraepelin's Victorian approach to taxonomy, Spitzer and his task force were, in effect, turning back the clock, making an end run around Freud and all insight-oriented psychotherapies, as if the legacy and carefully documented clinical experience of the last hundred years had never existed.

In Kraepelin-like fashion, Spitzer's revisions of the DSM purposely redefined mental illness by symptom groups, without ever having established what is normal and what is abnormal. The DSM-III requires the clinician to recognize the difference between normal states and abnormal symptoms solely by degree and by duration. Ironically, although the DSM-III was promoted as a modern replacement for antiquated non-scientific Freudian views, its own subjectivity in this crucial matter makes a mockery of the scientific method. Lane cites one particularly astonishing example in which Spitzer's taskforce decided that a particular set of symptoms must go on for at least two weeks before being classifiable as a mental illness. Why two weeks? "Well, because it looks more 'scientific.'"(10)

The reductio ad absurdum of this approach is a 2001 letter written by four psychiatrists to *Archives of General Psychiatry* in which they argue, semi-seriously, that the Biblical figure Samson (think Victor Mature) suffered from "antisocial personality disorder" (ASPD) because he met six out of seven criteria for the disorder, as defined in the DSM. (Only three of seven are required to confirm a diagnosis.) "It's pretty straightforward, pretty cut and dried," said Dr. Eric Altschuler, the lead author. "The study of the history of a disease can provide clues to its pathogenesis."(11) As Lane points out, however, this symptom-based diagnosis misses a few important contextual details—details that define the difference between a mysterious pathology and an understandable human reaction to life's blows:

> Now it's true that Samson didn't exactly plan ahead or 'conform to social norms.' His 'irritability and aggressiveness' also resulted in a 'reckless disregard for safety of self and others,' all of these being criteria in the DSM. But the Philistines had gouged out his eyes after Delilah repeatedly betrayed him—factors the scientists either didn't know or conveniently overlooked. You might think that having one's eyes gouged out after betrayal by a loved one would be enough reason to express a certain amount of fury. (12)

Clinical psychologists and many psychiatrists as well, objected strongly to the assumptions that had produced the DSM-III. "The poverty of thought that went into the decision-making process was frightening," said Renee Garfinkel of the American Psychological Association. (13) Lane continues, "When one leading psychiatrist was asked to define how he was using the term 'masochistic' during a meeting about its possible inclusion as a personality disorder, he replied: 'Oh, you know what I mean, a whiny individual . . . the Jewish mother type.'" Additionally, Leonore Walker, another psychologist said: "I couldn't believe my eyes, here were professional people making decisions based on feelings or impressions, not facts.

In some cases, the people revising DSM-III [were] making a mental illness out of adaptive behavior."(14)

The DSM-III's pathologizing of normal human variance was particularly apparent in regard to a subject that will assume considerable importance in the second half of *Overcoming Depression*: introversion . . . what Lane refers to as shyness. Initially, Spitzer wanted to define introversion as a mental illness. As might have been expected, there were howls of objection, to which Spitzer was heard to comment: "There are more Jungians in this country than I had realized."(15) When the objections continued, Spitzer reluctantly agreed to drop the term he had proposed, "Introverted Personality Disorder," substituting instead the term "Schizoid Personality Disorder." Because "Schizoid Personality Disorder" might need to be distinguished from something more morbid, Spitzer and his crew also invented a new category: "Schizoaffective Personality Disorder"—more of the same but worse. All that remained was to agree on a term other than "introverted" to describe behavior that all the participants agreed was "introversion."

This was a particularly perplexing part of the DSM-III for me. As psychology residents, we had been assigned the task of finding our nearest likely fit in the classification of mental disorders. Pouring over Arieti's three volumes, I could eliminate *psychosis*. I did not believe I was out of touch with any reality that mattered. I could get past *neurosis*, since I was confident that my therapist was enough of a resource in that arena. *Personality Disorder* seemed more likely, because, I figured whatever disorder I had should have something to do with who I was as a person. Of possible personality disorders, *Schizoid* seemed the best fit, particularly as the term was used in those humanistic days before the DSM-III: it simply meant a person whose default position in life was independence and who valued time alone. Such people choose to relate to others, if possible, only when the relationship is authentic and meaningful. They have a strong aversion to meaningless social chitchat and superficial social relationships. Not a very alarming orientation, it seemed to me. After Spitzer got through with it, however, *Schizoid* became positively pathological. It was as if a gestalt switch had been flipped on the Rubin vase, and the two human faces had disappeared, leaving only an object. Personality types were now symptoms of disease.

In this respect and many others, the process of creating the DSM-III was a triumph of Groupthink. Although there were some slight concessions on turf areas here and there, Lane shows how Spitzer and his fellow biopsychiatrists reached consensus by the simple expedient of leaving out all dissenters. Dr. Paul Fink, then-chair of psychiatry at Thomas Jefferson University, fumed: "I do not know who determined that this small group of people should try to reorganize psychiatric thinking in the United States, but I am somewhat concerned that they have such an arrogant view of their mission and are not willing to incorporate some of the things which we have learned over the past 70 years."(16) In fact, it turns out Dr. Fink was being too kind. Almost overnight, the DSM-III was successful in obliterating an entire century of clinical practice and thought about mental and emotional distress and it was successful in excluding all insight-oriented psychotherapy as valid treatment for people in emotional distress.

Over the years in my struggle to place my clients in the diagnostic pigeonholes that insurance companies will accept, I have looked in vain to the DSM for help. Introversion among artists poses particular problems. There is nothing in the DSM to authorize psychotherapy for troubled, sensitive people who are struggling to understand their need to withdraw from meaningless social intercourse on the one hand, and, on the other hand, to support the dramatic swings of mood so essential to their creativity—mood swings that were, after the DSM-III, regarded as symptoms of *bipolar disorder*. The closest fit in the DSM is the diagnosis of "Social Avoidance Personality Disorder," but that label carries with it the assumption of *brain dysfunction*, for which the treatment of choice is no longer psychotherapy. As Peter Breggin says often, "the DSM succeeds in separating those in need from those they need."

The big winner in this process was not Robert Spitzer, of course. It was the US pharmaceutical industry. The drug companies had been openly backing the DSM-III revisions from the start, for obvious reasons: if Spitzer could roll a bunch of symptoms up into a disease, then they could compound a pill to treat the disease (i.e., the symptoms)—a pill that *any* doctor could prescribe. The process worked even better if Spitzer and his team found pathology in emotional states/symptoms that the drug companies could *already* alter with the pills they had in stock. Which is exactly what happened on more than one occasion. Years later, Spitzer told Lane,

They (Upjohn) were delighted that we had the category panic disorder, because they felt they had a drug for it . . . . When I later steered the interview toward the future approval of other disorders in the DSM, he conceded quite matter-of-factly that such an outcome was partly "a function of 'Do you have a treatment?' If you have no treatment for it, there's not as much pressure to put the thing in. (17)

The drug companies were quite open about what they wanted from the psychiatric community. At one Boston conference, the chief executive of Upjohn introduced his presentation by saying, "Look, there are three reasons why Upjohn is here (and paying for this conference) taking an interest in these diagnoses. The first is money. The second is money. And the third is money."(18)

They got what they paid for. Since 1974, the pharmaceutical industry has made billions of dollars on antidepressants alone. The profits from the sale of these psychopharmacological drugs have, in turn, funded a hugely successful mass media campaign to convince the public that intense feelings are dangerous and that pills are safe—that sadness is caused by brain dysfunction—which these wonderful drugs can cure. Nobody has to feel sad any more. This widespread belief has, in turn, affected clinical practice. Even though the DSM-IV-TR of 2000, attempting to correct earlier laxity, stresses that there needs to be "clinically significant distress or impairment in social, occupational or other important areas of functioning" before a diagnosis of pathology can be made, this judgment remains subjective. What is normal and what is abnormal often gets lost when the physician is presented with a suffering person demanding a quick pharmacological solution. Pressed for time by the strictures of managed care that limit the length of each consultation and pressed as well by feelings of helplessness in the face of pain and despair, a doctor who would otherwise be more scrupulous about his Hippocratic Oath ("do no harm") can all too easily give in and prescribe a drug like Paxil to alleviate apparent symptoms of depression, despite the fact that the drug often leads to "self-harm or harm to others" as well as emotional lability, hostility, aggression, impotence, insomnia, anxiety about public bathrooms, and fear of being criticized—all of which, the TV drug advertisements inform us, are *symptoms* of depression!

The drug companies haven't persuaded everybody, of course. Nor has psychotherapy entirely disappeared. (I have had a thriving practice for the last 40 years!) Indeed, a cognitive-behavioral form of psychotherapy, originally developed by Dr Albert Ellis in the 1950's, has made something of a comeback recently, largely by marketing itself as "evidence-based." The US Department of Veterans Affairs uses cognitive-behavioral therapy to treat what the DSM calls "post traumatic stress disorder" . . . but with several important caveats: psychotherapy is generally used as an *adjunct* to antidepressant medication, despite the fact that,

> According to emerging evidence, patients with PTSD symptoms tend to prefer psychotherapy treatment over medication when given a choice. (19)

Moreover, treatment is limited in duration (usually 12 weeks) and focused almost entirely on behavioral coping (e.g. "anger management or stress management"). Like the purges at the Kellogg's Battle Creek sanitarium or Dr. Freeman's ice pick, the goal of modern medication and cognitive management alike is to *get rid* of intense "emotional disturbances" rather than to move *with* and *through* troubling feelings to a place of greater emotional insight and satisfaction. That kind of psychotherapy—a rich interactive listening process that the therapist and client weave together over a period of years—still exists; because it is not covered by medical insurance, however, it is available only to people who have sufficient means to pay for it themselves. In effect, we have come full circle, back to the 18th century when the upper and middle classes can navigate through their "storms of murk" in the equivalent of the Quakers' York Retreat while the poor and foreign born are dumped into the pharmaceutical equivalent of Bedlam.

CHAPTER THREE
OBJECTING TO FEELINGS:
THE ANTIDEPRESSANT FIX

People wish to be settled; only as they are unsettled is there any hope for them.—Ralph Waldo Emerson

"Few Americans are aware that the 'chemical imbalance' theory is purposely promoted by drug companies in order to further a drug-based approach to treating mental problems. Few are aware of the permanent brain damage and other long-term health effects we now know result from taking mind drugs. Few are aware that, among drug researchers, job promotions, tenure, grants and intimidation are all factors which encourage faith in one of the most harmful lies ever to become widely believed—Timothy Scott, *America Fooled*

"IT'S AN OLD STORY," Barbara Ehrenreich explains with a wink. "If you want to sell something, first find the terrible affliction that it cures"—

In the 1980's, as silicone implants were taking off, the doctors discovered "micromastia"—the 'disease' of small-breastedness. More recently, as big pharma searches furiously for a female Viagra, an amazingly high 43 percent of women have been found to suffer from "Female Sexual Dysfunction," or FSD. (1)

For the last thirty years, the most terrible of the Terrible Afflictions has been sadness, repackaged by the DSM-III in five flavors: *adjustment disorder with depressed mood, bipolar depression, major depression, dysthymic disorder,* and *atypical depression.* These terms sound like the names of diseases, but they are not, any more than a fever is a disease. They are simply conveniently labeled groups of symptoms, each with its own diagnostic checklist. *New Yorker* writer Louis Menand explains:

> If you have a fever, the doctor runs some tests in order to find out what your problem is. The tests, not the fever, identify the disease. The tests determine, in fact, that there is a disease. In the case of mood disorders, it is difficult to find a test to distinguish mental illness from normal mood changes. The brains of people who are suffering from mild depression look the same on a scan as the brains of people whose football team has just lost the Super Bowl. They even look the same as the brains of people who have been asked to think sad thoughts. (2)

This crucial issue was largely ignored in the flurry that followed the publication of the DSM-III in February 1980—February being an especially appropriate month since the radically revised DSM was an essentially a Valentine's gift from the academic psychiatric community to the pharmaceutical industry. Almost overnight, intuitive diagnosis and insight psychotherapy were replaced by code-driven psychopharmacology: SYMPTOM: "sadness most of the day, nearly every day, for two weeks." DIAGNOSIS: DSM—III code 309.00. TREATMENT: fluoxetine . . . better known as Prozac. The Era of Antidepressants had arrived. (3)

Before the Era of Antidepressants, US consumers had been through a thirty-year Age of Anxiety for which the universal cure was the tranquilizer—Miltown, then Librium and Valium—all marketed directly to potential users who, breaking with earlier tradition, now entered their doctor's offices with the names of the drugs they wanted already in their hands. In 1955, Carter-Wallace began selling meprobamate as an anti-anxiety drug under the brand name Miltown—"the first psychotropic blockbuster and the fastest-selling drug in U.S. history."

> Within a year, one out of every twenty Americans had taken Miltown; within two years, a billion tablets had been manufactured. By the end of the decade, Miltown and Equanil . . . accounted for a third of all prescriptions written by American physicians. These drugs were eclipsed in the nineteen-sixties by . . . Librium and Valium . . . Between 1968 and 1981, Valium was the most frequently prescribed medication in the Western world. In 1972, stock in its manufacturer, Hoffmann-La Roche, traded at seventy-three thousand dollars a share. (4)

All thanks to DSM diagnostic code 300.00 (*generalized anxiety disorder*).

Patients who had strong objections to some of their feelings were supported in their objection and reassured that they need not move toward any uncomfortable places in their emotional lives. Checklist based diagnosis and prescription made life easier for doctors, eliminating ambiguity and complexity and giving them time to see more patients. More patients per doctor-hour were exactly what insurance companies wanted, so they were big winners, too.

This tranquilizer gravy train threatened to derail in 1961 when it became clear that Thalidomide, an all-purpose sedative/tranquilizer, had caused over 10,000 tragic birth defects worldwide. By the time Robert Spitzer began work on the DSM-III, US tranquilizers were under attack, the subject of high-profile congressional hearings. It had become clear that tranquilizers (benzodiazepines) as a class were much more dangerous than the American public had been told and much more highly addictive. In 1980, the year the DSM-III appeared, the FDA required that tranquilizers begin carrying a warning, including the statement that "anxiety or tension associated with the stress of everyday life usually does not require treatment with an anxiolytic."(5)

The pharmaceutical industry had a survival strategy already in the works, however. Spitzer and the DSM-III taskforce did the crucial groundwork by expanding the definition of the term "depression"—i.e. *narrowing* the definition of what is "normal." And that leads us to the other half of the drug company survival strategy: "rebranding." In a recent interview with *Salon*, Robert Whitaker explains this concept from the industry point of view:

> We have this market of people who feel discomfort in their lives, which we used to call anxiety. If we can rebrand it as depression, then we can bring a new antidepressant to market. (6)

Enter Prozac.

Antidepressants had been around for decades, but until the tranquilizer market crashed, the general public knew little about them. The reasons for this are instructive and deserve some attention. In 1951, an article appeared in *Life* magazine about the success of two new miracle drugs from Hoffman-La Roche (isoniazid and iproniazid) in treating tuberculosis. Noting that the drugs had a stimulating psychological effect, in 1952 psychiatrists Max Lurie and Harry Salzer began using isoniazid to treat patients suffering from depression. (Lurie probably coined the term *antidepressant*.) Similar experiments took place in France. However, because depression (as it was defined in the pre-DSM-III era) was regarded as a relatively *rare* condition, affecting perhaps only 50 out of every 1 million people—initially the big drug companies were not very interested in antidepressants. (7) They were much more concerned with marketing their new class of anti-anxiety drugs which were bringing in billions and reshaping Americas' views about "negative emotions." Once the addictive nature of tranquilizers became public knowledge and sales began to drop, the pharmaceutical industry changed course rapidly. Many of the antidepressants that began to appear after 1980 might have been marketed as anti-anxiety drugs in an earlier era, a use for which they are often prescribed today, "off label." But tranquilizers had acquired a bad reputation, so the industry shifted its focus to a new Terrible Affliction, systematically enlarging the definition, scope, and severity of the neglected illness known as *depression.*

Antidepressants became the gold standard treatment for depression, along with Electric Shock Treatments if the depression was deemed truly serious. By 2000, the American Psychiatric Association *Practice Guideline for the Treatment of Patients with Major Depressive Disorder* had begun recommending the use of antidepressant medications for patients with even relatively mild symptoms. Then, in an effort to enlarge the market further, the concept of subclinical depression was invented to justify prescribing antidepressants to people who did not meet the standard criteria for major depressive disorder. As Dr. Marcia Angell noted recently, this was part of an ongoing effort to expand the criteria for mental illness so that, eventually, nearly everyone can be defined as needing psychotropic medication. (8).

By 2008, ten of the fifty most prescribed drugs in the United States were "antidepressants." In *one* year in the U.S., 2008, there were 26.3 million prescriptions of Lexapro written, grossing $2,410,000,000. There were 16.9 million prescriptionsofEffexor,grossing2.66billiondollars;Sertraline, 29.5 million prescriptions, 648 million dollars; Floxitine, 23.3

million prescriptions, 349 million dollars; Citalopram, 21.6 million prescriptions, 260 million dollars; and Trazodone, 16.7 million prescriptions, 140 million dollars. Mysteriously, the number of people afflicted with a hitherto-fore *rare* form of mental illness (depression) had almost doubled in a single decade, reaching 27 million by 2005 and still climbing. (9)

Today, over 30 million people in the US alone, one in every ten Americans, are taking prescription antidepressants. Every one of those 30 million people has a right to assume—and presumably *does* assume—that the drugs they are putting into their bodies are proven, appropriate, effective, and safe from serious side effects. Otherwise, the FDA surely would not authorize their use nor would the APA and DSM advise doctors to prescribe them. And, indeed, at first glance there seems to be an enormous body of scientific evidence—thousands of double blind clinical trials—that supports the efficacy and safety of antidepressants, individually and as a class. If we look closer, however, cracks start to appear in the facade of this psychopharmacological belief system. Like the DSM-III, which is much less rigorously scientific that it purports to be, the evidence in favor of antidepressants is surprisingly thin and fragile.

The story I am going to relate in the next few pages has become fairly well known in the last few years, the subject of more than a dozen recent books that reflect the growing sense in this country that the US pharmaceutical industry is not to be trusted with our lives and happiness. It is a story is worth retelling, however, because so many people are at risk—and because everything I am going to say later about what *works* in treating depression depends on a clear understanding of what *doesn't* work, and why.

Over the last 30 years, the pharmaceutical industry, in concert with the psychiatric community, has aggressively promoted the notion that depression is caused by an inadequate supply of certain neurotransmitters in the human brain, especially serotonin, and that a class of drugs called selective serotonin reuptake inhibitors (SSRIs) corrects this problem, thus curing depression. Careful examination of the scientific evidence, however, suggests that there is little support for either of these claims. (10) For one thing, drugs that *lower* serotonin levels do *not* lower mood. (11) Dr. David D. Burns, an award-winning Stanford psychiatric researcher, summarizes the dissident view:

> I spent the first several years of my career doing full-time research on brain serotonin metabolism, but I never saw any convincing evidence that any psychiatric disorder, including depression, results from a deficiency of brain serotonin. In fact, we cannot measure brain serotonin levels in living human beings so there is no way to test this theory. Some neuroscientists would question whether the theory is even viable, since the brain does not function in this way, as a hydraulic system. (12)

Another psychiatrist, Dr. Grace E. Jackson, says that in reality no psychiatric disorder is demonstrable or diagnosable by brain scans or any other medical or biological means and that "depression is an episodic phenomenon that has been turned into a lifelong disease by pharmacology" (*Rethinking Psychiatric Drugs*). Peter Breggin makes an even stronger case: "At present, there are no known biochemical imbalances in the brain of typical psychiatric patients—until they are given psychiatric drugs." (13) That is, instead of developing a drug to treat an abnormality, pharmacology has defined a pathology to fit a drug. As Dr. Marcia Angell points out, it is entirely possible that drugs affecting neurotransmitters levels can relieve symptoms, even if the neurotransmitters had nothing to do with the condition in the first place. On that basis, one could argue that fevers are caused by too little aspirin. (14) Irish psychiatrist David Healy puts the whole neurotransmitter issue even more bluntly: "The serotonin theory of depression is comparable to the masturbation theory of insanity." (15)

The theory of "bad brain chemistry dates back to a 1965 article by Harvard medical school psychopharmacologist Joseph Schildkraut. Although his paper has been widely cited as proof of the theory, Schildkraut himself, writing in 1978, was much more cautious:

> Even in 1965, it was clearly recognized that abnormalities in catecholamine metabolism alone could not conceivably account for all of the diverse clinical and biological phenomena in all types of affective disorders. Thus, in my review, I stressed that this hypothesis was 'at best a reductionistic oversimplification of a very complex biological

state' that undoubtedly involved many other biochemical abnormalities . . . as well as physiological and psychological factors. (16)

Scientific qualifications of this sort were carefully removed in the promotional materials that, beginning in 1980, relentlessly marketed SSRIs to doctors and, directly, to the general public. More importantly, the pharmaceutical industry and the academic researchers who conduct clinical trials (often *supported by* the pharmaceutical industry and occasionally even "ghost-written" by them) systematically colluded in suppressing the mounting evidence that, in most cases, antidepressants are little more effective than placebos (sugar pills) in relieving depression that antidepressants have frequent, serious side effects—including, paradoxically, suicidal depression; and that they create long-term addiction, trapping users in a permanent pharmacological hell. Writing in 2007 in *The New York Review of Books*, Frederick Crews summarizes the situation thus:

> . . . the drug firms were pushing a simplistic "biobabble" myth whereby depression supposedly results straightforwardly from a shortfall of the neurotransmitter serotonin in the brain. No such causation has been established, and the proposal is no more reasonable than claiming that headaches arise from aspirin deprivation. But by insistently urging this idea upon physicians and the public, Big Pharma widened its net for recruiting patients, who could be counted upon to reason

as follows: "I feel bad; I must lack serotonin in my brain; these serotonin-boosting pills will surely do the trick." Thus millions of people who might have needed only counseling were exposed to incompletely explained risks. (17)

Defenders of the serotonin theory sometimes argue that it doesn't matter that we don't know exactly *how* Serotonin works as long as it *does* work and we have valid measures of input and output: 1) patient rated for depression on a standard scale before taking antidepressant; 2) patient takes antidepressant for a prescribed period of time (12 weeks); 3) patient's rating on the standard scale for depression improves. Since most suffering people who come into a doctor's office are more interested in getting relief than in getting scientific explanations, this stance seems reasonable. But is it? What *is* the evidence that SSRIs and other antidepressants actually provide some sort of healing of depression? Again, the answer is surprising . . . and disturbing.

Pay attention to item number three above, the measure used to determine whether or not the antidepressant medication is working. Note that the only data comes from a report by the patient. Granted, self-reported patient data plays an important part in treating any illness—but only a part. If I were being treated for diabetes, my doctor would undoubtedly be pleased if I told him that I was feeling better; but he would also insist on a blood test to measure my glucose level. He would not rely solely on my subjective report. For one thing, placebo effects are very powerful. The mere act of taking a pill often makes people feel better, even when the medication turns out to be sugar. That is why the FDA insists on double blind drug trials. Moreover, patients on antidepressants are even more unreliable because they are under the influence of a powerful psychotropic substance—a substance that, by very definition, causes changes in perception, mood, thinking, and behavior. Peter Breggin argues that antidepressants cause *intoxication anosognosia*, a medical term used to describe the way in which a damaged brain denies the loss of function it has suffered. That is, patients subjected to biopsychiatric interventions often display poor judgment about the positive and negative effects of the treatment. (18) There is considerable evidence that most psychiatric drugs "work" by producing a kind of anesthesia of the mind, spirit, or feelings. (19) Even more insidiously, serious impairment of mental functioning can occur before anyone recognizes that anything is the matter. Neither the patient nor the doctor may realize that thinking is slowed or that emotions are dulled. Breggin calls this "medication spellbinding." (20) This mental disconnect is similar to the way in which people describe their feelings while drinking alcohol or smoking marijuana. They feel better when their brain is impaired; life is good. Antidepressant medication can cause similar intoxication. As Breggin points out, patients feel that they are mentally improved when in reality they have been chemically lobotomized. They are "feeling no pain" because they are not feeling anything at all. (21) Clearly, no self-respecting medical doctor would base a treatment regimen on the reports of an intoxicated, mentally impaired patient. When we rely on such reports to establish the efficacy of antidepressants, we make a mockery of science.

Grace Jackson says that antidepressants are a result of evidence *biased* medicine. The design of FDA trials has been manipulated to obscure the drugs' inefficacy and harmful side effects.

There are at least four good reasons to doubt the efficacy of antidepressants: 1) Overwhelming evidence of pervasive conflict of interest among the academic and government scientists who conduct and evaluate antidepressant drug trials; 2) the low bar that the FDA sets for new drug approvals; 3) the FDA policy of discarding and blocking the publication of negative drug trials; 4) the unblinding effects of the inert placebos often used in antidepressant trials; and, even if we discount all four of the reasons I have just cited, the *results of the drug trials themselves.* Let's take a closer look at each one of these reasons in order, starting with conflict of interest.

A few pages ago, I listed the kind of profits the pharmaceutical industry is making from antidepressant sales. In 2008 alone, they totaled $9.6 billion—more than three times the gross national product of the country of Burundi. $9.6 billion is not much when it comes to GNP, but it buys a lot of free drinks for medical researchers at academic conferences. It buys much more as well. In his 2010 book *Anatomy of an Epidemic,* Robert Whitaker follows the money trail, establishing definitively how the drug industry has used its vast wealth to co-opt both the scientific community and the regulatory process. Academic psychiatrists—paid by the drug companies to serve as consultants on advisory boards and as speakers—act essentially as salesmen. E.g. the chair of the psychiatric department at Emory Medical School earned at least $2.8 million as a speaker and consultant for drug firms. (22) There are the direct gifts to physicians as well. A California survey found that GlaxoSmithKline is quite willing to give $2,500 in freebies to each physician it deals with; Eli Lilly gives $3,000. In 2008, Senator Chuck Grassley, a Republication from Iowa, made headlines when he exposed hidden financial ties between a number of leading academic researchers and the drug companies whose antidepressants they were evaluating. (23) Summarizing the Grassley findings and previous analyses of problematic academe-industry relationships in biomedical research, Dr. Marcia Angell, Senior Lecturer at the Harvard Medical School and former editor-in-chief of *the New England Journal of Medicine* (NEJM), concludes that, "It is simply no longer possible to believe much of the clinical research that is published, or to rely on the judgment of trusted physicians or authoritative medical guidelines."

... Most doctors take money or gifts from drug companies in one way or another. Many are paid consultants, speakers at company-sponsored meetings, ghost-authors of papers written by drug companies or their agents ... and ostensible "researchers" whose contribution often consists merely of putting their patients on a drug and transmitting some token information to the company. Still more doctors are recipients of free meals and other out-and-out gifts. In addition, drug companies subsidize most meetings of professional organizations and most of the continuing medical education needed by doctors to maintain their state licenses . . . . By such means, the pharmaceutical industry has gained enormous control over how doctors evaluate and use its own products. Its extensive ties to physicians, particularly senior faculty at prestigious medical schools, affect the results of research, the way medicine is practiced, and even the definition of what constitutes a disease. (24)

Most of us have confidence in the efficacy of antidepressants because we have confidence in the FDA. As Angell's sweeping indictment suggests, however, the pharmaceutical industry is so powerful that it defines the very universe in which FDA regulators live and work. Large-scale clinical trials tend to be very expensive, so scientists and regulators frequently look to the drug companies for sponsorship. Thus the investigator, who is conducting the trial of a given drug, is often being financially supported by the very company whose potential product she is testing. One of the fruits of this enormous industry climate control is the relatively low bar that the FDA sets in its approval process. Although new drugs do go through many trials, as we would expect, only two of those trials need to yield positive results for a drug to get FDA authorization. The negative trials, even if there are many, are simply ignored. Eli Lilly had to run five large-scale trials of Prozac in order to get the two positive results the FDA required. GlaxoSmithKline had to run even more trials on Paxil, which later was required to carry a Black Box warning that it may cause suicide in children and adolescents. (25)

The results of successful clinical trials are published in prestigious medical journals and later appear in the PR materials that the company uses to interest doctors and consumers in its product. What happens to the results of *unsuccessful* trials? Unfortunately nothing. Indeed, less than nothing. The FDA does not require that studies showing *lack* of efficacy be published, and the pharmaceutical industry makes sure that they are not published. In a particularly egregious case, Andrew Mosholder, an FDA drug safety officer, concluded early on that antidepressants doubled the risk of suicidal thinking in children, but he was initially prevented from publishing his findings. (26)

The suppression of adverse data about antidepressant performance has been a fundamental drug industry strategy from the first. Turner, Matthews, Linardatos, and Rosenthal (2008) demonstrate that the selective publication of antidepressant trials has significantly reinforced the widespread belief among both healthcare professionals and the general public that antidepressants have been scientifically proven to be effective in treating depression. In short, by systematically suppressing the publication of clinical trials that show that antidepressants perform little better than sugar pills, the pharmaceutical industry, working in concert with psychiatric academe, has fundamentally misled the American public, using all of us as guinea pigs in what is essentially a vast, unregulated medical experiment. Dr. Marcia Angell writes:

> I witnessed firsthand the influence of the industry on medical research during my two decades at *The New England Journal of Medicine* . . . Sometimes companies don't allow researchers to publish their results at all if they are unfavorable to the companies' drugs. As I saw industry influence grow, I became increasingly troubled by the possibility that much published research is seriously flawed, leading doctors to believe new drugs are generally more effective and safer than they actually are. (27)

Moreover, even apparently *successful* clinical trials, whose results have been published in prestigious journals, are suspect for reasons that have to do with the inherently tricky nature of psychotropic drug testing. As you probably know, drug trials follow a rigorous "double blind" protocol. The subjects of the experiment are divided into two groups, the treatment group and the control group. The treatment group gets the medication being tested; the control group gets an identical-looking pill (placebo) that contains no drug. (The classic "inert placebo" is a sugar pill.) Because decades of research has clearly demonstrated that in any experiment involving people, conscious and unconscious human bias can significantly affect the results, neither the researchers or the subjects are allowed to know who is in the treatment group and who is in the control group. However, as Moncrieff,

Wessely, and Hardy demonstrate in an important 2004 study, double blinds don't always work very well in antidepressant trials. Antidepressants have significant adverse side effects. Researchers know this, and many subjects know it as well. Thus "the appearance of side effects may reveal the identity of medication to participants or investigators and thus may bias the results of conventional trials using inert placebos." Analyzing nine drug trials involving 751 participants, Moncrieff and his team concluded differences between antidepressants and active placebos were small. This suggests that unblinding effects may inflate the efficacy of antidepressants in trials using inert placebos."

Recently, even more damning evidence that antidepressants are ineffective has surfaced. It comes from a surprising source: the results of *industry-sponsored* FDA clinical trials. Irving Kirsch and an international team of researchers used the US Freedom of Information act to obtain data from 47 pre-approval FDA trials of various antidepressants tested between 1987 and 1999. (Forty percent of these studies, most of them negative, had never been published, twice the usual average.) Combining the results of the published and unpublished studies, Kirsch's team conducted a meta-analysis to assess the effectiveness of antidepressants as a class versus the effectiveness of placebos. Their conclusions:

> These findings suggest that, compared with placebo, the new-generation antidepressants do not produce clinically significant improvements in depression in patients who

initially have moderate or even very severe depression, but show significant effects only in the most severely depressed patients. The findings also show that the effect for these patients seems to be due to decreased responsiveness to placebo, rather than increased responsiveness to medication. Given these results, the researchers conclude that there is little reason to prescribe new-generation antidepressant medications to any but the most severely depressed patients unless alternative treatments have been ineffective. (28)

In short, "The belief that antidepressants can cure depression chemically is simply wrong," Kirsch told *Newsweek* writer Sharon Begley in 2010. "The dirty little secret" of psychopharmacology, once known only to FDA and industry insiders, was now out in the open.

But not entirely. Kirsch entitled his recent book *The Emperor's New* Drugs, a wry reference to the Hans Christian Anderson story about a monarch who is hoodwinked by his tailors into believing that he is wearing a magic suit when he is really wearing nothing at all. When a little boy in the crowd shouts out the truth, the emperor walks on as if he has not heard, unwilling to admit the magnitude of his deception. Kirsch got a similar response to his own scholarly expose. Although the news media disseminated the results of the 2008 Kirsch study fairly widely, and anti-antidepressant chatter in the blogosphere increased exponentially, the medical community, especially prescribing psychiatrists, closed ranks around the drug industry and its products. For many doctors, Kirsch's conclusions challenged their observation that their patients *did* seem to get better after being given antidepressants. Kirsch responded, observing that since doctors don't normally prescribe placebos, they have no basis for comparison. "When they prescribe a treatment and it works," says Kirsch, "their natural tendency is to attribute the cure to the treatment" rather than to the act of pill-giving itself . . . or to the fact, as other studies demonstrate, that even major depressive episodes often resolve over time whether or not they are treated. The consensus is four to six months.

Despite the best efforts of the biopsychiatric community, doubts about the efficacy of antidepressants have gained a foothold in the mass media in the years since Kirsch's initial study. In July of 2011, for example, Dr Marcia Angell published a widely-circulated two-part article in *The New York Review of Books* that uses the work of Kirsch and others to mount a devastating critique of psychopharmacology, extending the thrust of her own 2004 book *The Truth About the Drug Companies: How They Deceive Us and What to Do About It.* (29)

The New York Times, generally supportive of biopsychiatry in its Science Times pages, recruited Dr. Peter Kramer, author of the 1993 best-seller *Listening to Prozac,* to rebut Angell and Kirsch, but Kramer's pre-emptive Op Ed piece ("In Defense of Antidepressants," 10 July 2011) relies largely on ex-cathedra assertions: "Antidepressants work—ordinarily well, on a par with other medications doctors prescribe." At various points, Kramer seems to be recommending antidepressants as a kind of elixir of life (Good for what ails 'ya!)—e.g. "antidepressants bolster confidence or diminish emotional vulnerability—for people with depression but also for healthy people . . . they do seem to make the brain more flexible." He dismisses studies that dispute the efficacy of antidepressants as being based on "shaky data." However, as Robert Whitaker and others in the blogosphere immediately noted, Kramer inaccurately describes the key findings of each of these studies. More telling still, buried at the end of his piece is a disclaimer of sorts. Despite his rousing "defense" of antidepressants, in his own practice, Kramer prefers psychotherapy! ("I aim to use drugs sparingly.") Why? "They have side effects, some of them serious." (30)

This point tends to elude many of Kirsch's other critics in the research community. Even those who have strong doubts about antidepressants have been reluctant to give up on drug therapy entirely, in large part because they see no obvious alternative to it. (There *is* one actually, as I will explain.) For example, in a 2008 *British Journal of Medicine* editorial, Erick Turner and Robert Rosenthal cite the results of their own study, agreeing with Kirsch that "antidepressant drugs are much less effective than is apparent from journal articles." However, they nevertheless insist that "each drug was superior to placebo," arguing that the criteria for clinical significance Kirsch used are flawed, despite the fact that those criteria are recommended by the UK's National Institute for Health and Clinical Excellence (NICE). Resorting to a "you're one, too" argument, Turner and Rosenthal defend biopsychiatry against its implicit opponent, psychotherapy, reminding us that "for psychotherapy trials, there is no equivalent of the FDA whose records we can examine, so how can we be sure that selective publication is not occurring here *as well*?" [my italics]Ultimately, they revert to anecdotal evidence and face value arguments—the same kind of non-scientific reasoning psychiatry has accused psychotherapy of using ever since the DSM-III: "Our clinical recommendation is that when considering the potential benefits of treatment with antidepressants, be circumspect but not dismissive. Efficacy measured in clinical trials does not necessarily translate into effectiveness in clinical practice." In effect, they are saying that even a little bit of pharmacological help is better than nothing at all.

Turner and Rosenthal miss one obvious point, however. The alternatives to antidepressant treatment, whether sugar pills or psychotherapy, have no adverse side effects. ADs have plenty! In deciding whether or not to prescribe a drug for depression, doctors need to carefully weigh the possible benefits (which are, according to most studies, quite small) against the possible risks (which are quite large). Otherwise, they are essentially violating their Hippocratic Oath. Kirsch explains the calculation this way:

> Imagine having a choice between ... treatments. Treatment A produces a large therapeutic response but also a large number of adverse effects, including diarrhea, nausea, anorexia, sweating, forgetfulness, bleeding, seizures, anxiety, mania,

> sleep disruption, and sexual dysfunction . . . . Treatment D has been assessed in many comparative studies, in which it has been found to be as effective as Treatment A in the short term and more effective in the long term. It does not produce adverse effects. Given a choice between these alternatives, which would you choose? (31)

"Depression hurts," the Eli Lilly Company tells us in its TV ads for Cymbalta. Unfortunately, taking antidepressants hurts worse. Let's start with one of the more serious side effects: sudden death. Monoamine Oxidase Inhibitors, an older class of antidepressants that are nevertheless still prescribed, sometimes off-label, can produce a potentially lethal spike in blood pressure if they are taken by mouth along with foods containing tyramine. I.e. if you pop your MAOI and then go out for a salami and cheese sandwich, you'd better have your will in order.

Children, who are often treated with antidepressants off-label for a variety of conditions including anxiety, attention deficit hyperactivity disorder, are at special risk for another fatal side effect: suicide. A 2006 meta-analysis of 24 FDA drug trials involving nine different antidepressants concluded that children and adolescents treated with antidepressants were nearly twice as likely to exhibit suicidal thinking and behavior than similar children in the control groups. The FDA now requires all antidepressants to carry a Black Box warning that reads, in part:

Antidepressants increased the risk of suicidal thinking and behavior (suicidality) in short-term studies in children and adolescents with Major Depressive Disorder (MDD) and other psychiatric disorders. Anyone considering the use of [Insert established name] or any other antidepressant in a child or adolescent must balance this risk with the clinical need. (32)

The most common, well-documented, and subtly devastating side effect of antidepressants is a radical lowering of libido. ADs not only block sexual performance—an effect that, in men at least, might be countered with Viagra—they erase *interest* in sex. They destroy passion. The absence of loving physical intimacy, in turn, destroys relationships. And without intimate relationships, life itself often becomes unbearable. As Harvard psychiatrist John Ratey reminds us, "Sexual feelings and passions are primary drivers in all of us, and muzzling them can leave us without a general passion for life." (33) Moreover, the loss of interest in sex doesn't always stop when the patient stops taking antidepressants. Post SSRI Sexual Dysfunction can go on for years. (34)

All classes of antidepressants inhibit REM sleep. (MAOIs eliminate it entirely.) No one knows precisely what function REM sleep performs, although many researchers think it is crucial to memory consolidation and creative thinking; however, its importance is clearly indicated by recent studies of REM sleep deprivation:

... Long-term REM sleep deprivation is lethal, as it would also perturb primitive networks involved in energy homeostasis and basic functions. The importance of sleep is illustrated by the effects of sleep deprivation in humans . . . Cognition becomes impaired . . . and mood labile . . . Selective REM sleep deprivation produces similar behavioral effects over a longer time frame. In this case, increased attempts to enter REM sleep are noted, suggesting the development of a REM sleep debt. (35)

REM sleep deprivation may account for the subtle cognitive losses that long-term antidepressant users often report to me and other therapists, a dulling of mental acuity, a diminution of creativity and inspiration.

Loss of sexual passion and loss of creative fire are linked to the most common, paradoxical, and appalling side effect of antidepressants: the loss of *emotion*. In a crucial 2002 study of SSRI-induced sexual dysfunction, Adam Opbroek and his research team noted that 80% of their sample also reported "clinically significant blunting of several emotions." Opbroek concludes that "emotional blunting" may be an under-appreciated side-effect of SSRIs that may contribute to . . . reduced quality of life." (36) The "emotional blunting" Opbroek describes—loss of intensity, excitement, passion, joy—is quite familiar to me personally: I observed it in my Aunt Edith after she had her frontal lobotomy. It was a loss from which she never recovered. She survived but, in fundamental ways, she ceased to live. And I see it in clients who are using up all of their life energy trying not to feel what they feel—people who are *depressing* themselves, turning down the volume on the music inside them. In short, antidepressants *cause* depression!

This becomes clear in a more recent qualitative study by British psychiatrists Jonathan Price and Guy Goodwin (*Medicographia* 2009) in which they summarize and analyze the well-documented emotional deficits induced by SSRI use, including loss of the ability to cry; irritation; loss of empathy; loss of erotic dreaming; loss of creativity; loss of the ability to express feelings or to recognize them in others; decreased interest in sex and decreased sexual pleasure; *increased* worry; *increased* sadness.

> Some patients taking antidepressants report that while they feel less emotional pain than before commencing their antidepressant medication, they also experience a restricted range of emotions and, in particular, cannot get a "normal" emotional response to everyday events that would usually be associated with, for example, joy or sadness) . . . "Just not caring" had an unhelpful effect on everyday responsibilities, resulting in financial problems and problems at work or college. Emotional detachment from family and reduced emotional responsiveness had an unhelpful impact on family life, and on perceived quality of parenting. Reduced inspiration, reduced imagination, reduced motivation, and reduced passion for and enjoyment of creative activities, had adversely affected some participants' creativity.

In some participants, emotional side effects had led to reduced sociability. Finally, emotional flattening, emotional detachment from other people, and reduced concern for other people's needs and feelings had unhelpful effects on relationships within families, with a significant other, and at work. (37)

Price and Goodwin put a face on these generalizations by filling their paper with quotes from antidepressant users themselves:

"I'm on this constant emotional plain of blank-blank—not happiness but OK-ness"

"I'd be . . . aware that I was in a situation or doing something that . . . should make me happy but it would just have no real effect."

"I am able to comfort and cuddle [my children] but I feel that . . . like there is no emotion behind it."

"I . . . felt slightly removed from everything . . . I just left things, you know . . . things didn't really matter somehow."

"You feel that your personality has been shifted sideways or been unbalanced somehow."

Clearly, if this is what the *cure* does for you, most people would prefer the disease! And so, despite their doctor's advice or sometimes with their doctor's support, many people decide to stop taking antidepressants. Or rather, they try to stop. The little thing that the pharmaceutical industry forgot to mention about tranquilizers turns out to be true of antidepressants as well: they are powerfully addictive. (38)

For many years, I and the therapists and psychiatrists that I supervise have observed emotional flattening in patients who come to us already using antidepressants. Many of these people are deeply troubled by the way their ADs make them feel (or *not* feel) and have tried to go off the drugs, often without success. One especially poignant client comes to mind. Let's call her Barbara. As a young woman, she was diagnosed with depression after the birth of her child. Post-partum depression is one of several instances in which low mood clearly has a physiological basis. There is no question that the hormonal changes women experience following childbirth have a strong emotional component. (Other instances of physiologically induced depression include hypothyroidism and diabetes, viral disorders such as infectious mononucleosis and hepatitis, and neurological diseases such as multiple sclerosis and Parkinsonism.) (39) Because many women have trusted me with their feelings, I know the depression is often not *simply* hormonal, however. There is often a psychological component as well. A woman may have considerable ambivalence about the whole business of having babies, feelings that she may try to push down because they are not socially sanctioned or are inconsistent with her self-image. New mothers can be overwhelmed by feelings of responsibility, feelings of fear and helplessness, worry about how they will juggle their family and their career, feelings of enormous resentment when their own dependency needs get pushed aside, dread of the life changes that motherhood will mean. "I'll never feel free again," is a phrase I have heard more than once. "I feel like I might have made a terrible mistake." "I feel so scared and trapped, I just want to curl up in a ball and die." "I could kill X, he supported and encouraged this and he doesn't plan to make any changes in his life." These days, when new mothers express these feelings (or depress themselves in order *not* to feel), they are often prescribed antidepressant medication.

That is what happened to Barbara. Initially, she had to cycle through many different brands, each with wildly unpredictable side effects, until she finally found an antidepressant she could tolerate. Later, when she tried to stop taking the drug, she was plunged into a depression much worse than the post-partum blues she had started with. This cruel phenomenon—tactfully termed "SSRI discontinuation syndrome"—includes both classic physical drug withdrawal symptoms (dizziness, sweating, nausea, insomnia) and a range of emotional symptoms as well, among them cognitive confusion, terrifying nightmares, psychosis, suicidal thoughts and actions, not to mention a perpetual "storm of murk." Studies over the last eight years clearly demonstrate that these symptoms "cannot be explained as a remanifestation of the original disorder." (40) Nor are they as rare as we all first thought; indeed, they are now so well known that they have acquired a slang nickname, "brain zaps." If the patient can tolerate the zaps for long enough without going back on medication, the symptoms often dissipate . . . but not always. Sometimes, the SSRI "syndrome" lasts long after the "discontinuation." Sometimes it lasts forever.

This seems to be what happened to Barbara. Because of withdrawal problems, her doctors kept her on drugs for years. She now suffers from severe untreatable headaches apparently caused by the "cure" she was given. Attempts to discontinue the drugs, even gradually, result in an uncontrollable deep depression. She had no history of even mild depression before the post-partum episode.

Nor is Barbara an exception. Her cruel experience has been repeated over and over again. Science writer Robert Whitaker travelled the country for years amassing such anecdotal evidence of harm, which he reports in his comprehensive study of antidepressant addiction and corporate greed, *Anatomy of an Epidemic* (2010). Moreover, he documents how the pattern of AD-induced suffering has been deliberately obscured. He concludes:

> Over the short term, those who take and antidepressant will likely see these symptoms lessen. They will see this as proof that the drugs work, as will their doctors. However, this short-term amelioration of symptoms is not markedly greater than what is seen in patients treated with a placebo, and this initial use also puts them onto a problematic

long-term course. If they stop taking the medicine, they are at risk of relapsing. But if they stay on the drugs, they will likely suffer recurrent episodes of depression, and this chronicity increases the risk they will become disabled. (41)

Whitaker's data tells a story that the drug companies who market ADs and the doctors who casually dispense them have withheld from the public: antidepressants don't *cure* chemical imbalances in the brain; they *cause* chemical imbalances in the brain—changes that help turn first-time customers into long-time users. We're hooked.

In his 2010 *New Yorker* essay, Louis Menand summarizes the current situation as follows:

> There is suspicion that the pharmaceutical industry is cooking the studies that prove that antidepressant drugs are safe and effective, and that the industry's direct-to-consumer advertising is encouraging people to demand pills to cure conditions that are not diseases (like shyness) or to get through ordinary life problems (like being laid off). The Food and Drug Administration has been accused of setting the bar too low for the approval of brand-name drugs. Critics claim that health-care organizations are corrupted by industry largesse, and that conflict-of-interest rules are lax or nonexistent. Within the profession, the manual that prescribes the criteria for official diagnoses, the Diagnostic and Statistical Manual of Mental Disorders . . . has been under criticism for decades. And doctors prescribe

antidepressants for patients who are not suffering from depression. People take antidepressants for eating disorders, panic attacks, premature ejaculation, and alcoholism . . . . As a branch of medicine, depression seems to be a mess. Business, however, is extremely good. Between 1988, the year after Prozac was approved by the F.D.A., and 2000, adult use of antidepressants almost tripled . . . In 2008 a hundred and sixty-four million prescriptions were written for antidepressants, and sales totaled $9.6 billion. As a depressed person might ask, What does it all mean? (42)

Let me try to answer that question. Among the many AD patient quotes that Price and Goodwin assemble in their 2009 paper on "emotional blunting," one quote especially caught my attention:

A feeling of being depressed was like cycling over cobble stones and you're feeling things a bit too intensely and too sharply . . . and the sort of flattening out effect [of antidepressants] is something which is cushioning that . . . (43)

Those cobble stones are a fruitful metaphor. Emotional life is indeed a bumpy ride, full of jarring, unexpected turns and constant ups and downs. Here's what it looks like at street level:

. . . a bumpy road, a roller coaster, a musical line on an oscilloscope, the wave of emotion as it flows through our brain-body loop. It perfectly understandable that we might object to being tossed around on this strange carnival ride, object to the sinking feeling as we go down, down, down. If we object so much that we try to "flatten" the ride, we get ourselves in trouble, however. As in a wave form, in life one thing leads to another. If we try to stop ourselves from going down—from experiencing "dark" feelings (mislabeled as "negative" feelings)—then there is no way we can get up. The same thing applies to the top of the wave: if we object to the anxiety that inevitably accompanies emotional highs—the feeling that we might fly apart—then we get stuck as well. We have flatlined ourselves, dying a little in the midst of life.

Antidepressants do not cure this problem. They perpetuate it. They are a chemical version of the tinkering we do on our own when we object so much to what we feel that we use up all of our energy trying not to feel it. When we move away from intense emotion—especially from anxiety—we inevitably move toward depression. There is literally no other way to go. When we use antidepressants to cushion the ride, the same thing happens. Only with antidepressants, the move toward depression is often irreversible, resulting in permanent emotional flattening . . . the chemical equivalent of a frontal lobotomy.

What is the alternative? Move the other way! As I said in the Introduction, the operative question I ask my clients is simple but powerful: *"What are you are trying not to feel?"* Once we can locate that estranged feeling, then we know which way to go: *toward* it . . . toward anxiety, toward discomfort, toward the darkness and the helplessness, into the "swamplands of the soul." (44)

This will seem like perverse advice at first. All of our lives, we have been told to move away from anxiety (a so-called "negative feeling"), just as we have been told to step back from the edge of a cliff lest we fall. But sometimes we need to fall a little in order to rise. As a pilot I know that when an airplane "stalls" (the wing stops providing lift) and the plane threatens to fall to earth, the correct move is to point the nose *down* toward the earth. I remember how scary and counterintuitive this was the first time I experienced it (indeed, every time I experience it!)—how hard it is to trust that the spiral downward will end and the wing will regain its lift once you deliberately push forward on the yoke and put the plane into a dive. But it works. Going down, I go up. There is no other way. If a pilot in a stalled airplane becomes so frightened of going down, panics and pulls the nose *up*, he puts the plane in "a grave-yard" spiral and crashes. Being too frightened to move toward our uncomfortable feelings (our anxiety, our pain) can be just as dangerous.

CHAPTER FOUR

OBJECTING TO FEELINGS: AGITATED DEPRESSION

> *". . . I write of melancholy, by I being busy to avoid melancholy. There is no greater cause of melancholy than' idleness, "no better cure than business . . ."*—Robert Burton (1)

WRITING IN 1621, Robert Burton was drawing on a tradition that goes back to Aristotle when he nominated "busy-ness" as an antidote to melancholy. Terms have changed. What Burton thought of as *melancholia* is now DSM-IV code 300.4 (*Dysthymic Disorder*). However, the association of busy-ness with mental health and sadness or anxiety with mental illness has remained remarkably consistent over the last 400 years, as has the corollary tendency to view introversion with suspicion. In the first decade of the 21st century, with our Blackberries and IPods attached to our bodies at all times, always on the move, inseparable from the clocks and screens imbedded in each of our Household Gods—we live in a whirlwind of busyness so intense and cacophonous that we cannot hear ourselves think. Or, more to the point, we cannot hear ourselves *feel*. In this vortex of data noise and virtual networking, people who like to be alone a lot—people who are quiet and inward-looking—are odd men out indeed, likely candidates for a little Fluoxetine pick-me-up.

In this brief, transitional chapter, I want to make a case for quiet men and women, an argument that that I will develop more fully later in relationship to Gustav Mahler. Let me start by making a case *against* busyness. Burton was wrong: busyness is not an antidote to depression; it is a form of depression in and of itself. It is all the more insidious because its pathology is so utterly invisible in our hard-wired culture, whose norms value "putting out" and denigrate "taking in." The most useful term for the psychic state I am describing is "agitated depression," but this requires some explanation since the DSM-IV and the DSM-IV-TR have eliminated this dysfunction altogether. These manuals only obliquely refer to "agitated depression" as "Psychomotor Agitation" and as the flip side of "Psychomotor Retardation" (what we used to call "catatonic stupor"). Both phenomena get lost in the symptom group that defines "Major Depressive Disorder."

Psychomotor changes include agitation (e.g., the inability to sit still, pacing, hand-wringing; or pulling or rubbing the skin, clothing, or other objects) or retardation (e.g., slowed speech, thinking, and body movements; increased pauses before answering; speech that is increased in volume, inflection, amount, or variety of content, or muteness). (DSM IV, 321)

Anybody who has ridden the New York City subway in the last 50 years (post "deinstitutionalization") has seen plenty of this behavior, as did I during my residency at St. Elizabeth's. I saw it in my Jesus Men who alternated ("manic-depressively") from feeling like God (omnipotent) to feeling like shit (impotent); from "speech that is pressured, loud, rapid and difficult to interrupt (DSM-IV)" to catatonic silence. The staff found them hard to deal with in their agitated modality and heavily medicated them on chlorpromazine or Thorazine SR, medications that are still used today to deliberately create "emotional blunting."

What do these obviously Crazy People have to do with Us? Quite a bit, actually. Indeed, if we put wireless headsets on them and released them into the city streets today, my guess is that it would take quite some time before anyone would notice that their word salad was different from the word salad we speak and text to each other all day long. (The Jesus Men would have *loved* the gadgetry.) That is, the agitatedly depressed people inside the asylum walls have a lot more in common with the agitated people outside the walls (us) than we like to admit. They illustrate something of an extreme in the dark art of feeling avoidance, an art that many of us practice as well without realizing it. Let me explain.

At the end of the last chapter, I defined the root cause of depression as feeling avoidance. That is, depression is not a disease we *have*; it is something that we are *doing* to ourselves. It is an active process. Imagine that you live in a large airy house full of light and warmth. You hear a knock at the door, then a rattle of the handle. It makes you a little uncomfortable. (You're not sure why.) So instead of moving toward the door (toward the discomfort), you retreat, first to one room, then to another, finally ending up in a windowless, airless attic. (You're safe, but you're missing out on a lot.) Then you hear the rattle again, this time coming from the trapdoor in the floor. It starts to open! You push it closed, but there is no lock. You have to keep pushing all day long and all night long, pushing with all your might, using every bit of life energy you have. You have to keep pushing forever.

That's what we do when we depress ourselves. And little wonder that it makes us tired—prevents us from sleeping and concentrating and enjoying sex. Who has energy left for sex? We've used it all up keeping the damned trapdoor closed! What antidepressants do (if they do anything at all) is put a lock on the door and plugs in our ears so we won't hear the rattle. We don't have to work so hard—and that brings a measure of relief—the kind of relief we feel when we stop hitting ourselves in the head with a hammer. But we're still stuck in a dark windowless attic. (And it's a lovely spring day outside!) Worse than that: we will never know that on the other side of the dreaded door is, not the Grim Reaper, but the very person we have been longing most to meet and embrace: our authentic feeling self. We are on *both* sides of the door. We are the door. And the house. And the lovely spring garden outside. But we don't know that from our hiding place in the attic. If we take antidepressants, we will never know.

The solution to this locked room problem is obvious: open the door! But it takes a lot of courage to do that. It takes a lot of courage just to walk across the attic floor toward the door. We have to open the door ourselves. (It's our door after all.) But it helps if somebody is there to talk to, to hold our hand. That is what a psychotherapist is for, not to cure us (we're not sick, just anxious) but to support us, to empathize with us, to help us reach out to the estranged parts of ourselves (our doppelgangers) and embrace them.

What I have been describing metaphorically is the most easily recognized mode of depression, whose primary symptoms appear in the DSM as chronic fatigue, listlessness, low mood. To illustrate how *agitated* depression works as a feeling avoidance strategy, I need to edit the story a bit. Imagine that you live in the same large airy house. You hear the same knock at the door, then a rattle of the handle. It makes you a little uncomfortable. (You're not sure why.) So instead of moving toward the door (toward the discomfort), you retreat into another room. But this time, you don't go all the way up to the attic. Instead, you go into the family room and turn on the TV, something really loud and upbeat like *American Idol* or *Dancing with the Stars*.

You turn up the volume on the set so that you won't hear the disturbing rattle at the door. It works for a while, but then the rattle gets louder, so you turn on the CD player, too. Maybe some reggae. That works for a while, but then . . . . So you start walking around singing to yourself, stamping your feet. But still, even through the din . . . So you put on your IPod earbuds and start cleaning your closet, organizing all your clothes by color and the year you bought them. You partition your hard-drive while baking a soufflé, reread all 742 emails in your Inbox, and invite 56 of your closest friends over for an all-night dance party. (They come in through a different door.) And yet, even then, you hear that rattle, so . . . And so on and so on, until you are dancing in circles as fast as you can, and it's still not fast enough. That's agitated depression. Or one metaphorical version of it at least. In real life (as opposed to metaphor) agitated depression looks very different, on the surface, from what I am going to call "listless depression." But it is not. Both modalities are feeling-avoidance strategies, and both result in a profound and pervasive loss of life energy, libido, and joy . . . and often a loss of intimate relationships as well. If you're dancing in circles like a broken windup doll you don't have any more capacity for love than you do if you are locked alone in an attic. The difference is that, in a culture where busyness is associated with capitalist-style productivity and productivity with social worth and status, agitated depression won't appear to be dysfunctional until it becomes very extreme. (Compulsive hair-twisting and pacing is pathological; compulsive Blackberry use is not.)

I have a client whose wife illustrates this point. Let's call her Jane. She is an extremely successful attorney, a partner in a major law firm. Few of the people who know her socially would categorize her as depressed, but she is. The only dimension of the universe that has any meaning to her is time. She is driven by the clock, driven by a constant pressure to organize, structure, and plan. There is no room in her tight schedule for feeling. Feelings get in the way of getting things done. She relates to her husband and children as if she were their manager. She keeps them organized, assigns weekend tasks, and keeps them focused on what she knows that needs to get done, lawn work, home work, cleaning the basement. Recently, when she found her husband, Bill, having a special moment of closeness with their thirteen-year-old son, she barged in angrily, "Don't you know it's 10 minutes past his bed time? He needs to be asleep!" But nobody sees her as depressed (least of all Jane) because she is so successful in the corporate world and seems so full of energy all the time. Nobody seems to notice how empty she is in every other respect. Except Bill, of course. He notices.

There is another factor at work here as well: in the US today, as in the distant past, the extroverts make the rules for all of us. That means that anyone who invites 56 friends over for an all night party is likely to seem normal (indeed better than normal) while someone who stays home alone listening to Mahler's Second Symphony ("The Resurrection") is likely to seem a little peculiar, perhaps requiring psychopharmacological uplift.

This cultural bias in favor of extroversion—something that Carl Jung noticed nearly 100 years ago in his own culture—was much in evidence during the debates in the late 1970's that ultimately produced the DSM-III. As I noted in Chapter Two, there was a prolonged and heated discussion about how the new DSM would view introversion. Most insight-oriented psychotherapists (myself included) regarded introversion as a normal human personality type. The biopsychiatrists, led by Robert Spitzer, tended to see it as pathological, a tendency that persists today. (The DSM-IV views a restricted number of friendships as a medical symptom. See 301.20 and 301.22). Christopher Lane reports that at one point in the discussion, Spitzer was pressed on the matter of extroversion. If extreme forms of introversion were to be labeled as mental disorders, then what about extreme forms of extroversion? Shouldn't they be regarded as pathological as well? Spitzer stumbled around a bit, considering, but finally responded that he was simply unable to imagine any pathological condition related to extroversion. He would have liked to have done so, he added, if only for the sake of symmetry, but "nature" was not symmetrical in this matter, so the new DSM was not going to be either. End of discussion. (2) On to the next issue. After all, Spitzer was a busy man, having taken virtually sole responsibility for controlling every detail of the new classificatory system, a system that would tightly pigeonhole many millions of people for decades to come. A busy, busy, busy man.

In my experience, agitated depression (of the busy, busy type I have been describing) is the most common form of depression, yet it receives barely a passing mention in the DSM-III or in any of the later versions. In contrast, the principal characteristic of introverts—a desire to spend considerable time alone—is consistently marked as problematic. This requires a little more explanation.

The terms *extrovert* and *introvert* are not arcane; they are familiar to everyone; and yet there is considerable misunderstanding about what they mean as psychological constructs. Indeed, psychologists disagree among themselves. There are those of us who believe that introversion and extroversion need to be understood together as end points on a sliding scale. Each of us falls somewhere on that scale, possessing both extroverted and introverted characteristics, albeit leaning toward one end of the scale rather than the other. Carl Jung had a rather different view of extroversion and introversion, a view that, in somewhat dumbed-down form, is still enshrined in the well-known Myers Briggs "personality test." (Your guidance counselor probably made you take it in high school.) For Jung, a relentlessly binary thinker and a thorough-going essentialist, all of humanity was divided into two complimentary but fundamentally opposite personality types based on how people habitually directed their Life Energy. People who directed their energy out into the world around them, finding satisfaction there, he called *extroverts*. People who directed their energy inward into their own psyche and soul, finding satisfaction there, he called *introverts*. (As readers of the recently released *Red Book* will know, Jung himself was ferociously inward looking.)

Although many people today regard Jung's view as excessively reductionist, it provides a useful framework for understanding why agitated depression is at once prevalent but invisible while introversion is strongly marked as deviant. Imagine for a moment that personality type is equivalent to handedness (which is pretty much what Jung thought, actually).

Fig. 7 Psychologist Carl Jung, 1910

Most people are born with two hands and can use each hand to do many tasks; however, very early in life, we develop a strong preference for one hand, using it for many more tasks than the other. This preference is hardwired and apparently linked to brain hemisphere dominance as well. In Jung's view, although we all possess the capacity for both extroversion and introversion (just as we have two hands), each of us has a strong, inborn preference for one orientation or the other. Some people habitually look outward; some people habitually look inward. The problem for inward-looking people is, analogically, the same as the problems left-handers experience. As those of you who are left-handed know all too well, the built environment is designed by and for right-handed people, people who assume that they constitute the human norm. (Similarly, before the Disability Rights Movement, the built environment was designed by and for so-called "able bodied" people who never considered that what suited them might not work for a person with disabilities.) Like left-handers living in a right-handed world that doesn't fit them very well, introverts live in a world that has been designed by and for extroverts. In such a context, introverts are deviant by default. (3)

It is important to remember here that there is nothing wrong with either extroversion or introversion. But because extroverts tend to make the rules and define the social norms—precisely because they like to do that kind of stuff—introverts end up seeming a little weird, sometimes even to themselves. It is easy to falsely conflate introversion and pathological shyness (*social anxiety disorder* in the DSM) in which people experience anxiety in social situations, fearing that everybody is looking at them and judging them. But introverts are not especially afraid of other people, just unusually sensitive. They are not cold. Indeed, they are capable of deep attachment and great passion. But only with a few people with whom they have satisfying authentic relationships. Social chitchat gives them no satisfaction. A social networking event designed to facilitate business card exchange is an introvert's vision of hell. Sitting quietly listening to Mahler's Second Symphony is a million times more satisfying. For an extrovert, sitting at home when you could be out partying simply doesn't make sense. It seems like a sad choice to make—which it would be if an extrovert were making it. But not for the introvert. Alone time is not sad time. It is precious. Indeed, it is essential. Thus when extroverts (busy, busy) write the diagnostic manuals—and who else would bother—it is inevitable that introverts come off looking weird and sad. Without the cultural equivalent of a corpus callosum, the left brain simply can't understand what the right brain is doing.

In extreme introversion, it is clear that one of the things the right brain is doing is diving down into the dark swamplands of the soul and coming up with art. Although not all introverts are artists, a great many of the world's greatest artists are introverts, for reasons that are fairly obvious. Art comes from deep inside us, formal complexity and emotional expression inextricably woven together. The process of creating art requires enormous, sustained, inward concentration. As anyone knows who has lived with a writer or composer (or been one), when the muse arrives, our beloved friend simply disappears for a while. Sitting at their desk or piano, they are there but not there. For them, the outer world has dropped away and vanished. This is not psychosis. It is not sadness. It is bliss. (At least for the artist. The partner often has another story to tell!) If you doubt this, simply think of Beethoven (an obvious candidate for Prozac), suffering from the illness that would kill him a few years later, tormented by maddening tinnitus, and nearly stone deaf, composing the Ninth Symphony and later the Misa Solemnis *entirely inside his head*. Freude! Freude!

What has this "inner music" to do with depression? Quite a lot, I would submit. To illustrate what I mean, I want to return to a quote from famed neuroscientist Antonio Damasio that I used in my Introduction. In the opening to his 2003 book *Looking for Spinoza: Joy, Sorrow, and the Feeling Brain*, Damasio writes:

> Feelings of pain or pleasure or some quality in between are the bedrock of our minds. We often fail to notice this simple reality because the mental images of the objects and events that surround us, along with the images of the words and sentences that describe them, use up so much of our overburdened attention. But there they are, feelings of myriad emotions and related states, the continuous musical line of our minds, the unstoppable humming of the most universal of melodies that only dies down when we go to sleep, a humming that turns into all-out singing when we

are occupied by joy, or a mournful requiem when sorrow takes over. (4)

Elsewhere Damasio explains that this "continuous musical line" of emotion is not separate from cognitive processes but integral to them, just as brain/mind and body are integrated in a continuous loop: ". . . The body and brain are engaged in a continuous interaction that unfolds in time, within different regions of the body and within mental space as well. Mental states cause brain states, which cause body states; body states are then mapped in the brain and incorporated into the ongoing mental states." (5) In other words, people are not mechanisms, Rube Goldberg devices controlled, magically, by an extra-physical mind. We are a process. And emotions are essential to that process. They keep us in balance, providing a means for the brain and mind to evaluate the environment within and around us and respond adaptively.

"For the first time in human history, we will be in position to design our own brain," neuropsychiatrist Richard Restak recently proclaimed in praise of antidepressants. (6) It is easy to see the appeal of this approach: cosmetic surgery for our sagging eyelids and breasts; pharmacological surgery for our sagging spirits. As the frozen face of Joan Rivers reminds us, however, there is a price to pay for having "too much work done." Trying to cut out feelings we find unattractive is not only dangerous; it is impossible, if we want to feel anything at all. Feelings do not present themselves in discrete packets. They flow, in a "continuous musical line." The only way to stop hearing the frequencies that cause us discomfort (the so-called "negative" feelings . . . anxiety, sadness) is to tune down the volume as a whole until there is no sound at all, only the silence we call depression. We can do this through antidepressant drugs, lobotomizing ourselves into a state of emotional apathy. We can accomplish the same thing without drugs through repression, another way of turning down the volume. Or we can turn up the volume of our lives until it is so loud and distracting that the noise drowns out our inner music. Either way, we damage our entire organism, for which emotional flow is as essential as blood flow.

Agitated depression (turning up the noise) is especially insidious for us today because it has so much social support and is often misunderstood as a sign of healthy extroversion. Introverts, although they don't get much respect, are often much more resilient than they appear. Gustav Mahler is a crucial case in point. Small, grim-faced, afflicted by tics and an odd irregular gait, Mahler was perceived as eccentric by most people who knew him and as neurotic/bi-polar by generations of armchair psychiatrists after his death. Even people who admire the power of his music tend to regard him as emotionally frail: The program for Baltimore Orchestra's 2011 Mahler celebration speaks of his "his crippling fear of death." (7) Nothing could be further from the truth, as we shall see. Although beset by tragedy and stress from his earliest years to his early death, Mahler was emotionally robust and courageous. There were no attic hideouts in Mahler's soul. When he heard the knock at the door, he moved toward it, not away. There was no door inside himself that he was willing to keep closed. A card-carrying introvert (as any serious composer surely must be), he had no interest in the busy busy mechanisms essential to agitated depression. Faced with the worst crisis of his life, in terrible emotional pain, he considered the advice of his friends that he should "get away." But not for long.

> What is all this about the soul? And it's sickness? And how am I supposed to cure it?" he wrote to himself, "With a journey to Scandinavia? That would be another 'distraction'. Only here, in solitude, will I be able to come back to myself, and to consciousness of myself. For since that panic stricken terror came upon me I have only tried to look away and listen away. If I am to find my way back to myself, I must give myself over to the terrors of solitude. (8)

In the next chapter I want to explore those terrors with you more directly, using Mahler as our field guide.

PART II

MOVING TOWARD FEELINGS
(The Polka)

CHAPTER FIVE

LISTENING TO FEELINGS, LISTENING TO MAHLER

O red rose!

Man lies in greatest need!

Man lies in greatest pain!

—Mahler's Second Symphony

IN THE INITIAL CHAPTERS of this book, I have argued that, for the last thirty years, "depression" has become a catch-all term, over-medicated, over-diagnosed and over-treated with antidepressants, medications that do much more harm than good. This does not mean that depression doesn't exist, however. Serious debilitating depression affects very few people, but those people suffer enormously, so deeply hidden within their own minds that they are virtually unreachable. They drag their souls behind them, like the living dead. For some psychiatrists, the one treatment that really seems to make a difference is, not antidepressants, but ECT (Electro-convulsive-therapy). People supposedly can be shocked out of their stupor, become able to gain insight through psychotherapy, and eventually resume rather normal lives. The way ECT is administered today, under anesthesia, it is supposed to be tolerable for most people, although a careful evaluation of the brain trauma involved justifies the horror that clings to ECT in the popular imagination. You can actually use that horror as a crude guide to self-diagnosis, if you wish. If you think you are depressed, before you start taking antidepressants, consider whether you might be willing to undergo electro-shock-therapy. If you don't think you are in *that* bad shape, then you probably are not depressed in any true clinical sense and don't need antidepressants either. Before subjecting your brain to a lobotomy or the trauma of electro-shock surely you would at least consider the possibility that you are simply not listening to some of your feelings and that they are clamoring for attention (the rattle of the door)—feelings that you hate feeling, feelings you have been trying your best not to hear. You should consider the same possibility before taking antidepressants because they, like a lobotomy or ECT, are likely to do irreparable damage to your brain.

Like any new skill, listening for feelings (your own or others') requires considerable practice, preferably working side by side with someone who has already mastered the skill. I know this first hand. When I started out as a therapist, the only thing I was good at was talking. Paradoxically, the person who taught me how to truly listen for feelings was one of the craziest inmates at St. Elizabeth's Hospital, known to the staff as "Mr. H." I came there to cure him; instead, he cured me.

My supervisor at St. Elizabeth's was a Norwegian man. I thought he was a little weird and worried that he had it in for me. In retrospect, I realized that he was smart and uncommonly creative. He had a secret plan for me. One of the first assignments he gave me was to interview Mr. H, who had been diagnosed as Schizophrenic, Catatonic Type. According to the hospital records, he had not spoken or related to anyone for more than fifteen years. Interviewing Mr. H meant taking two attendants on the ward with me (he was considered dangerous), leading Mr. H to an interview room, and placing him in a chair. It was an excruciating experience for me to sit there and talk "to" him without getting any response, no acknowledgement of my presence at all, not even a flicker of an eyelid. I might as well have been invisible. I do not know what I talked about—probably the weather, what was going on in the world, and other nonsense, trying to fill the void of silence from Mr. H. Fifteen minutes seemed like hours. It was as much as I could stand.

I had no idea what this assignment was about, but I dutifully reported to my supervisor that I had completed the task. He replied, "Fine, and you will need to be doing that every day for a while." My exact reply was probably, "the hell you say!" He said, "It is either this or you are out of the program." I think at the time I probably said, "OK, then I'm out." This was the best clinical psychological internship in the country, however; so, having slept on it, I came back, determined to endure what I believed was cruel and unusual punishment. I did the best I could in the time I spent with Mr. H and gradually became more comfortable with his silence, having given up any expectation of response. This had been going on every day for about three weeks, when during the "interview," Mr. H suddenly moved his eyes ever so slightly to look at me. It's strange now to remember how something so slight could have felt so exciting. Afterwards, of course, I wondered if I had simply imagined that miniscule acknowledgment. But the next day, as I sat with my legs crossed, Mr. H. reached over and squeezed my shoe. "I once had some dancing shoes," he said. It was the first thing he had said to anyone in 15 years.

From that day on, Mr. H began talking with me regularly. He explained that he did not care much for what people said. Instead, he said, "I listen for feelings." Later he revealed that he had chosen to talk to me because he sensed that I cared what he felt. He was right. Somehow, despite the silences, I had begun to care for the man. I asked him to join my weekly therapy group with the Jesus-men, and he agreed. It turned out to be a great idea. When I got lost trying to follow what was happening in the group, I could ask Mr. H what was really going on. Without much of the usual "word salad," he could often say who was disturbed and why.

In the psychiatric records, Mr. H was listed as unpredictable in his behavior, perhaps dangerous. There had been times when he had suddenly hugged or kissed someone who came on the ward. Occasionally, he had slapped people. Mr. H explained that he kept very still and quiet so that he could tell what others around him were feeling. When he encountered people filled with unusually strong love or hatred, he could not help but react.

Later on, this started to make more sense to me. I learned from his records that Mr. H had grown up with a volatile mother who would, without provocation, fly into uncontrolled rages. She had abused Mr. H as a child. It seemed clear to me that he had trained himself to be utterly still, listening for feelings, in hope that he could anticipate his mother's rages and get out of the way. His extreme sensitivity was an adaptation to a harsh environment. His silence was a survival strategy.

After we had gotten to know each other a bit, he remarked to me one day, "You know, Dr. Snyder, these psychiatrists here are crazy." In some cases I had my suspicions, but I was more than a little curious about why Mr. H would say so. When I asked, he said simply, "They believe what people say with words. I don't listen to words; I listen to feelings."

By this time I was beginning to understand why my supervisor had assigned me to Mr. H. When I came to St. Elizabeth's, I was an intellectual guy, habitually operating from the left side of my brain, always measuring, evaluating, and staying in control. I was focused on all the things I needed to accomplish in my internship. Attending to feelings would have gotten in the way. Even at the beginning, however, I had a sense that Mr. H could teach me something that was important. In an uncharacteristic move, I decided to take a risk and trust that Mr. H was not really "crazy." I asked him to teach me how to be still and pick up the feelings of others. (In effect, I became his apprentice!) I remember my lessons. I would be sitting beside him on the ward, as still as I knew how, and hear him, without so much as a quiver of recognition of my presence, say, "You're moving too much." Being stupid about the process, I at first thought he was referring to my physical posture. Later I realized that he meant my own feelings were not quiet enough. I had particular difficulty ridding myself of anxiety . . . i.e., the fear that my professional colleagues might think I'd gone round the bend. In a good sense, I had.

Looking back on this experience now, I recognize that my time with Mr. H taught me one of the most profound lessons of my life, the importance of listening to feelings in ourselves and in others. As an insight-oriented psychotherapist, I have been practicing that lesson for over forty years now, listening to the feelings of troubled men and women and encouraging them to listen to themselves. My experience confirms for me that paying attention to feelings, rather than to thoughts and behaviors, and supporting the expression of feelings—guilt, shame, fear, anxiety, resentment, pain—is the best medicine for the human heart and soul. The most practical approach to treating depression is actually the simplest: to assume that the symptoms my clients present—apathy, listlessness, despair—are, not the result of a mysterious chemical imbalance, but the result of their strenuous efforts not to feel feelings that are crying out for attention. When they are able to welcome these estranged feelings back into their lives, their relief is transformative. They are able to stop merely surviving and begin to live much more full and joyous lives.

Because emotion is so important to my work as a psychotherapist, as well as to my own life, I have always thought it strange that human feelings have received so little scientific attention. Emotion has been marginalized in Western philosophy from the very beginning, connected with our bodies which, in turn, connect us to the "lower" animal world. From the perspective of Cartesian dualism, the mind/soul is separate from the body/emotion—higher, transcendent. Thoughts are what make us human, not feelings. The biopsychiatrists who create the diagnostic codes operate from a modern version of this perspective. Having successfully removed the term "emotional" from serious study, they fantasize about designer brains of the future.

There are signs that this perspective is changing, however. Over the last 15 years, there has been a dramatic surge of interest in affect among humanists, social scientists, and media theorists. This interest has been stimulated by exciting new work being done by a number neuroscientists (Joseph LeDoux, Vilayanur Ramachandran, Antonio Damasio, e.g.) who use brain imaging techniques to study the biological basis of emotion. As I suggested earlier, I have been especially intrigued by the "body-minded brain" concept of Damasio, whose research-based attack on Cartesian dualism offers us an opportunity to reposition emotion as central to our human experience.

Damasio confesses that he spent years studying everything but feelings, believing that feelings were somehow intangible and not the providence of science. However, his work with patients who had suffered brain damage changed his mind, and he began to see that the neurology of feelings was no less viable a subject for investigation than the study of vision or memory. With the help of scanning techniques that allowed him to create real-time images of neural activity, he began to map the geography of the feeling brain.

Fig. 8 Neuroscientist Antonio Damasio

Damasio and his research team at the Brain and Creativity Institute at the University of Southern California have been able to demonstrate that when previously normal individuals sustain damage to brain regions necessary for emotions and feelings, their ability to make appropriate decisions is compromised. They seem to be able to think normally, but they end up losing their money, their jobs, and their marriages. Without emotions, they become cognitively dysfunctional. Damage to the prefrontal lobes of the brain—the area on which antidepressant drugs act—has long-term consequences. Damasio is quite direct about this matter: impairment of the "normal operation of the serotonin system . . . can be quite dangerous."(1)

There is more than a cautionary tale here, however. Damasio's work helps us understand why apparently trivial events can trigger emotions so strong and disturbing that we try to block them out of our awareness, using up our life energy to depress ourselves. "The body, in most of its aspects, is continuously represented in the brain," he writes. He calls this the "body loop." Each of these brain-body states is transitory, succeeding each other in a flow; however, some states are recorded, as if we were taking a freeze-frame screen shot of ourselves, for the record:

> A remarkable activity of the human brain consists of creating mapped representations of reality in its sensory cortices, such as visual, auditory or somatosensory, and permitting the experience of those maps in the form of mental images. A no

less remarkable activity consists of creating memory records of the sensory maps and playing back an approximation of their original content during recall. (2)

The machinery behind feelings enables the biological corrections necessary for survival by offering explicit and highlighted information as to the state of different components of the organism at each given moment. Feelings label the related neural maps with a stamp that reads: "Mark that!" (3)

In addition to the body loop, there is what Damasio calls the "as-if body loop."

. . . The brain can simulate a certain body state as if it were occurring; and because our perception of any body state is rooted in the body maps of the somatosensing regions, we perceive the body state as actually occurring even if it is not. (4)

This capacity—an ongoing Theatre of the Mind—has important implications for psychotherapy, as Damasio explains in a vivid example:

Think of the house where once, as a child, you may have had an experience of intense fear. When you visit that house today you may feel uncomfortable without any cause for the discomfort other than the fact that, long ago you had a powerful negative emotion in those same surroundings. It may even happen that in a different but somewhat similar house you experience the same discomfort, again for no reason other than you can detect the brain's record of a comparable object and situation . . . *Emotionally competent objects* . . . whether actually present, as a freshly minted image, or as a reconstructed image recalled from memory, [have the same effect]. (5)

In other words, in the Theatre of the Mind, there is no way to know the difference between a dream tiger and a real one.

Damasio's work gives strong scientific support to a simple but powerful concept that I continually re-enforce when I am working with troubled people: namely, that *all feelings are transitory*. Like notes in a melodic line, they come and they go, one after another. Some of the notes are high, some are low; none of them last forever. We know this when it comes to joy. No matter how much we want to hold on to our happiness, it passes away, all too quickly. It is more difficult to remember that the same thing is true of uncomfortable feelings as well. Pain, anxiety, sadness—the emotions we object to and despise in ourselves—will also pass away if we simply let ourselves feel them. Indeed, the more we are able to tolerate their intensity, the quicker they will dissipate.

Any of us are likely to feel overwhelmed by grief when someone dear to us dies or we lose a satisfying job or, worse, lose our physical mobility from disease or accident, or even when we lose a pet. Under these circumstances, it is normal to retreat to dark places of the soul where the thought of going on living seems unbearable. The feelings underlying depression invariably involve *loss* and incipient *helplessness*—loss of control, loss of dreams, loss of intimacy and love. We feel hopelessness, unable to picture anything ever being any better. We have lost our power to make things right; we have lost our path back to a place of security. The circumstances of life and the breakdown of relationships have conspired to ruin our day. We thought we had everything managed, everything under control; but suddenly, we cannot pay the mortgage this month; our trust in someone close has been betrayed; someone very dear has died; even our body is letting us down, prey to acute or chronic ills; and besides all that, there are the terrorists at the door. In a real sense, we have become separated, estranged, from ourselves and others, from everything positive or meaningful. We feel hopeless about ever feeling good, healthy, joyous, or loving. We would like to simply collapse and drown in our tears. These are intense feelings, dark feelings, overwhelming feelings. However, as Peter Breggin points out, *none* of them constitute a "disease" simply because they are extreme. And all of these emotional states are transitory, if we allow them to be.

This is easier said than done, however. When dark stormy moods arrive, blocking out the sun, we often forget that emotional weather, like atmospheric weather, is changeable. We try to retreat from the storm, distracting ourselves with tasks and plans, so we are too busy to feel what we feel. This avoidance is understandable, but it doesn't really work. Being alive, fully alive, means that we have to go with the flow of our feelings, just as a plane sometimes has to go through rough weather to reach its destination.

I was flying my little airplane from North Dakota to the Eastern Shore of Maryland after a visit with my daughter and her family. Before I took off, I had studied the weather carefully and had planned my route to avoid a line of severe thunderstorms that stretched from the Canadian border to Chicago. In little planes or in big planes, every pilot does whatever he can to avoid flying into stormy weather. I thought my plan was foolproof. I was wrong.

As I neared Chicago, I could see ahead of me two towering cumulus clouds that were obviously above my cruising altitude of 11,000 feet. I had a clear path between the two, but suddenly the Chicago Air Traffic Controller issued a new clearance that would turn me toward the potential storm on my left. I objected: "Chicago, Zero Foxtrot Quebec (my abbreviated call sign), Unable, need five degree deviation from present course to the right, weather." But the air traffic controller was adamant: there was too much traffic in the area. I had no choice but to fly toward the big cloud.

I wasn't scared at first. I had flown through the tops of cumulus clouds many times before, and while there was always some unpleasant turbulence, the experience was never dreadful. I expected it to be like that. I did not expect it to be the most frightening experience of my life.

*I had barely nosed into the white fluffiness when everything went totally black, and extreme turbulence began. I was tossed a thousand feet up, the seat belt and shoulder harness threatening to cut me in two, and then dropped a thousand feet down, my head missing the cabin top by a whisker. Then came the hail, striking the aluminum skin of my craft with deafening noise, and the blinding flashes of lightening. Little yellow and purple tongues danced along the cowling, and the acrid smell of ozone wafted into the cabin. I was terrified that all this gyrating, bouncing and banging around would break the little plane apart and send it, and me, crashing to earth. I desperately wanted to turn around and go back where I had been in that calm safe blue sky, but the voice of my training spoke loudly in my head: "Do not attempt any turns! YOU WILL COME THROUGH ON THE OTHER SIDE. Let the plane go. Any control inputs will simply tear the wings off or put the plane in a graveyard spin. Just try, very gently, to keep the wings level. You **will** come through on the other side!"*

I didn't really believe that I would come through; but then, as suddenly as it all began, it ended. I broke out of the awful cloud into the most beautiful sight I will likely ever see: deep blue sky, white fluffy clouds scattered below me, and below them, the lush green earth of Northern Indiana. Heading east, with the lowering sun behind casting colors of yellow and orange toward the horizon, I could see clearly all the way to Ohio. I began my slow descent, coasting downhill, and suddenly some thirty miles ahead I spotted the little Ohio town, and the gorgeous little airport, that was to be my safe haven for the night.

The emotional storms of life are like this. The only way to avoid them is to depress ourselves, or anti-depress ourselves, into a kind of living death. If we want to experience the ecstasy of soaring and sing life in the key of joy, then we have to fly into dark clouds and learn to sing in the key of pain. There are times when thunderstorms cannot be avoided. When those times come, we need to hold on to the sure and certain truth that black moods, like black clouds, are transitory, as transitory as the ecstatic moods we like to store in a bottle. When we are in a dark and dreadful place, hurting and afraid, time passes very slowly, and it is easy to despair. We need to remind ourselves that we WILL COME THROUGH ON THE OTHER SIDE as long as we don't try to control what we can't control. In emotional life, as in flying, control inputs are not only ineffectual; they are dangerous. (Taking an antidepressant can put us in a graveyard spiral from which we cannot recover.) Paradoxically, *surrendering* control is necessary for survival. The most important thing to do is to do nothing. Simply ride the storm. Get tossed about. You will be frightened, but you will survive. YOU WILL COME THROUGH ON THE OTHER SIDE.

From first to last, the music of Gustav Mahler embodies with great power and originality this, the most fundamental fact of emotional life: that, like storm clouds, feelings come and feelings go. The fourth movement of his Second Symphony begins in agony and despair:

> O red rose!
>
> Man lies in greatest need!
>
> Man lies in greatest pain!
>
> How I would rather be in heaven.

Music Selection Four: *The Fourth Movement of Mahler's Second begins without pause from the "fearful scream of the soul" of the Third Movement. The human voice appears as if the cry of disgust demands a verbal response. Humanity no longer looks repulsive. Instead it looks simply needy: "Man lies in greatest need." The voice and the music are intensely soothing. It is as if there enters a love that is intensely personal and yet embraces the entire world, as music can do. The verse and music continues along a path, blocked by an angel. The "Ach nein!" is passionate, but firm. It represents Mahler's objection to conventional piety – I will be the person I am, and I will travel the path I choose. What is more, God will help me. Martha Nussbaum adds: "The creative soul will follow the light that is its life and that will prove more powerful than all angelic dismissals."*

Otto Klemperer, Royal Concertgebouw Orch., 1951.

http://www.overcomingdepressionwithoutdrugs.com/music

Then I came upon a broad path.

Then an angel came and wanted to dismiss me.

Ah no! I did not allow myself to be dismissed.

I am from God and I would go again to God!

Dear God will give me a lamp,

will light my way to eternal blessed life! (6)

The song moves from darkness to light and hope, the torment seeming to resolve. (I am from God and shall return to God!). Then, suddenly, the strings interrupt; there are violent drum rolls and a cry of despair. In his life, as in his music, Mahler let the storms inside come and go. The exceptionally wide range of emotions he allowed himself to experience finds direct expression in the dramatic shifts of tone and tempo characteristic of his idiosyncratic style, at once Romantic and Modern.

When feelings of loss and helplessness threatened to overwhelm him, as they did more than once in his life, Mahler's response was to turn inward, seek solitude and a connection with the natural world, a sense of connection he sometimes referred to as being in the "The Eternal Feminine." There he was able to let go of everything associated with "The Eternal Masculine" (the effort to control and manage) and surrender completely to his feelings. The forests and the lakes in northern Austria where he spent his summers, and to which he returned when in distress, were, in Damasio's sense, "emotionally competent objects." In their presence—and the music that flowed from their presence—he was able to remap his somatic state and recover his emotional balance.

"The depth of our despair often reflects the contrasting desire that we have to live a more joyful, creative, and meaningful life," writes Peter Breggin. (7) For Mahler, emotional surrender into the dark depths of feeling was the pathway to an experience of oneness with the universe, a soul-satisfying sense of peace and contentment. He often recorded these experiences in words—words in which the music inside him is already aborning:

> I have stood high on the mountains, where the Spirit of God breathes; I have walked in the meadows, lulled by the sound of the cowbells. However, I have been unable to flee from my destiny. Doubt pursues me along every road. Nothing makes me really happy and tears accompany my most blissful smile . . . Toward evening I go out into the meadow and climb the great lime tree that stands there alone, and contemplate the world from its summit. Before my eyes the Danube follows its eternal course and the gleam of the setting sun is caught by its waves. Behind me in the village the bells of evening ring. They are borne to me by a friendly breeze and gently stir the branches of the tree which rock me to sleep . . . , while the flowers and leaves of my beloved lime tree brush against my cheeks! Everything is peaceful. A sacred peace! From a distance only the melancholy call of the frog resounds sadly among the reeds. (8)

The emotional highs and lows that Mahler permitted in himself—his capacity for utter surrender—is difficult for most of us to tolerate. It is incredibly hard to change the habits we have employed to keep such feelings at bay. In my own life and in the lives of others I have supported, the choice to experience repressed feelings is invariably accompanied by extreme anxiety.

"If I go there I will never come out," people often tell me. "I'll go insane, they will take me to the 'funny farm.'" "I'll be sick the rest of my life." The emotions inside us make us feel that we have swallowed something we cannot digest. It sits there making us sick. If we don't throw up, we will die. Pioneering hospital chaplain Anton Boisen, having survived a collapse into an extremely regressed emotional state, says we must bring into the open whatever is causing the inner disharmony and not only recognize it ourselves but acknowledge it to those whose love is necessary for us. We must not be afraid to tell. There are no short cuts, no magic bullets, no cosmetic surgery for the soul. (9) There is no way to remove the anxiety that attends us as we walk this path. But it doesn't last forever. And the more we are able to retrieve the feelings we dread, the more whole and free we become.

Fig. 9 Gustav Mahler, 1892

CHAPTER SIX

INTROVERSION AND THE FEELING LIFE

Our time is hungry in spirit. In some unnoticed way we have managed to inflict severe surgery on ourselves. We have . . . become utterly taken up with the outside world and allowed the interior life to shrink. When we devote no time to the inner life . . . we become accustomed to keeping things at surface level. The deeper questions about who we are and what we are here for visit us less and less, and we remain strangers in our own lives. —John O'Donohue (1)

THE SECRET to Mahler's emotional resilience was his introversion. He did not move toward depression, even in overwhelmingly depressing circumstances, because he was able to withdraw from the world and move inward toward the places where his deepest feelings lay. This formula sounds paradoxical to us today because, in our Antidepressant Era, circumscribed by DSM diagnostic codes, *withdrawal* and *introversion* are generally regarded as pathological. They are symptoms of mental illness rather than mental health. As I discussed at length in Chapter Two, Robert Spitzer and his DSM-III taskforce wanted to use the term *introversion*, previously merely a description of a normal personality type, to define a cluster of supposed emotional disorders. Spitzer didn't get his way entirely, but he was able to slip the diagnosis in sideways. In the DSM-III, many of the characteristics of introversion—e.g. preferring to spend time alone, being "self-absorbed"—were grouped under a new label, "schizoid personality disorder,"(2) a condition that sounds very dangerous and is often misunderstood by lay people as being related to *schizophrenia*. (It isn't!)

Using standard measures of personality type, about 60% of the US population could be classified as extroverted. Precisely because they are the majority, they tend to define the norm. In the last 30 years in particular, psychiatric intervention has focused primarily on moving introverted people toward the norm. There has been virtually no effort to move extroverted people toward greater introversion. A limit case like Mr. H. illustrates why this approach is problematic. Although hardly a model of mental health, Mr. H's extreme sensitivity to emotional nuance was directly related to his extreme withdrawal. It was his radical stillness and silence that made him such an acute listener. In a world where verbal noise and frenetic activity are the norms, it is increasingly difficult for us to *make time to feel*—time apart from others, time alone.

Here I want to turn from precept to example and begin to focus more directly on Gustav Mahler, a man whose very ability to survive flowed from his ability to be alone, to make time for feeling.

Mahler was born on July 7, 1860, in a grubby *shtetl* called Kalischt on the border of Bohemia and Moravia, then part of the Austro-Hungarian Empire, one of the most anti-Semitic regions of Europe. (Until 1781, Moravian Jews were required to wear a yellow badge marking them as outcasts, as if they were carriers of the plague.) Mahler's father Bernhardt, the son of itinerant cloth peddlers, sold liquor out of a cart and later ran the village tavern. He was hot-tempered but literate—indeed, bookish—and dreamed of better things. (The locals nicknamed him the "coachman-scholar.") Mahler's mother Marie (nee Hermann) was the daughter of a soap manufacturer and above Bernhardt in social class, as well as considerably younger. (She was 19; he 29.) She objected to the match her parents had made for her, saying she was in love with someone younger than Mahler, but she was lame and probably had little choice in the matter. Eventually, she did what she was told.

This was not a recipe for marital bliss, and Bernhardt and Marie quarreled frequently. ("They belonged together like fire and water," Mahler later said of his parents.) (3) The stress increased when Bernhardt and Marie's first child, Isidor, was killed in an accident when he was barely one year old. Gustav, who arrived a year later, was a replacement child, born into a family already shadowed by death. It was a shadow that would never leave. Seven of the fourteen children born to Bernhard and Marie Mahler would die in infancy.

Fig. 10 Mahler's father Bernhardt

Fig. 11 Mahler's mother Marie

An eighth child, Gustav's younger brother, Ernst, to whom he was very close, died at age 12, as mentioned earlier, literally in Mahler's arms. Even by 19th century standards, where graveyards were filled with tiny tombs, the prevalence of death and loss in the Mahler household was extraordinary and ghastly. Nor did the dying stop at childhood. In 1889, Mahler's mother, father, and sister Leopoldine all died within a matter of months of each other. Four years later his brother Otto committed suicide by shooting himself in the heart. By the time Mahler was 35, 13 out of the 16 members of his family were gone. By the time he was 47, he had lost his first-born child as well.

1860, the year of Mahler's birth, was auspicious. The Emperor Franz Joseph had just decreed that Jews could own property, lifting centuries of constraint. Bernhardt Mahler responded by moving his young family to Iglau (pop. 17,000), a military garrison town where there were greater opportunities. Hard-driven and hard driving, he had considerable success. He bought a house and outbuildings on the town square across from the soldiers' barracks and built a distillery, running a bustling tavern business out of the ground floor of his home. He eventually bought out most of his competition and rose in socio-economic status, despite the stigma of his position as a German-speaking Jew. By the time Gustav was 19, his household included a nurse, a servant, and a cook, as well as the tavern's bookkeeper and full-time waitress. Like many self-educated men, Bernhardt Mahler was determined to give his children the education that he had not received. Gustav was the primary beneficiary of this impulse. Bernhardt made his son's studies a priority and found the best music teachers Iglau could provide. (4)

Mahler's sensitivity to music manifested itself early on. At the age of three, in his mother's arms, he shouted out in synagogue for the cantor to stop his singing: "Be quiet! That's horrible!" He suggested instead "Eits a Binkel Kasi," a rather bawdy peddler's polka, hardly suited for a house of worship. His father encouraged his precocity. When he was still a toddler, Mahler was given a tiny accordion. He played by ear, accurately duplicating the drinking songs he heard in his father's tavern and the marching music that wafted over from the military parade grounds. Mahler's toy accordion figures in another legendary story related by Mahler's principal biographer, Henry-Louis de La Grange:

> He was not yet four when one day a band playing the military music that enchanted his childhood passed the house. Gustav was not even dressed, but he slipped outside in his night shirt and followed the soldiers with his little accordion. It was only when he reached the market place and began to be frightened at having gone out alone that two neighbors recognized him. The women agreed to take him home, but only after he had played for them, on his accordion, his entire repertoire of military music. Seated on a fruit vendor's counter, he enchanted a large audience of housewives and passers-by. After this, amid applause and

laughter, he was taken back to his parents, who were by then considerably worried by his disappearance. (5)

By the age of five, Mahler was being given piano lessons. His parents and siblings gathered around to hear him play. Although his talent was undoubtedly inborn, it was clearly reinforced by the attention it brought him, a commodity that was probably in short supply given Marie's perpetual cycle of birthing and burying and Bernhardt's focus on his business. In danger of being lost in the shuffle, music made Mahler the star of his family.

"Getting lost," in an introverted way, is a recurring theme of the vignettes Mahler later told about his childhood, as is his characteristic preference for being alone. Mahler recalls,

> As an amusing example of my silent reveries, I was once told that while I was a small boy, my parents spent several hours looking in vain for me while I was in the pigsty. I had wandered in accidentally and, discovering that I could not open the door, had just stayed there, God knows for how long, without uttering a word or a cry until someone who had come to look for me passed nearby. When I heard them call 'Gustav, Gustav!' I answered quite happily, 'Here I am.'
>
> Another time my father took me for a long walk in the woods around Iglau and ordered me to sit on a bench until I was called. In the meantime he forgot about me. But I did not

get tired waiting and remained in my place, without moving and very happy. To everyone's great amazement I was found in just that way several hours later. (6)

In similar circumstances, most children would have felt abandoned and anxious, not "very happy," although they, too, might have stayed put, out of fearful obedience. Was Mahler lying to himself about what he felt? Yes and no, I think. Given the dynamics of his family, it's quite possible that Mahler felt he had been abandoned elementally a long time ago and responded by learning how to abandon the world. He was born barely a year after the tragic death of his brother Isidor. With grief fresh in her heart, his mother may have refused to bond with her new son, protecting herself from additional disappointment. Or perhaps not. In later years, Mahler expressed very little affection for his father, despite all the advantages Bernhardt had given him; but he always described his mother as loving and supportive. "He [Bernhardt] was all stubbornness, she gentleness itself."(7) Perhaps once Marie became confident that Gustav was not going to die, he became quite special to her. Her letters to him, her first surviving child, suggest good humor and affection.

When somebody asked him as a small boy what he wanted to be when he grew up, he replied, "a martyr."(8) Perhaps this is because he identified with the image of his mother that he carried in his mind. The site of Marie Mahler's martyrdom was her marriage. Her husband was domineering, demanding and prone to rages. Gustav Mahler grew up in tumult, the inevitable angry quarrels in the tavern below mingling with the angry quarrels in the family rooms above. Inherently sensitive to sound and the emotional content of sound, Mahler early on sought out places of silent refuge where he could cocoon himself. Alma Mahler would later insist that Mahler had "dreamed his way through family life and childhood. He saw nothing of the unending tortures his mother had to endure from the brutality of his father."(9) Alma's second sentence is clearly untrue, however. During their brief consultation, Mahler told Freud a story about a seminal incident in his childhood in which he fled from his house to escape the sound of his parents arguing, ran out into the streets, and heard a barrel organ playing "Ach, du lieber Augustin." Freud reported that *Mahler* believed that "the conjunction of high tragedy and light amusement was from then on inextricably fixed in his mind."(10)

As an analysis of Mahler's music, this is much too pat, despite the authoritative source; but it suggests that Mahler had learned the hard way, and very early on, that life is full of uncontrollable ups and downs, joined to each other in a continuous flow. The song itself conveys that message: "Ach, du lieber Augustin" is about the bubonic plague. Its refrain "Alles ist hin" ("all is lost") evokes a universal death and despair. The tune itself is rather jolly, however, and so is the figure whom the lyrics address. "Augustin" is a legendary 17th century Viennese street musician who reputedly passed out drunk and was tossed into a common burial pit with victims of the plague. Unaffected by the disease because his blood alcohol was so high, he awoke amid the rotting corpses and began playing a tune, in celebration of his resurrection! (11)

In the graveyard of his family life, Mahler, copying Augustin, learned how to protect and resurrect himself through music. In the Augustin anecdote, Mahler flees outward into the streets; but his habitual flight path was inward. Another vignette from Mahler's childhood illustrates this strategy. Like his father, Mahler adored books and the ability they gave him to live entirely in his imagination. "I devised the following scheme," he remembered . . . .

> With my treasure of books in my pocket, I climbed onto the roof through the attic window . . . There I read away blissful hours, until someone spied me from the house opposite to ours. Terrified, they informed my father, who ran up to the attic. For perhaps an hour he stood at the garret window in mortal fear, not daring to call, lest I should fall. Finally, I crawled down and was given a terrible beating. To my great sorrow the window was soon walled up. (12)

It seems clear that Mahler was less troubled by the beating he received than by the fact that he was now cut off from his secret space.

Fig. 12 Gustav Mahler circa
"Polka with Introductory Funeral March"

From the beginning of his life, Mahler had the ability to transform pain and grief into "creative issue" by living in his imagination. For Alma Mahler, who subtly and not so subtly trashes her dead husband's image in her memoirs, Mahler's "dreaminess" was sign of weakness, even sickness. Thoroughly outward-looking in her orientation, seeking signs of her own worth in social status and social attention, Alma was continually frustrated and mystified by her husband's introversion. She equated it with pathology. If she and Mahler had lived at the turn of *this* century (the 21st) instead of the turn of the last one, Alma would have found overwhelming support for her point of view . . . and Gustav would have found very little. In 1910, at Alma's insistence, Mahler consulted with Freud. They had a four-hour talk as they walked around the town of Leiden, then parted amicably. It is not clear that very much was gained from this conversation, but nothing much was lost either. Had the year been 2010 rather than 1910, the cost would have been much higher. Alma would have sent Gustav to Dr. Robert Spitzer (or his clone) who would have written the number 301.20 on Mahler's forehead ("Schizoid Personality Disorder") and sent him home with a big bottle of pills.

The term *schizoid* was coined in 1908 by Eugen Bleuler to designate a *natural* human tendency to direct attention toward one's inner life and away from the external world. Conceptually, the term was meant to be close to *introversion* in that Bleuler did not view it as a psychopathology. I am using *schizoid* in the same way, convinced that turning one's attention toward the inner life and away from the external world is essentially a creative act that gives us access to the feeling side of life. We wouldn't have Mahler's symphonies without it. As I have suggested, however, there is frequent confusion, even among mental health professionals, between the term *schizoid* and the term *schizophrenic.* Schizophrenia is one of the major diagnostic categories for serious mental illness. It describes someone who is fundamentally out of touch with reality, hearing voices, in layman's terms just plain crazy. The Schizoid personality is sometimes cut off, too but only in the sense that all the libidinal desire and striving is directed inward, and one lives an intense inner life often revealed in an astonishing wealth of fantasy and imagination. Obviously, this orientation is essential to successful artists.

"Solitude is essential to me when I am composing; as a creative artist I require it without condition," Mahler wrote to a friend. (13) However, he knew that he needed to live in the external world as well and was able to do so for long periods. "I need *practical* exercise for my musical ability to counterbalance the enormous creative activity that goes on within." (14) Ambitious and immensely hard-working, Mahler built a successful career as conductor, primarily of operas, often functioning as art designer and director as well. He began this career in 1880 at a small theater in the spa of Bad Hall in upper Austria and soon realized that he had found his calling. Mahler steadily moved up the ladder to larger theaters. For three years, he served as music director of the Royal Hungarian Opera, often conducting as many as 19 different operas a month. After converting to Catholicism—a formality whose significance the secular Mahler largely shrugged off—he was offered the directorship of the Vienna State Opera, considered to be the most prestigious musical position in the Austrian Empire. In his ten years at the opera, he transformed its repertoire and raised its artistic standards, achieving an international reputation for himself in the process. When he resigned in frustration in May of 1907, he was immediately offered the directorship of the Metropolitan Opera in New York. The 1908 and 1909 seasons were a great success for him. In 1909, Mahler accepted a position as conductor of a revamped New York Philharmonic Orchestra and toughed out a series of battles with the house's financial backers. He planned to return to New York, but by the time he reached Europe in April 1911, he was mortally ill and had only a few weeks to live.

Throughout his thirty-year career as a conductor, Mahler's close attention to detail pleased his audiences but drove his singers and musicians mad. They found him tyrannical, over-demanding, and often brutal in his criticisms. His collaborators' comments about his perfectionism have prompted armchair psychiatrists to diagnose him as having *Obsessive-Compulsive Disorder* or *Obsessive-Compulsive Personality Disorder*, another couple of numbers on his forehead (300.3 and 301.4). The great *fin de siecle* contralto Ernestine Schumann-Heink was disturbed by Mahler's apparent perfectionism as well but saw it in larger context:

. . . Poor Mahler! He was thin and nervous and sensitive, trembling to all music . . . [He] wanted and sought endlessly for perfection. He forgot that there is no perfection in this world . . . He forgot that when the orchestra was before him it was only eighty or a hundred men who were not geniuses like himself, but simply good workers. They often irritated him so terribly that he couldn't bear it; then he became a musical tyrant. And this people couldn't understand or forgive. They didn't see why he was so merciless, and so it was that he was misjudged wherever he went. It was a tragedy for him, this attitude, for deep in his heart he had charity, and he was the most loveable and kindest creature you could imagine—except when he as conducting . . . He was an idealist in every way. He enjoyed every living thing. Why, the shining of the sun, a tree, even the smallest flower, could make ecstasy for him. (15)

What Schumann-Heink moves toward here, but does not quite reach, is an understanding of why Mahler was so difficult when conducting. It was not because he had a mental *disorder* but because he had such an exquisite sense of mental *order*. He needed, deeply needed, for the music the orchestra produced in the external world ("reality") to match exactly the music that he heard in his head (another, even more potent reality). He wanted to reproduce his inner music so that his audiences could feel what he felt. Those overwhelming feelings (ecstasies in sound) were his gift to them, his calling. And he couldn't stand to work with anybody who didn't see their job that way.

This drive to make the internal external continually put him up against the messy collaborative nature of theatrical life, a problem he shared with many equally tyrannical Hollywood film directors (Fritz Lang, Billy Wilder, e.g.) who, decades later, drove their actors nuts (and produced great films in the process) by dictating every line reading and every bit of business. They weren't simply being "Teutonic." They were trying to get their inner vision up on the screen intact.

The artistic struggles inherent in the collaborative process often drained Mahler. He knew that he needed the balance that came from working with others (as well as the money and fame), but he needed to be alone even more. "I am as 'swamped' as only a theatrical director can be," he wrote to a friend:

> A dreadful, consuming life it is! All of my senses and emotions are turned outward. I am becoming more and more a stranger to myself. How will it end? . . . Remember me as one usually remembers those who have died. (16)

He was not entirely being sarcastic. Too much time in the external social world really was deadly for him.

Fig. 13 Caricature of Mahler conducting

Mahler's default position was to value his inner life, his solitude. In consequence, he was sometimes emotionally disconnected, a typical "schizoid" characteristic. He could appear withdrawn, a state that, especially today, might seem to be synonymous with being depressed but is actually quite different. Like most schizoid sensibilities (introverts) Mahler was a nonconformist, indifferent to what people judge to be normal and appropriate in social intercourse. He chose to relate to people authentically or not at all, with no apologies for walking away. This sometimes was misinterpreted as congenital coldness, but Mahler wasn't cold at all. Far from it. Natalie Bauer-Lechner, who knew him well, writes: "Mahler always threw himself vehemently into a friendship whenever he felt especially attracted to a person." If there was no attraction—no authenticity—then he didn't pretend there was.

German-born conductor Bruno Walter, who as a young man became a Mahler protégé, describes Mahler's emotional intensity and range:

> . . . small in stature, pale and thin: the lofty forehead of his long face framed in blue-black hair, and behind glasses, remarkable eyes; lines of sadness and of humor furrowed a countenance across which an astonishing range of expression passed as he spoke to the various people round him . . . Never had I encountered so intense a human being . . . As we were coming off the stage, I was about to take my leave when he stopped me, and said: "Walk a

bit of the way with me." . . . It fascinated me to find the same intensity and high intellectual pitch in his talk as in his rehearsing. The violence with which he rebuffed my insufficient remarks—how shyly I made them! His sudden plunge into reflective silence, then the friendly glance with which he picked up a sensible observation; the unexpected twitches of furtive pain across his face; even the curious irregularity of his walk—now he would stamp; now stand stock-still; now rush ahead . . . (17)

Fig. 14 Mahler at the Vienna Opera, 1902

Everybody noticed these tics, his odd step-stop-stomp gait, characteristics that marked him as eccentric in his own era and as pathological in ours (300.3). Following the Freudian breadcrumb trail, some analysts have suggested that Mahler's gait was an unconscious imitation of his mother's limp, a way of possessing her by incorporating her into his own body. Others interpret his strange movements as Saint Vitus Dance, the result of a chronic bacterial infection he contracted during a childhood bout of rheumatic fever. Both of these theories are plausible but miss the point. Mahler could apparently control his jerking foot when he focused on it. It was only when he was swept away by his own thoughts and feelings that it became noticeable. The stop-start gait was even more clearly linked to mental transport. It was as if his entire motor system were being piloted by his imagination. Nor is this peculiarity confined to Mahler. When lost in imagination, many artists exhibit similar eccentricities. A dear friend of mine, a poet and musician (now dead, alas), would completely forget what he was doing when the muse struck, which it did often and unpredictably. I would be walking down the street with him, volubly making some important conversational point, only to discover that I was talking to empty air. He was a half a block behind, frozen to the spot, his hand raised in the air, conducting a piece of new music that had suddenly popped into his head. He often told a joke on himself, recalling a time when he stood rapt on the sidewalk composing a poem. Only when he was finished did he look down and notice that he was standing in wet concrete that was rapidly hardening around his shoes!

The most visible manifestations of Mahler's need to detach himself were his summer composing huts (*Komponierhäuschen*) in which he wrote much of his greatest music. Their design was an architectonic expression of his entire personality structure. Small spaces (barely 12 feet square) they cloistered Mahler from the external world, allowing him to vastly expand the space of his inner world and connect it to the natural rhythms of the water and the earth. Because he worked so hard during the opera season, often "swamped" by alienated labor, summers were infinitely precious to Mahler, his seasonal alone time, the only time he was free to do nothing but create. The *Komponierhäuschen* were guardhouses, in effect.

There were three of them. The first was at Steinbach am Attersee, about 30 miles east of Salzburg. Mahler and his entourage (his sisters Justine and Emma and his friends Natalie Bauer-Lechner and Bruno Walter) came to Steinbach in 1893 where, working from a room in the inn facing the water, he was able to break his composer's block and make crucial progress on his Second Symphony. Troubled by the noise from the road, the following year Mahler had a small hut built away from the inn, across a flower-filled meadow on the shore of Lake Atter. A simple whitewashed structure with a red tile roof, the hut consisted of a single room, sparsely furnished with a table, a chair, a wood-burning stove, and a piano. There were double windows on three sides and a glass panel door to let in the light and the sounds of the moving water. "Mahler would always say that the lake had its own language, the lake talked to him. From up at the inn, he couldn't hear it," remembered the man who built the hut. (18)

Fig. 15 Mahler's Komponierhäuschen in Sekirn

Mahler completed his Second Symphony at Steinbach in 1894 and drafted the Third Symphony the following year. In 1899, his sisters persuaded him to build a summer house of his own, and work began on an elaborate villa at Maiernigg on the south shore of the Wörthersee. He had a hut constructed on a wooded hill near the lake, accessible only via a steep path. Cloistered in this guard house, from 1900 to 1907, Mahler composed most of his major work, including the fourth, fifth, sixth, seventh, and eighth symphonies. From 1901 on, his young wife Alma joined him at Maiernigg. "He said he could compose only when she was close to his side; but not too close: for actual composition, he demanded complete silence, and he would not even let her play the piano down in the house."(19) Mahler regulated his daily routine protectively, just as he had done at Steinbach. Alma recalls:

> Mahler got up at six or six-thirty every day. As soon as he was awake, he rang for the cook, who promptly prepared his breakfast and carried it up a steep, slippery trail to his forest study, two hundred feet above the house. (She was forbidden to use the regular road, lest he meet her on his way up; before work he could not stand seeing anyone.) The study was a one-room brick hut with a door and three windows, a grand piano, a bookshelf with the collected works of Kant and Goethe. No music but Bach's. About noon he came down, changed and went for a swim . . . . I would sit on the steps and he would climb out to chat, lie on the sun deck until his body was crimson, and jump in again . . . until

he felt reinvigorated. Then we walked back through the garden . . . and sat down to lunch. The soup had to be on the table. Our afternoons were spent walking. Rain or shine, we walked for three or four hours, or rowed around the gleaming, heat-spewing lake. Nor did Mahler stop composing during the afternoon respite: Often he stopped and stood with the sun burning down on his hatless skull, drew out a notebook, wrote, thought, wrote some more. Sometimes he beat time in the air before writing the notes down. This could go on for an hour or more, with me sitting on a tree trunk or in the grass, not daring to look at him. (20)

When Mahler was sequestered in his inner world, any intrusion from the outer world was profoundly disturbing to him. Alma reports:

Once he came back (from the cabin) boiling with rage. I had to dismiss the chambermaid instantly (he said) and he threw himself onto the bed, practically in a swoon. What had happened? Someone had knocked on the door, and the girl had opened it to a stranger asking for 'Mister Mahler'. Under strict orders not to show anyone in, the girl replied: 'the Director is at work and is not to be disturbed by anyone.' The man asked where he was working and the stupid girl indicated in the direction of his Arbeitshaus. The man, representative of a big American piano company, went off calmly into the forest to propose two pianos to 'Mister Mahler', although we already had two grands in New York. He stepped up to the fence and called out in a loud voice: 'How do you do?' Mahler, who was working with the utmost concentration, jumped up and out of the house, threw the man out and staggered back into the studio with a cardiac spasm. He was sobbing when he found me. He said that he felt as though he had been precipitated from the top of St. Stephen's Cathedral. (21)

From 1901 to 1904, working in the hut at Maiernigg, Mahler composed his extraordinary *Kindertotenleider* ("Songs of the Death of Children"), a song cycle based on poems by Friedrich Rückert (1788-1866) written in response to the deaths of Rückert's young son and daughter. Years later, Alma said that she had warned Mahler not to tempt fate, but that, characteristically, he hadn't listened to her. Like so many things that Alma remembered, this may or may not be true. In any case, in July of 1907, the first of three hammer blows of fate knocked at the door of Mahler's woodland cloister. Three days after they had arrived at Maiernigg, the Mahlers' two little girls contracted scarlet fever and diphtheria. The younger of the two, Anna, 3, recovered. The older, Maria ("Putzi," age 5) lingered for two terrible weeks and then died. Mahler, who adored both children, especially Putzi, "hid himself in his room" (Alma remembers) sobbing uncontrollably, unable to bear the sound of Putzi's strangled breathing. (22)

Alma's account makes her the implicit hero of this terrible story, and its victim: *he* ran away, leaving her to manage things alone. *She* is the strong one; he, the weak. In fact, the opposite was true, and not just on this occasion. As a child, Alma had been extremely close to her father, Viennese landscape painter Emil Jakob Schindler, and was devastated when he died suddenly when she was 13. She idealized him in much the same manner that Mahler idealized his mother. In marrying Mahler, an artist 19 years her senior, Alma was seeking to reanimate her lost "family romance," one might conclude. (Mahler even resembled Schindler in build.) There were other forces at work as well, however. "The loveliest girl in Vienna was Alma, the smartest as well," Tom Lehrer begins his immortal song. By 1901 when they first met, though only 22, Alma was smart enough to know that Gustav Mahler was one of the most famous men in Vienna. Passersby pointed him out on the street. Even the anti-Semites who called him "the Jewish monkey" fought for tickets to hear him conduct. And fame mattered for Alma. It was one of many *external* measures she required to validate her own worth. Fame was an aphrodisiac.

Before they married, Mahler, with characteristic tactlessness and honesty, told her what she was in for, more or less. Alma, who fancied herself an artist like her father, had studied music and had competently composed several songs. Mahler was totally unsupportive of her ambitions, however. He wanted a mother-wife-lover who would be in the world solely to support him in *his* art, drawing a magic circle around his need to be alone:

> You could be or become the dearest and most sublime object of my life, my wife, the loyal companion who understands and promotes me . . . Would it be possible for you, from now on, to regard my music as yours? . . . How do you

picture the married life of a husband and wife who are both composers? Have you any idea how ridiculous and, in time, how degrading for both of us such a peculiarly competitive relationship would inevitably become? What will happen if . . . you're 'in the mood,' you're obliged to attend to the house or to something I might happen to need . . . Would it mean the destruction of your life . . . if you were to give up your music entirely in order to possess and also to be mine instead? . . . This point must be settled between us before we can even contemplate a union for life . . . You have only one profession from now on: to make me happy. The role of 'composer,' the 'worker's' role falls to me—yours that of the loving companion and understanding partner. (23)

Alma's initial response was to call the whole thing off, but she says she could not because she realized she loved him. In the end, she reluctantly agreed to Mahler's terms. For years after, she poured out her increasing unhappiness to her diary, blaming Mahler's ban on her artistic career for her suffering:

I don't know what to do. There's such a struggle going on in me! And a miserable longing for someone who thinks OF ME, who helps me to find MYSELF! I've sunk to the level of a housekeeper! . . . I am so tired. If only the one thing was left to me—my music! If only I could still learn. Nothing can be changed! I vegetate. I'm so tired! Gustav is so solitary, so distant! Everything in him is so deeply buried . . . Before, when I felt lonely, there were so many people there to protect me. (24)

Fig. 16 Alma Schindler, 1899

Jealous of Mahler's attentions to Putzi, Alma suffered a serious post-partum depression after the birth of their second daughter in 1904, a Storm of Murk that never entirely lifted. After the death of Putzi, and perhaps before, she began to abuse alcohol.

Was Mahler's Schizoid Personality to blame for Alma's angst? In some respects, yes. Like the marriage of his parents, Alma and Gustav "belonged together like fire and water." He was not an easy man to live with, to put it mildly! Mahler despised the conventions of society and sometimes neglected the conventions of affection as well, passing his closest friends in the street without noticing them. On one occasion, in the midst of a conversation with a musician, he leapt from the street into a tram without finishing his sentence. He once walked and bicycled for four days without addressing a word to anyone. (25) Being one of his friends was never an easy matter. Being his wife was even harder.

There are numerous examples of how the intensity of Mahler's inner world made him oblivious to the demands and customs of the outer world. Alma recalled that in restaurants he would often stand up, point, and call out loudly: "Waiter! What is that gentleman over there eating?" He once stirred his coffee with a cigarette and then puffed a stream of liquid onto the table. One evening in Budapest, he took Justine to have coffee at the Stadtwaldchen, one of the city's most elegant cafes. They sat at a table on the highest terrace in order to enjoy the view. His attention taken up by the conversation, Mahler casually tossed the contents of his water glass over the balustrade, onto an elegant group on the lower terrace. Another scene occurred when the Mahlers were invited to dine at the house of a wealthy family. As usual, Gustav arrived late from the opera; the other guests were already at table. No sooner had he taken his place than he selected an apple from one of the decorative fruit-dishes garnishing the table, sniffed its perfume and put it down next to his plate, much to the astonishment of the other guests. He quickly polished off the main course, then, without waiting for the dessert, got up and went into the smoking room. (26) In Vienna, where good manners were considered essential, Mahler was off the charts—and oblivious to the embarrassment he habitually caused his social-conscious wife.

And yet, as Alma's own diary outpourings suggest, the real problems she had lay within herself—or, rather, with her inability to find herself inside herself. For Mahler, an introvert, to be alone was to be connected, at peace. For Alma, an extrovert practiced in the art of agitated depression, to be alone was terrifying. Disconnected from the social world that gave her value (the constant stream of compliments about her beauty and intelligence), she had no resources. She came up empty. Disguising that emptiness (her Hollow Fortress Self) became her life's work. She continued it long after Mahler's death, taking posthumous revenge on him by portraying him as a neurotic megalomaniac. It is worth noting, of course, that she never gave up his name and the increasing fame that attended it. Although she had at least one lover during their marriage and many lovers thereafter, to her death she billed herself as his widow, Alma *Mahler*-Werfel.

Is this account too hard on Alma? Probably so. But it underscores an important theme in this chapter, namely that, in a crisis, introverts often have greater emotional resilience than extroverts because they are looking the right way to begin with: inward, toward the place where the feelings are. This was clearly true in the Mahlers' lives after the death of Putzi. Alma, already suffering from chronic endogenous depression, became unable to shake her apathy and despair. Mahler, in contrast, plunged into an abyss of grief and emerged emotionally intact. With one stroke," he wrote to Bruno Walter, "I have lost everything I have gained in terms of who I thought I was, and have to learn my first steps again like a newborn." Although neither Mahler nor Alma could bear returning to Maiernigg, they found a house in Alt-Schluderbach, near Toblach in the South Tyrol. Mahler had another small hut built in the woods with a panoramic view across the valley to the mountains. There, in the summer of 1908, he began to compose *Das Lied von der Erde*.

CHAPTER SEVEN
JOY AND ANGST

Mahler's compositions are huge mystery plays, starting from earth and climbing to heaven, when choruses of angels and the light of the Almighty hail the newcomer, while in the depths Death plays on a strident violin and hell screams.

—Max Graf (1)

HOW CAN WE BE REBORN in the face of life's inevitable disappointments and tragedies? The Danish philosopher Søren Kierkegaard (1813-1855) believed that the first step is the acceptance of anxiety. Knowing from his own experience how difficult this is to do, he also suggested a bit wistfully that it is probably better to be an extrovert and live tucked into others, embedded in a safe framework of social and cultural obligations and duties, than to feel so anxious. When we are born, we are thrust out into a hostile environment that is not necessarily conducive to our survival. We will never fully recover from the existential anxiety of this separation, the loss of the comfort of the womb, the disconnection from our mother and from Mother Earth—and from the rest of the universe that surrounds us. Mahler experienced this disconnection quite profoundly at times and carried at the core of his being a desire to reconnect. We are of the earth and to the earth we return. We are born; we have our precious human being-ness; and we die. The you and me we know ceases to be. No matter what fantasies we have about the continued existence of the "soul," the "resurrection of the body," or "a heaven full of virgins," the truth is the truth. Death is hard-wired into life. Ernst Becker puts it succinctly:

> [Man] is out of nature and hopelessly in it; he is dual, up in the stars and yet housed in a heart-pumping, breath-gasping body that once belonged to a fish and still carries the gill-marks to prove it. His body is a material fleshy casing that is alien to him in many ways the strangest and most repugnant being that aches and bleeds and will decay and die. Man is literally split in two: he has an awareness of his own splendid uniqueness in that he sticks out of nature with a towering majesty, and yet he goes back into the ground a few feet in order blindly and dumbly to rot and disappear forever. (2)

All of us know this by the time we are five, but we don't like to be reminded. It is our open secret. I, too, dislike being reminded, especially if what follows is some philosophical or theological discussion designed to make me feel better. No discussion is going to make me feel better, thank you! I resent having been given a life and then having it taken away. I dislike feeling helpless under any circumstances, and the vulnerability and impotency I feel when I remember that I am going to lose *everything*, the entire wonder and beauty of the universe, is too much to bear. These elemental feelings of separation and estrangement create a desperate longing for closeness with another person, or with people in general, or for some sense of connection to the earth, the water, and the energy of the universe. Because overcoming this basic estrangement is never complete, it is easy for us to become overwhelmed with a painful sense of aloneness and abandonment.

Fig. 17 Søren Kierkegaard (1813-1855)

Music Selection Five: *To describe this First Movement of Mahler's Fourth Symphony, his words are best: "What I had in mind here was unbelievably difficult to do. Imagine the uniform blue of the skies, which is more difficult to paint than all changing and contrasting shades. This is the fundamental mood of the whole. Only sometimes it darkens and becomes ghostly, gruesome. But heaven itself is not so darkened; it shines on in an eternal blue. Only to us it suddenly seems gruesome, just as on the most beautiful day in the woods, flooded with light, we are often gripped by panic and fear. The Scherzo (second movement) is mystical, confused and eerie so that your hair will stand on end. But in the following Adagio you will soon see that things were not so bad – everything is resolved."*

Bruno Walter, NY Philharmonic, 1945.
http://www.overcomingdepressionwithoutdrugs.com/music

As long as we are alive, we are never without the anxiety associated with these primordial feelings of helplessness and estrangement. It is the background noise of our existence. The existentialists tell us that we are foolish to try to deny the terror that our impending nonbeing provokes. Agitated depression is one form of denial. We keep ourselves busy, busy, busy with nothing that has any real significance; we relate frenetically without risking authentic intimacy; we seek security but can never find enough of it because, ultimately, only vulnerability and impotence are real. Something terrible can happen to us at any moment, and deep down inside, we know it. Kierkegaard believed that the only people who are truly free are those who can look life in the face and realize that everything is problematic—that we are shipwrecked. The only genuine thoughts are the ideas of the shipwrecked, and only from that existential position can we possibly bring any order into the chaos of life. All else is farce. "The idea of death, the fear of it, haunts the human animal like nothing else," Becker says. "It is the mainspring of human activity—activity designed largely to avoid the finality of death, to overcome it by denying in some way that it is the final destiny of man." (3)

Does this mean that we should spend our lives reminding ourselves that we are going to die, keeping skulls on our desks like medieval monks? No! Precisely because life is short, uncertain, and precious, we shouldn't spoil a single second of it. I simply want to suggest that the best way *not* to spoil it is to spend very little time and energy on a quest for security. (That includes religious dogma that promises us immortality.) Seeking security saps the energy we need for joyful living, leaving us depressed: we die to keep from dying. Whether or not we have a skull on our desk, our primordial anxiety is always there humming along just below the waterline of our civilized existence. The trick is not to react too much when, on occasion, it pops up to the surface.

Unfortunately, most people on earth don't need a decorative skull to remind them of their mortality. For millions of men, women and children, the specter of death appears daily in many guises—thirst, hunger, earthquakes, murder, torture.

For soldiers in a war zone, death is routine. For men and women in extended care facilities, death may seem like a good idea, especially if they are ill or zonked out on antidepressants. For most adolescents, death seems quite distant. But not always. A teenager I know quite well lost her mother when she was only sixteen. For Gustav Mahler, the death of children was a regularly scheduled event. He never got used to it; but it became a familiar feature of his experience, as did the transitory nature of even the deepest grief. He didn't get over his losses, especially the loss of Putzi; but he got *through* them.

At times of great sorrow and loss, Mahler instinctively sought connection to the natural world, as if he could burrow back into Mother Earth. Being in the forest or near the water "grounded" him when he had lost his bearings. Watching Mahler play his new Third Symphony on the piano in his composing hut, Bruno Walter was reminded of Pan:

> Had he been an ordinary "nature lover," a devotee of gardens and animals, his music would have been more "civilized." Here however, the Dionysiac possession by nature, which I had learned to recognize, sounded through music that expressed the very root of his being. Now I seemed to see him in the round: I saw him as possessed alike by the stark power of the crags and by the tender flowers, as familiar with the dark secrets of the life of the animals in the woods . . . . He brought everything—aloofness and whimsy, cruelty and untamability—to life. I saw him as Pan . . . . Light streamed from him onto his work and from his work onto him. (4)

Mahler's powerful spirituality had nothing to do with conventional religious beliefs, which generally support depressive fantasies of escape rather than a sense of existential freedom. (Once we accept that we will lose everything, there is nothing left to lose, and we can adopt Alfred E. Newman's motto, "What, me worry?") There may be a place for religious experience in our lives if it begins and ends with feelings of wonder and awe, but doctrinal prescriptions about the steps to take to avoid death will only lead us to an emotional cul-de-sac. "The most beautiful emotion we can experience is the mysterious," said Einstein, "It is the fundamental emotion that stands at the cradle of all true art and science. He to whom this emotion is a stranger, who can no longer wonder and stand rapt in awe, is as good as dead, a snuffed-out candle."

Much of what passes for "faith" has nothing to do with awe and mystery. It is merely one of many unconsciously motivated habits designed to push away the feelings of vulnerability and helplessness. Insight into these patterns gives us the privilege of choice, a choice to go *into* the dark places of our souls when opportunity arises (and it will arise!) . . . and even to welcome the experience to become more connected with our primordial selves. An observing ego—a sense of humor—also helps. I'm continually amazed at all the unconscious maneuvers I use just so I can get myself into situations where I feel helpless. For example, for years I had a pattern of taking on difficult tasks that I knew full well I did not have the skill or the patience or the time to accomplish. I was setting myself up to be overwhelmed. I used to see this kind of behind-our-backs emotional entitlement as pathological, something to fix in therapy; but actually, it is incredibly freeing. Periodically, we need a dose of helplessness just to remind ourselves that we are human.

As Kierkegaard tells us, ". . . the curriculum of the 'school' of anxiety is the unlearning of repression . . ." (5) Every time we narrow the range of "acceptable" feelings, every time we avoid anxiety, we kill off part of ourselves. Eventually, we kill off so much of ourselves that we have little feeling left, transforming ourselves into emotional Zombies, totally depressed. We can do this as individuals at low cost by using repression. Or we can do it on a larger societal scale by using antidepressants. In the later case, the cost is higher in every respect.

In order to avoid these traps, we need to understand the distinction between anxiety and tension, which are often falsely conflated. Indeed, in advertizing copy, "anxiety and tension" are frequently grouped together it is as if they were one word. This confusion is exacerbated by the pharmaceutical industry because they have a wonderful drug that treats "anxiety and tension," a tranquilizer. Tranquilizers are muscle relaxers, among many other things, or so we are told. Since relaxing muscles is as effective in reducing anxiety as it is in reducing stress, there is little reason to make any distinction. However, if one does not go the drug route, the distinction is crucial. Tension has to do with conflict, the conflict between behavior and feeling. The stronger the feeling and the more discrepant the behavior, the greater the tension. Tension is bad. It raises your blood pressure. It stresses your heart. It can kill you.

There may be an appropriate use of tranquilizing drugs to break cycles of acute tension. However, they should only be used briefly because of the risk of addiction. Similarly, one might reasonably choose to use a low-dose tranquilizer briefly to support an anxiety-laden choice one would otherwise avoid. Flying is just such an experience for many people, it seems. Taking a tranquilizer to manage the experience might be the only way to make an important flight. As Dr. Breggin and others have pointed out, however, tranquilizers cause an early stage of central nervous system depression—sedation. The basic clinical effect on the mind cannot be distinguished from alcohol or barbiturates. Moreover, withdrawal is only one of the problems associated with tranquilizer use. "An even more terrifying specter haunts the long-term use of minor tranquilizers—the possibility of brain atrophy. The minor tranquilizers are like alcohol and when used long-term cause brain shrinkage." (6)

Feelings of anxiety are so intractable, and so fundamental to us as human beings, that to attempt to eliminate them through drugs will never succeed in allaying our dis-ease. From a therapeutic perspective, it is preferable to view any anxiety-laden experience as an opportunity to embrace existential truths and drop the defenses we unconsciously employ to obscure our essential vulnerability. I believe what we usually call *excitement* is really *embraced anxiety*. In other words, the *anxiety* sometimes associated with flying is the flip side of the *excitement* associated with flying. (As a pilot I experience both sides all the time!)

In short, anxiety, fear, and excitement are sister feelings. Our physiological experience is similar in each. Anxiety has a tendency to "regress toward" fear, fancy language that means we would rather be afraid than anxious. The difference is semantic: fear has an object, there is something definite of which we are afraid; anxiety is vague, undifferentiated apprehension. Excitement is an experience of vulnerability wherein the thrill is worth the risk (like skydiving). If there is a tiger in our path, we are afraid. If we don't see a tiger but are in an area where tigers might be, we are anxious. To be in an area where we might see a tiger in the wild, while having a reasonable escape route, is exciting!

Unfortunately, in the last thirty years, the belief that anxiety is a mental illness that drugs can cure has become almost universally accepted. The possibility that the experience of existential anxiety might be a normal human condition has become completely obscured in the marketing of drugs. However, as Carl Jung intuited more than a hundred years ago in his concept of the "collective unconscious" and as neuroscientist Antonio Damasio has demonstrated in his recent body-minded brain studies, feelings in general and anxiety in particular have crucial evolutionary functions. That is, *anxiety cannot be eliminated*. It is a fundamental part of what makes us human beings.

Every time we choose to avoid anxiety, we die a little in the midst of life. Moreover, every time we choose to avoid anxiety, we make it more difficult in the future to choose anything that could conceivably make us anxious. The result is that we paint ourselves into a psychological corner, withdrawing more and more from whatever might enable us to feel alive and vital and excited. In short, we move toward depression. The bottom line is simple: Every choice we make is either a movement toward life-affirming anxiety or a movement toward life-denying depression.

Once again, Gustav Mahler offers us a powerful example of the courage it takes to make affirming choices. When a physician was called to attend their dying daughter, Putzi, Alma thought to distract Mahler from his acute distress (or so she says) by suggesting that the doctor examine Mahler's heart. Her unconscious motivation would appear to be ambivalent since Mahler had had rheumatic fever as a child and there was undoubtedly some previous evidence of valve damage. Not surprisingly, the "distraction" turned out to be formidable. As he listened to Mahler's heart, the physician became alarmed and told Mahler that he was in immediate danger of heart failure. He suggested Mahler consult a specialist. Mahler did so, and the specialist confirmed the initial diagnosis: Mahler had an irregular heartbeat and might die at any moment if he exerted himself too much or became too excited.

Ironically, the diagnosis was incorrect. The irregular heartbeat was something that Mahler probably had had from birth. The danger was not exertion but *infection* that could enter his heart through the leaky valves. Apparently, Mahler didn't know this, however; and four years later, he contracted a streptococcal infection during a visit to a dentist in New York. It was the sort of thing can be easily cured today with penicillin. Unfortunately, penicillin wasn't discovered until 1928, 17 years after Mahler's death. He was 52.

During the four years between his daughter's death and his own, Mahler lived with the belief that his next heartbeat might be his last. Both his doctors and his wife treated him as sickly, re-enforcing a sense of immanent doom. Nevertheless, because the presence of death had been no stranger in his life—and because he had gone into the abyss before and come out whole—there were long stretches of his life in which he was remarkably free from worry.

During the first year after the diagnosis, he dutifully followed his doctors' orders to forego strenuous exercise. He gave up hiking, which he loved and which he needed to free the flow of music in his imagination. He gave up the bicycling he enjoyed, and he gave up swimming, a treasured daily activity during his summers in the Tyrol. Then he changed his mind. Throwing the dice, he decided that his doctors were wrong about his sick heart. He had been protecting himself to death. But not anymore. Un-pathologizing himself, he resumed his normal activities, doing the things that gave him joy, determined to *live* his life and not merely exist.

Although biographer Stuart Feder sees Mahler ultimately as a broken, neurotic man, recently discovered correspondence proves otherwise. In spite of everything that had happened to him, none of which he could control, to the end of his life, Mahler remained emotionally strong and vital. He continued to compose music with the same intensity. He continued to struggle with deep philosophical questions about the meaning of life and death. While it is unclear whether or not Mahler knew Kierkegaard, he would certainly have agreed with the philosopher when he says,

> In the eyes of the world, it is dangerous to venture. And why? Because one may lose . . . . And yet, by not venturing, it is so dreadfully easy to lose that which it would be difficult to lose in even the most venturesome venture—one's self. For if I have ventured amiss—very well, then life helps me by its punishment. But if I have not ventured at all—who then helps me when I lose myself? (7)

Fig. 18 Mahler's grave

CHAPTER EIGHT

REGRESSION IN THE SERVICE OF THE EGO

Fur dich leben! Fur dich sterben!

(To live for you! To die for you!) Almschi

—Gustav Mahler (1)

THE SUMMER OF 1910 began badly for Mahler. He had left New York for Europe but had agreed to return in the fall to conduct the Philharmonic. Having completed his Ninth Symphony in March, he had been looking forward to spending time in his composing Häuchen hut near Toblach working on a new symphony. His commitment to the Philharmonic shortened his summer break, however, threatening to deprive him of the isolation and freedom from interruption he needed in order to compose. As it turned out, this snag was the least of his problems. By the end of the summer, the loss of solitude would seem trivial compared to the new loss he would suddenly have to face: the loss of his wife to another man.

The long ocean voyage from New York had been especially difficult for Alma. She now dreaded the summertime. The blessing of isolation for Mahler meant loneliness for her. Never good company for herself, she had recently suffered a series of miscarriages that left her despondent. Unable to face the impending third anniversary of Putzi's death in July, she lost herself in a Storm of Murk. The official diagnosis was a "nervous disorder." Leaving Mahler in his Häuchen, Alma followed doctors' orders and went off for a "rest cure" at a fashionable sanatorium/spa in Tobelbad.

"My nerves were in a critical state and . . . I longed to plunge myself into love or life or anything that could release me from my icy constraints," she wrote. (2) Suffering from a number of psychosomatic illnesses and perhaps alcoholism, Alma at 31 was no longer so confident in the power of her beauty to bring her the reassuring attention from men that she craved. Gustav, creatively "lost to the world" most of the time, was unlikely to spend much effort shoring up her fragile ego with a shower of pretty compliments. In short, Alma was ripe for an affair.

She found a willing partner almost immediately in Walter Gropius, a handsome 27 year old architect and future founder of the Bauhaus school, who was "taking the waters" at Tobelbad when Alma arrived. In her memoirs, Alma describes herself as restrained: "I lived an utterly solitary life at Tobelbad, as I always did whenever I was by myself anywhere." (3) She acknowledged that the head of the sanatorium had been worried about her and introduced her to a young architect (Gropius) who was sympathetic. "I soon had little doubt he was in love with me and hoping I might return his love. So I left." (4)

Well, not quite! Mahler brought Alma to Tobelbad on 1 June. On 4 June, her physician introduced her to Gropius. Her "solitary life" had lasted two days. She and Gropius began making love almost immediately. The intensity of the experience is apparent in this passage from Alma's unpublished diary:

Fig. 19 Alma Mahler, 1910

"I remember one night that was troubled by the coming light of the morning and by the sweet singing of a nightingale—but beside me lay a beautiful young man—and on that night two souls met and the body was forgotten."(5)

Not surprisingly, Alma's letters to Gustav became less frequent and more distant in tone. Mahler, who Natalie observed was "sensitive to every tremor of his delicately strung soul," sensed Alma's distancing immediately but assumed she was simply not giving herself enough to the "cure." As was Mahler's custom, he began writing her lengthy philosophical tracts that, if anything, drove Alma even more passionately into the arms of Gropius. In her deeply depressed state, the excitement of the affair was life-saving for Alma. Gropius' ardent attentions were far more effective than purgative waters in diminishing her repressed feelings of helplessness and restoring her sense of self-worth. For Mahler, however, the affair was life-threatening. Even before he knew the truth, he began to feel abandoned by the one person with whom he was most seriously invested emotionally.

Mahler, like other introverts, did not habitually "tuck himself into other people" or cultivate a wide social support network. He had bonded with one significant person (his mother-wife-lover Alma), a relationship that therefore had ultimate significance. Because his marriage was so central to Mahler—his one real tie to the external world—when it began to disintegrate, *he* began to disintegrate, in the most literate sense. He fell apart, losing himself in a state of frightening depersonalization and regression. This process began even before Mahler knew of Gropius. Sensing that Alma was moving away from him, Mahler moved toward her. Sensing that he seemed more in love with her than ever before, she moved further away. In one of his visits, her greeting seemed to be confined to a complaint about his bad haircut.

Fig. 20 Walter Gropius

Alma's mother, Anna Moll, encouraged her daughter's relationship with Gropius. Anna was undoubtedly glad to see her daughter come back from the dead; and unconsciously she may have supported the liaison to justify an extramarital affair that she had had when married to Alma's father, about which Alma had been quite judgmental. In any case, after they left Tobelbad, Walter and Alma carried on a passionate correspondence using her mother as a blind. At the same time, Anna, whom Mahler loved and trusted, continued to act as his confidant, without revealing the secret she knew . . . the stuff of soap operas! Finally, it was Gropius (a big fan of Mahler's music, by the way) who broke the news. Apparently unwilling to maintain the deception—a game that didn't seem to bother Alma—Gropius made a classic Freudian slip and "misaddressed" a love letter to Alma to the attention of "Herr Director Mahler." The letter got Mahler's full attention. Alma remembers,

> Mahler was seated at the piano when he opened the letter. "What is this?" he asked in a choking voice and handed it to me. He was convinced at the time, and remained convinced ever after, that the architect had deliberately addressed the letter to him as his way of asking for my hand in marriage. And now—at last—I was able to tell him all. I told him I had longed for his love year after year and that he, in his fanatical concentration on his own life, had simply overlooked me . . . We sent for my mother to come to our aid, and until she came we could do nothing but walk about together all day

long in tears. [From that moment,] the doors of our two rooms, which were next to each other, had to be always open . . . I often woke in the night and found him standing by my bedside in the darkness . . . I had to fetch him from his studio every day for meals. I did so very cautiously. He was often on the floor weeping in his dread that he might lose me, had lost me perhaps already. On the floor, he said, he was nearer the earth. (6)

Alma now took the lead in a ghastly relational game that she and Mahler would play out, with varying degrees of intensity, for the remainder of his life. She held on fiercely to her passion for Gropius (whom she would marry in 1915, after Mahler's death and an intervening affair with artist Oskar Kokoschka). Whatever her passion for Mahler had been, it was dead. ("Now that my eyes had been opened by the impetuous assaults of a youthful lover . . . I knew that my marriage was no marriage.") However, to "spare [Mahler's] feelings," she concealed her feelings from him. Mahler, acutely sensitive to emotional nuance, intuited the truth, of course. ("He knew it as well as I did.") But he went along with the game rather than lose Alma outright. Thus "we played out the comedy to the end." This sort of disjunction between behavior and feelings generally puts people in the madhouse with a diagnosis of schizophrenia. ("I hate you so I bring you cookies.") And it nearly drove Mahler mad as well; but ultimately, he survived even this crisis, for reasons that are worth examining more closely.

Gropius—who seems to have been as interested in getting close to Mahler as he was in getting close to Alma—made the next move. One day while she was driving through town with Mahler, Alma spotted Gropius hiding under a bridge. He had been "lurking in the neighborhood" for some time, trying to clandestinely establish contact.

> My heart stopped, but only from freight, not joy. I told Mahler at once, and he said: 'I'll go and bring him along myself." He went straight down to Toblach and found him at once. "Come along," he said. Nothing more was said by either . . . . and in silence they walked all the way up to our house, Mahler in front with a lantern and [Gropius] following on behind. (7)

At this point in the drama, Mahler seems almost delusional. He adored Wagner and had a special fondness for *Die Meistersinger von Nürnberg* (1868), which he had directed and conducted many times. When first contemplating marriage to Alma, 19 years his junior, Mahler had made nervous references to Hans Sachs, the lead character in *Die Meistersinger*, who secretly loves a much younger woman, Eva. Spotting Walter Gropius under the bridge, Mahler now seems determined to act out the second half of Wagner's plot in which Sachs, sacrificing his own feelings, helps the young man named "Walther" win Eva's hand! Alma recalls,

> Mahler came in with a very serious air. I hesitated for a long time before going to speak to [Gropius], and I broke off

our interview after a few minutes from a sudden alarm on Mahler's account. I found Mahler walking up and down his room. Two candles were alight on his table. He was reading the Bible. "Whatever you do will be right," he said. "Make your decision." But I had no choice! (8)

Alma sent Gropius on his way that night, but she continued to play a double game. While promising the abject Mahler that she wouldn't leave him, she was simultaneously telling Gropius, "I feel you as my betrothed" and "I must now see whether I can put up with this life at least until I—that is to say you—call me to you . . . so that I can follow you in full confidence and you without any anxiety can take me home." Gropius must have "called" her immediately, because the next day Alma wrote him again, this time to keep him at bay: "'Our' future . . . can't come as quickly as you think—Gustav lay the whole day long at my feet, and kept asking me, sobbing: 'Are you going to stay with me?' Finally I promised that I would and he said that in doing that I had saved his life." (9)

Reading this correspondence, it is easy to adopt Tom Lehrer's cynical view of Alma as wholly manipulative, and so she was; but there is no need to enlarge Mahler's humanity by diminishing hers to caricature. Because Alma was so completely other-directed—so much invested in behaviors and words and no little invested in emotion—it is difficult to know what she was actually feeling at any given point. Her father Emil had suffered from bouts of severe depression that may or may not have been triggered by his wife's adultery.

During periods when he was depressing himself, as well as periods of artistic creativity, he could not have been very emotionally available to his daughter. Alma's idealization of her relationship with her father, its closeness, thus may have been based more on a *yearning* for an all-encompassing love than on the fact of it. (Mahler's idealization of his mother may have had a similar foundation.) Her choice of the inward-turning Mahler as a father-lover surrogate suggests that Alma was unconsciously setting herself up for an encore, i.e., putting herself in a situation in which she would be *entitled* to the feelings of helplessness, yearning, and abandonment she had felt as a child, feelings that she consciously protected herself from feeling.

Keeping both Gropius and Mahler on the string would have served to enlarge Alma's sense of control and desirability. Having two lovers made her a double woman. The fact that both men vying for her were artists would have magically erased, for a time, her primary sense of childhood marginalization, unable to get her artist-father's attention. All this gratification would have ended the moment she made a choice, however; which is probably why she refused to choose. Moreover, her bond with Mahler may have been deeper than her words suggest. Clearly, whatever emotion she got from Gropius paled in comparison to the emotion she used Gropius to get from Mahler. Lying prostrate and weeping at her feet, Mahler elevated her to a position of total control (or at least the illusion of control). At the same time, his helplessness *acted out* for her the feelings of helplessness that she could not own directly in herself. Mahler was *her* emotional surrogate and her father's surrogate at once. It was a remarkably efficient projective configuration. Little wonder that Alma held on to it for as long as she could.

From Mahler's perspective, the prospect of losing Alma plunged him into an abyss of primordial feelings of abandonment. That wasn't what drove him crazy, however. What maddened him was the contradictory emotional messages Alma was sending him. Most of the ostensibly psychotic people I worked with in St. Elizabeth's were there because of this kind of *schizophrenigenic* double bind: when the words say one thing and the feelings say another, there is no way we can win for losing. (Think of Charles Boyer and Ingrid Bergman in *Gaslight*.) At some deep level, Mahler knew that Alma was continuing her involvement with Gropius and that he should distrust her words. Not to know whether to trust the words and behavior or one's intuitive sense of feelings is what much of functional schizophrenia is all about. My Jesus Men taught me to trust the feelings. ("I don't listen to words, I listen to feelings," said my guru Mr. H.) Thomas Sasz agrees: "We need the sanity of the insane to show how insane our sanity is." In the summer of 1910, Mahler suddenly found himself trapped in an insane world with no way to ground himself in experiential reality. He responded by regressing to a state of childlike helplessness and terror.

The crisis precipitated by the possibility that Alma might abandon him was extreme. In the vernacular, Mahler "fell to pieces." Stuart Feder describes Mahler as suffering from a "decomposition of his accustomed mental functioning (which was normally excellent), commonly called a nervous breakdown. The episode proved to be brief but intense and involved severe anxiety, distortion of reality, and even frank suicidal ideation."(10) Indeed, there is no question that Mahler's symptoms qualify for a DSM-IV diagnosis of major depression (296.2x) and a large bottle of antidepressant medication. Luckily for Mahler, Prozac wouldn't appear on the market for another 77 years, so he had time to recover on his own. Which he eventually did, but not right away. He was feeling *a lot* of anxiety.

Again, *anxiety* means that we are experiencing primordial feelings of vulnerability, projecting (picturing) that something quite bad is likely to happen, something we feel helpless to control or prevent. Existentially, there is an underlying anxiety built into life itself, a product of our constant subliminal knowledge that we will eventually cease to be. In short, any time we feel anxious, we feel a lot. For Mahler, the sudden possibility that Alma could leave him precipitated a global existential crisis that temporarily shattered his adult identity.

In her later memoirs, Alma (nicked-named "Tiger Mami" by her daughter Anna) (11) portrayed Mahler as entirely responsible for her relationship with Gropius, insisting that Mahler's emotional neglect and sexual inadequacies had driven her to seek satisfaction elsewhere. She obviously had conveyed these views to Mahler as well, who completely internalized her judgments and became childlike and pathetically over-solicitous. She complained that she would sometimes find him standing outside her bedroom in the middle of the night just gazing at her as she slept. She once found a note by her bedside:

> My breath of life! I've kissed the little slippers a thousand times and stood by your door with longing. You took pity on me, glorious one, but the demons punished me again, for thinking again of myself and not of you, dearest. I can't move from your door; I'd like to stand there until I've heard the sweet sound of your living and breathing. (12)

"From now on," writes biographer Henri-Louis de LaGrange, "Gustav's one effort, invested with all the more intensity and passion because he believed the cause was a lost one, was to woo Alma as if she were an angry goddess." (13) Alma acknowledged that she had never experienced Mahler more loving or attentive to her, but she used his vulnerability to berate him for past failures and his unfair treatment of her. She focused particularly on the seething resentment she felt about his demand that she give up her music. In his new state of being, Mahler searched out the songs she had composed and played them for her, encouraging her to take up composition again. (The fact that Alma did not resume her musical career, even after Mahler's death, suggests that her conscious resentment may have been a proxy for other unconscious feelings, feelings that had much less to we Mahler than she might have imagined.)

At one point, Mahler's anxiety and vulnerability led him to suicidal despair. On the title page of the second Scherzo of his Tenth Symphony, his current project, he wrote:

> (The Devil is dancing it with me,
> Madness, seize me, the accursed!
> Destroy me
> Let me forget that I exist!
> So that I cease to be
> So that I . . .) (14)

"Over the last measures of the Finale, at a point where the music strikes a particularly harrowing note, with the searing upward melodic leap (B sharp—G sharp), these simple words utter Mahler's despair and his undying love" . . .

> 'Fur dich leben! (To live for you!)
> Fur dich sterben! (To die for you!)
> Almschi!'" (15)

Music Selection Six: *The opening viola solo of this First (and only completed) Movement of the Tenth Symphony expresses an absolute despair, unlike anything except the final coda of Mahler's Sixth Symphony. There could hardly be more eloquent evidence of Mahler's state of psychological distress than what he expressed in this music, composed during the month of August 1910, the month he took his afternoon stroll with Sigmund Freud. We have in this music an all-powerful emotional outburst, from the pitch black darkness of the introduction right through to the hymnic declaration of the closing bars. The exception is in the distant ray of hope that takes shape in the heavenly flute solo, one of the most inspired and moving melodies Mahler ever composed. Towards the end, this motif is tenderly reiterated, exchanged with the woodwinds and finally taken up by the horns. On the top of this passage Mahler wrote the tender words: "Fur dich leben! Fur dich sterben! Almischi!" De LaGrange adds, "but what torment, what anguish, what paroxysms of agony he suffered before reaching this ultimate state of blissful fulfillment!"*

🎧 **Hermann Scherchen, Wiener Staatsoper Orch, 1952.**
http://www.overcomingdepressionwithoutdrugs.com/music

For most armchair psychoanalysts, these intense outcries sound like symptoms of a dangerous clinical depression. As I have suggested, I find this view paradoxical. The people who appear in my office describing themselves as depressed do not generally complain that they feel too much; they complain that they don't feel very much at all anymore. In this sense, "intense outcries" are not symptoms of anything; they are expressions of feeling and as such, antithetical to depression in its most basic meaning ("pushing down"). Because he had spent so much of his creative life in touch with intense emotions, and because he knew that, in life and as in music, both the high notes and low notes are transitory, Mahler had the capacity to feel the full force of his feelings even when his sobbing threatened to tear him apart. He was shattered, but he was not depressed! There was no feeling he was pushing down. He felt it all. In fact, throughout these terrible months, his very weeping washed him clean of despair. Even in the midst of his agony, he felt that, in some strange way, he was being reborn, that he had begun to exist as a new and better human being.

Anton Boisen (1876-1965), a pioneering hospital chaplain, suffered a series of psychotic breaks as a young man. He was diagnosed with "catatonic dementia praecox," a condition that would later have been termed "catatonic schizophrenia." One of the main characteristics of this reaction was an almost total withdrawal from the external world and an absorption in what is going on within, a withdrawal that often takes the form of catatonic stupor. Boisen was involuntarily committed to a mental hospital in a catatonic state, having lost speech but not hearing. The attending physician, overlooking the possibility that Boisen might be able to hear him, said to an intern while doing rounds, "there is no need to spend much time with a patient in this condition, it's pretty hopeless." Boisen recovered suddenly a few weeks later, to everyone's surprise, most especially to his own. "To be plunged as a patient into a hospital for the insane may be a tragedy or it may be an opportunity. For me it has been an opportunity," he wrote later. (16)

Boisen described his exploration of his inner world in terms that are somewhat similar to Jung's conscious explorations reported in *Liber Novus* (the "Red Book"). Both men saw their terribly disorienting and frightful journey into the depths as having religious and psychological significance. Boisen believed that certain men of unquestionable religious genius could pass through a period of intense psychic regression or emotional breakdown and yet successfully return from these depths of despair to a new perspective on life, a new ordering of priorities. These explorations of the inner world could thus be thought of not as tragic "breaks" with reality but as problem solving experiences, make or break attempts at reorganizing the psyche that call forth hidden sources of power and succeed in bringing about a profound unification of the personality. Mahler's inner journey of 1910 did not take him as far down as Boisen's did; but he, too, used his experience of "falling apart" as an opportunity to put himself back together on new and better terms.

Much has been made of the ostensible role that Sigmund Freud played in Mahler's recovery. Without doubt, Mahler's four-hour afternoon stroll with Freud though the streets of Leiden was significant in turning Mahler's despair into hope, but that shift hardly was the result of some deep psychoanalysis. It was more like the placebo effect of an "antidepressant" drug. Mahler had faith in Freud because Freud had been instrumental in curing Mahler's friend Bruno Walter, and

Freud convinced Mahler that all was far from hopeless with Alma; he could win her back.

Prior to 1910, Mahler had often expressed disdain for Freud's psychoanalytic theories. However, Bruno Walter had recently had a very positive experience with Freud that apparently moderated Mahler's views. Walter had been experiencing pain in his right arm and was terrified that it might lead to the end of his career as a conductor. The doctors he consulted, one after another, diagnosed his problem with medical precision as "a professional cramp," but the problem kept getting worse. Finally, he went to see Sigmund Freud. To Walter's surprise, Freud did not ask him about his sexual life. Instead, he examined his arm briefly and then asked if he had ever been to Sicily. "In short, I was to leave that very evening, forget all about my arm and do nothing for a few weeks but use my eyes. I did what I was told." Walter came back not entirely cured, but Freud kept focusing on the times when Walter forgot about his arm, pointing out that he had no pain when he did. "But what if I should have to stop [while I am conducting]?" Walter asked. You won't have to stop, Freud reassured him. "Can I take upon myself the responsibility of possibly upsetting a performance?" Walter asked. "I'll take that responsibility," responded the guru, and Bruno Walter was healed. (17)

Interestingly, Freud seems less like a psychoanalyst and more like an existential-humanistic therapist in this encounter. Apparently Freud used much the same approach with Mahler. Mahler had endured his month-long crisis of August 1910 in complete isolation. The "splendid isolation" he had sought to nurture his inner soul now plagued him. He was facing the collapse of his private world and yet unable to reveal to anyone the terrible secret of his wife's betrayal. Alma had her mother with whom she could talk about the wonderful ways Gropius made her feel and her discomfort with Mahler's suffering. With her mother she could cry and scream. And, of course, she could pour out her heart to Walter Gropius. Mahler had nobody to talk to talk to about Alma except Alma, and she wasn't much help! In his despair, Mahler turned to Freud.

Fig. 21 Sigmund Freud, c. 1900

Freud was vacationing with his extended family in Leiden that summer, a charming Dutch coastal resort. Although he generally avoided professional business when on vacation, he agreed to a consult with Mahler. Freud expressed some resentment that Mahler made and cancelled three appointments but viewed these cancellations as a sign of his neurosis. In fact, the cancellations were the result of Mahler's ill health: he had been fighting acute tonsillitis (a recurrent ailment) and was trying to regain enough strength for the arduous three-day journey across Europe. In any case, on the afternoon of the 26th of August 1910, Gustav Mahler had a four-hour peripatetic conversation with Sigmund Freud. In *Gustav Mahler: a life in crisis* (2004), Stuart Feder paints a detailed portrait of their route through the town, imagining what that afternoon stroll might have been like, walking, talking, and sitting on a park bench, maybe taking tea in a café. I picture it a little differently. Mahler had a quite peculiar gait, as I have indicated; children would sometimes laugh behind his back. He seemed insensitive to walking companions who could never match his stride: he would speed up and slow down in response to his inner world. Bruno Walter, who dearly loved him, said he was impossible to walk with. It is not easy to picture how Freud and Mahler could have walked together in sync. Otherwise, as Feder and others observe, the two men undoubtedly were in sync and seem to have experienced instant rapport. They spoke German with a similar regional coloring. They both viewed themselves as assimilated Western Jews. Neither was observant, although Freud was proud of his association with B'nai B'rith. Mahler was entirely unaffiliated with Jewish groups but early in life had defined himself as Ahaseurus, the wandering Jew, always searching, never finding, the answers to the ultimate questions of existence.

Fig. 22 Mahler protégé, conductor Bruno Walter
(1876-1962)

What did the two men talk about? In fact we know very little. The most reliable source of information comes from a recently released diary of Marie Bonaparte, a patient of Freud's and later a member of his inner circle. Many years later, he described his afternoon consultation with Mahler to her, and she recorded the account in her diary. Bonaparte's story differs significantly from the version Alma told in her memoirs. "Freud did indeed seem to calm him down," Alma wrote, "After hearing his confession, he (Freud) showered him with the most violent reproaches: 'How can someone in such a state chain a young woman to himself?'" We do not need Marie Bonaparte's diary to guess that these reproaches simply represent what Alma would have *liked* Freud to have said, thus justifying her having taken a lover by depicting Mahler as a "prematurely aged, sick, and impotent man."

There is no clear indication that Mahler told Freud about the details of his plight, Alma's infatuation and intimate involvement with Gropius. Bonaparte's notes indicate that Freud believed that Mahler had come to him simply because "at the time [his] marriage was not going well." Like others, I do not believe that Freud would have described Mahler's plight in these terms had he known of Alma's adultery. In withholding this information, Mahler may have been protecting himself from embarrassment, but was also protecting Alma.

According to Bonaparte, Freud saw the problem between the couple, not as a matter of sexual betrayal but as related to what we today would say they *projected* onto each other: Mahler longing for his missing mother, and Alma longing for her missing father. Characteristically, Freud sized up the Mahler's problems in terms of his oedipal theories: Alma was strongly attracted to the creative masculinity of her father and wished to act out her desires with Gustav; and Gustav, strongly attracted to a mother who he could count on never to abandon him, wanted Alma to be that mother. This is a perfectly reasonable approach to the couple, especially since Freud didn't have a lot of time with Mahler. Clearly Mahler did see Alma too much as a nurturing person and not enough as a young woman needing to feel sexually desirable, especially now that she was thirty-something.

In addition to what we know of Mahler's visit to Freud from Alma and Marie Bonaparte, we also have a letter Freud wrote to a psychologist-colleague, Theodore Reik, in which Freud says "this visit appeared necessary to him, because his wife at the time rebelled against the fact that he withdrew his libido from her." This line is often interpreted to indicate that Mahler had told Freud that he was impotent with Alma, but this is a misreading. At the time Freud was still developing his concept of libido as a primitive life-affirming drive essential to the preservation of the species. Libido could be sublimated into creative expression, Freud thought, but that could lead to mental illness. I.e., What Freud concluded was that Mahler simply spent too much of his life energy in composing music and not enough time romancing his wife. And that constitutes all we need to know about Mahler, Freud and libido.

Following his visit with Freud, Gustav wrote to Alma on September 4, 1910:

> Freud is quite right—you were always for me the light and
> the central point! . . . But what torment and what pain that
> you can no longer respond. But as surely as love must wake
> to love, and faith find faith again, and as long as Eros is the
> ruler of men and gods, so surely will I make a fresh conquest
> of all, of the heart which once was mine. (18)

It seems clear that Mahler knew where to redirect some
"libido." LaGrange observes that "throughout these terrible
months, Mahler felt that he was in some way reborn, and that
he had begun to exist as a new and better human being . . .
Mahler had already survived many crisis during his life and he
would surely have succeeded in restoring equilibrium to his
marriage, given the opportunity." (19)

Mahler's suicidal thoughts had ceased. He still thought
about death, for obvious biographical reasons; he was a man
for whom "Friend Death" was ever present. But in a sense, the
frightful presence of death served as a great blessing for him.
Because he was always conscious of death, literally unable to
deny it, he was able to access and work through the feelings
of anxiety and vulnerability that mortality occasions. He
regressed, but he did not *depress* himself. His intense outcries
(*Fur dich leben! Fur dich sterben!*) were the signs of a man
feeling his feelings and then moving on. The crisis of summer
1910 was not an end point but a *reculer pour mieux sauter.*

Reculer pour mieux sauter means that one sometimes
has to go back a bit in order to make a better leap forward.
In Shrink-talk, we call this "regression in the service of the

ego." The last time I heard the phrase used was at a national psychological convention. After many rounds of drinks, a group of male psychologists began talking about "chasing some skirts," justifying their inclination as "regression in the service of the ego." What they meant was that there was nothing wrong with being childishly immature occasionally. In fact, it might be healthy. The jury is still out on "skirt-chasing," but the general principal is valid, especially when it comes to tears. We need to overcome our culturally supported resistance to crying and allow ourselves to cry as we did when we were children whenever we felt scared or hurt or frustrated. It would be nice if spontaneous crying were as permissible for adults as spontaneous laughter is, and that rapid child-like shifts in mood were deemed as normal for us as they are for toddlers. Growing up does not mean we have outgrown feelings of despair and hopelessness; we have simply outgrown our access to them. The defenses we have built up to keep from feeling primordial feelings of fear, hurt and helplessness actually imperil our physical and emotional health. In short—when life provides you with an opportunity to feel these feelings, go there! . . . Go there as fully and completely as you can. I promise you will come out on the other side, and will come out more whole. You will have retrieved important pieces of yourself that you have you had left behind. For all of us, and in our culture especially for men, it is important to maybe picture for a moment dropping all defenses, all pretenses, and surrender to a deep longing to say to someone through uncontrolled tears: Please, don't ever leave me!

CHAPTER NINE

DEATH AND THE PRECIOUSNESS OF LIFE

The big questions: Wherefore hast thou lived? Wherefore hast thou suffered? Is it all some great, fearful joke? We must answer these questions in some way if we are to continue living—yes, even if we must only continue dying.

—Gustav Mahler (1)

BECAUSE OF THE DIRECT CONNECTION between introversion and the ability to live in an inner world of feelings, creative people like Mahler can take us to hidden places in ourselves. Through art, we can access estranged emotions, feelings that we have pushed down (depressed) because we object so much to feeling them. Objectionable feelings come in four primary categories: (one) primordial fear of abandonment and estrangement; (two) feelings of vulnerability and helplessness; (three) regression to the rapidly changing intense feelings of childhood; and (four) existential anxiety occasioned by our finite existence and inevitable death. We have seen the first three emotional states illustrated in Mahler's life. We come now to Mahler and thoughts about death.

All of the feelings we object to in ourselves (abandonment, vulnerability, emotional lability) ultimately collapse into the fear we experience in the face of our upcoming death. "Everything that man does in his symbolic world is an attempt to deny and overcome his grotesque fate," the 17th century philosopher Blaise Pascal reminded us. For Pascal, the whole of civilization was a kind of "shared madness," a series of "social games" and personal "psychological tricks" designed to distract us from our mortality. That's the bad news. The good news is that embracing death as an essential aspect of life itself enables us to overcome all fear of feelings.

Morbidity—a much-misunderstood term—is an *objection* to the feelings that arise in discussions of death and dying. It is not "morbid" to recognize that death is a fact of life. Accepting the reality of our finite nature should also be distinguished from an understandable desire to avoid the physical suffering often associated with the process of dying. A client of mine said it quite well: "I'm not afraid of dying. I just don't want to be there when it happens!"

It is Christmas, 1910. The Mahler family is in New York for the Philharmonic season, pretending that nothing much had happened over the summer. From the large windows of their corner hotel suite, Alma can see Mahler across the plaza in Central Park making snowballs with their seven-year-old daughter "Gucki" (Anna). The room is overflowing with pink roses, one of many lavish gifts from her still-solicitous husband. Things seem to be going reasonably well, on the surface. Then, on the 20th of February 1911, after a stressful meeting with the Philharmonic executive committee, Mahler comes down with one of his frequent sore throats. The next day, his fever is spiking. He insists on conducting anyhow, so they wrap him in blankets and drive him to Carnegie Hall. He nearly collapses during the intermission, but he gets through it. It is his last concert. (2)

For the next three months, Mahler's condition fluctuated, his fever coming and going; but the direction of the spiral was down. He was mortally ill with a streptococcal infection that would eventually enter his vulnerable heart. Alma remembers,

> His ups and downs kept us on the rack; he was often convinced of his recovery; often again he despaired and was in mortal dread. When he felt better he joked about his approaching death.
>
> 'You will be in great demand when I am gone, with your youth and looks. Now who shall it be?'
>
> 'No one,' I said. 'Don't talk of it.'
>
> 'Yes, but let's see, who is there?'
>
> He went through his list, and always ended up with: 'It'll be better, after all, if I stay with you.' I had to laugh with tears in my eyes. (3)

Throughout his life, Mahler had had ample opportunity to be philosophical about death. By the time he was 12, seven of his brothers had died, arriving and departing in rapid succession like the seasons. The worst of these early losses was the death of an eighth brother, Ernst, a blow that marked the end of Mahler's childhood. Ernst was born when Mahler was not quite one year old. It would be many years before there was another surviving brother, and the two boys related to each other as if they were twins. They were exceptionally close. Of all his brothers and sisters, Mahler loved Ernst the most. Ernst was his companion in all of his games. Ernst was chosen to listen when Mahler played the piano. He was the one exception to Mahler's rule of solitude, a life partner. But not for long.

Theodor Fischer, a childhood friend and later a biographer of Mahler, was struck by the almost maternal affection Mahler showed to Ernst and the friendly way he lectured him when he was disobedient. In return, Ernst was the loyal sidekick who tended to many of Mahler's practical needs. Ernst's heart was weak, however, perhaps from rheumatic fever, and he became an invalid. Eventually, he contracted pericarditis, a bacterial-driven inflammation of the sac surrounding the heart, similar to the illness that killed Mahler 37 years later. LaGrange writes:

> This brother, the most intelligent and gifted of his brothers, to whom he had been so close since infancy, died after a long illness. Gustav followed the phases of its progress with terror, and for many months scarcely left the dying boy's bedside. He was always inventing new stories to cheer him up and take his mind off his sufferings. (4)

In 1874, Ernst died in Mahler's arms. Mahler was fourteen years old.

Not surprisingly, Mahler revisits these defining experiences of death many times in his musical compositions. In *Das Klagende Lied* (Song of Lamentation), a cantata begun when

Mahler was 18, death is already part of his idiosyncratic creative fabric. Even earlier, when he was barely six, Mahler wrote (or at least conceptualized) a musical composition he called *Polka with Introductory Funeral March*. The title says it all, not only about Mahler—who grew up amidst tavern songs and dirges in equal measure—but also about the dance of life, in which one emotional tempo succeeds the other in an unpredictable flow.

If Mahler was no stranger to loss, neither was he to fear. His vulnerable body kept reminding him he was mortal. Subject to various ailments throughout his life (migraine headaches, recurring throat infections), in the late 1880's, Mahler began to suffer from a severe hemorrhoid problem, delicately referred to as his "subterranean troubles." This problem became acute during 1889, the year of his sister's and his parents deaths, a time when he had to assume many burdensome responsibilities, *in loco parentis*. His torment reached a crisis on 24 February 1901, while Mahler was conducting a performance of Mozart's *Magic Flute*. As the opera went on, Mahler began to experience increasing pain. Alma Schindler, 21, was in the audience for the performance. She recalls, "In the afternoon at the Philharmonic and then, in the evening [at the opera], he looked Lucifer like, a face as white as chalk, eyes burning like coals. I felt sorry for him and said to people I was with: 'It's more than he can stand.'" In his dressing room later that night, Mahler began to hemorrhage. His sister called a doctor:

As he lost more blood, the whiteness of his face that Alma had noted earlier in the evening became more pronounced; equally alarming was the attendant quickening of Mahler's pulse. Another doctor was called in, this time a surgeon who managed, with considerable difficulty, to arrest the bleeding. He gave Mahler to understand that he could have bled to death . . . Whether there had in fact been a genuine threat to his life on the night of 24-25 February—and it was certainly possible—Mahler firmly believed this to have been the case. (5)

Understandably, given his childhood experiences of sudden death, Mahler was overwhelmed by feelings of anxiety and vulnerability during this event. His physical recovery was protracted and never entirely complete. However, his *emotional* recuperation was remarkably swift. By the next morning, he had entirely recovered his perspective and sense of humor. Lying in bed, he drafted a mock obituary: "Gustav Mahler has finally met the fate that his many crimes deserve." His body was a wreck, but his healthy "observing ego" was intact.

This near death experience dramatically affected Mahler's orientation to life. Having spent the last dozen years dutifully taking care of his surviving siblings and a few close friends—an arrangement that gave him companionship but not intimacy—he suddenly shifted his focus to founding a family of his own. When he met Alma Schindler later that year, he decided she should be his wife almost immediately, barely taking time to inform her of his plans. His proposal was characteristically inner-directed. As they walked up a hill in silence, Mahler suddenly turned to Alma and said, "It's not easy to marry a man like me! I must be entirely free. I can't allow myself to be hampered by any material responsibilities." Alma was stunned, but Mahler seemed unaware of the effect his blunt declaration had had on her. He walked on through the snow, apparently pleased that matters had been settled.

> When they got back to the house, he went up to Alma's room with her and kissed her for the first time. Thereupon, he began to talk about getting married as soon as possible 'as though it were a simple and obvious thing, as though it had all been settled by the few words he'd uttered along the way—so why wait? (6)

Mahler's courtship of Alma had lasted barely 20 days. When they were officially married a few months later, she was already pregnant. Having had enough of death, for the moment, Mahler had decided to live, and his tempo was *allegro appassionato*.

The next few years were the best time of Mahler's life. His early compositional style, exemplified in the *Wunderhorn* symphonies, shifted to a more classical yet highly innovative mode, evident in the Fifth Symphony and even more in the unusual and powerfully "tragic" Sixth. In the summer of 1901, shortly before he met Alma, he also began to compose a cycle of songs, the extraordinary *Kindertotenlieder* ("Songs on the Death of Children"). By the time he finished the cycle, in the summer of 1904, he was a happily married man with two little girls.

Many critics have wondered why Mahler would have been moved to write such a dark symphony as the Sixth, not to mention sad songs about the death of children, at a time in his life that was filled with domestic bliss. In the summer of 1904 when Mahler was working on the orchestration of the last of the *Kindertotenlieder* songs, his "two girls played happily outside the cottage." (7)

Alma reputedly accused Mahler of tempting fate. Later, after Putzi's death, she became convinced that Mahler had had a premonition of the coming tragedy when he composed the song cycle. Mahler disagreed. "I put myself in my thoughts into the situation of a man whose own child has died," he wrote to a friend. "When I really lost my daughter, I could not have written these songs anymore." Theodor Reik comments:

> It was, of course, unavoidable that he had to think that he anticipated the catastrophe five years before when he composed the *Kindertotenlieder*. He had to think that he had already experienced those intense feelings of mourning and grief when his little girl died. He really had experienced them, but not at the composition of the Ruckert songs, but long before it when he himself was a child and identified with his father. (8)

For me, the most important feature of this period is not what happened before Putzi's death but what *didn't* happen after.

Fig. 23 Mahler and Putzi

Although overwhelmed by grief—he had adored Putzi—Mahler did *not* experience a serious depression following her death. (Alma did.) In these circumstances, Mahler's very familiarity with the feelings of grief, and his acceptance of these feelings, were fundamentally protective. He allowed himself to experience the full poignancy of his loss without objection. He did not try to push his feelings down out of sight. Instead, he expressed them in his music, intuitively going to the darkest places within him. As Mahler told his friend Natalie Bauer-Lechner, there was an unconscious, mysterious power that manifested itself in the most difficult and significant passages of his compositions: "Usually, they are the ones which I don't want to come to grips with, which I would like to get around, yet which continue to hold me up and finally force their way to expression."(9)

Of the *Kindertotenlieder*, LaGrange writes in his understated style: "There exists little music where suffering has more communicative force." Protected inside the magic circle of his new family (as least for the moment) Mahler finally felt free to release the feelings of grief he had buried since his childhood—the sight of all those little coffins going out the door. It is when we cannot find this kind of release that we begin to depress ourselves. Every time we bury a feeling instead of feeling it, we leave pieces of ourselves behind. If we lose enough of ourselves in this manner, we experience a void inside—the emptiness we call depression. This is the crucial point in understanding depression, but it is essential that it not be simply something we know but, rather, something we *feel*.

Fig. 24 Natalie Bauer-Lechner

Natalie Bauer-Lechner, who was devoted to Mahler, lived with him and his sisters in the 1890's. Understandably, she had difficulty being a part of the new family Mahler created with Alma. However, in the summer of 1901 when Mahler was beginning to compose the *Kindertotenlieder*, Natalie was on hand to take detailed notes:

He told me that the last mentioned song came into being as follows. It occurred to him literally between one step and the next—that is, just as he was walking out of the dining room. He sketched it immediately in the dark anteroom, and ran with it to the spring—his favorite place, which often gives him aural inspiration. Here, he had the music completed very quickly. But now he saw that it was no symphonic theme—such as he had been after—but a song! . . . He said that he felt sorry for himself that he should have to write . . . the *Kindertotenlieder*, and he felt sorry for the world that would have to hear them one day, so terribly sad was their content. (10)

In the summer of 1901 when Mahler was composing three of his *Kindertotenlieder* songs, he was also composing three other lieder very different in emotional tone. The most quintessentially Mahleresque of these songs is "Ich bin der Welt abhanden gekommen" (*I am lost to the world*):

> I have lost touch with the world
> where I once wasted too much of my time.
> Nothing has been heard of me for so long
> that they may well think me dead.
> Indeed, I hardly care
> if the world thinks that I am dead.
> Neither can I deny it,
> for I am truly dead to the world.

I am dead to the bustle of the world
and repose in tranquil realms.
I live alone in my heaven,
in my devotion, in my song.

If Robert Spitzer were diagnosing Mahler based on the emotionally disjunctive work he was writing during this period, he would probably give him a 301.20 (Schizoid Personality Disorder) or perhaps a 296.89 (Bi-Polar II Disorder). In either case, Mahler would go home to his Hütchen with another big bottle of pills. If we erase all the numbers, however, we can see much more clearly that Mahler's domestic happiness simply freed him to explore his full emotional range. He could go down into the grave and get lost in the stars during a single afternoon at Maiernigg. The gorgeous sadness of the *Kindertotenlieder* is a sign of Mahler's emotional freedom, not a symptom of his morbidity or pathology.

Fig. 25 Score of *Kindertotenlieder Five*

Mahler was adamant that the five *Kindertotenlieder* songs be regarded as a complete and indivisible whole. The first song, always sung in the middle register, as if the afflicted father lacked the strength to raise his voice, establishes a situation that the last song resolves. There are rays of light in the first *lied* that look forward to the solace at the end. The *Kindertotenlieder* thus juxtapose personal loss and universal salvation, expressing Mahler's view that intrinsic human suffering requires a vision of the created universe as eternally present. LaGrange writes, "Mahler relied on song in all its purity, song that always seems to flow from the very heart of things . . . The orchestral accompaniment only brightens the emotions without ever destroying the effect of intimacy. A soul is being laid bare in these transparent sounds." The words of the fifth song are especially poignant:

> In this weather, in this tumult,
> I would never have sent the children out, they have been carried, carried out.
> I could say nothing about it.

> In this weather, in this storm,
> I would never have sent the children out.
> I feared they would fall sick,
> those are now vain thoughts.

In this weather, in this horror!

I would never have sent the children out.

They have been carried out.

I could say nothing about it!

In this weather, in this storm, in this tumult

they are sleeping as if in their mother's house,

frightened by no storm,

sheltered by God's hand,

they are sleeping as if in their mother's house!

The cycle ends with a radiant vision of eternal renewal, without which this deeply mystical, if not conventionally religious man, could not have borne the reality of human suffering—the reality of his *own* suffering, past and yet to come. It is significant that, in the original score of the *Kindertotenlieder*, Mahler replaced the word *Haus* (house) with *Schoss* (lap or womb) in the last line of the cycle. ("They are resting, they are resting in their mother's lap/womb.") This suggests a struggle between fidelity to Ruckert and adherence to his own philosophy. This conflict seems to show up in the music itself. Critics say that the song ends in the ostensible tonic key, D, but this ending seems unjustified. The music strongly implies a modulation to the dominant A. The resolution to D sounds like a temporary resting place in this subdominant of A, yet the modulation to A is never completed.

Music Selection Seven: *Kindertotenlieder, Number Five. The external storm, in which the children are being carried off to their funeral, is also an internal storm of anguish. Storms, one might expect, but how could one prepare for the terrible grief in the loss of a beloved child? Mahler knew that pain, and remarked to Alma that he could never have written this Lied after losing his own daughter. He said to Natalie that he felt sorry for those who would have to listen to such sad music. Yet I say, listen we must. The Baritone sings mit ruhelos schmerzvollen Ausdruck (with restless, pain-filled expression). Nussbaum adds that the music itself gives the impression of something sharp and malign digging or burrowing its way into the flesh. From personal experience I know that to leave this painful, grieving part of oneself behind is to invite the most serious of all depressions. The helplessness in the face of such tragedy needs to be embraced, as does the guilt that maybe I could have done something to have prevented it. In the experience of such grief one could attempt to tear the flesh from ones bones with ones fingernails. Or one could listen to this music as the need arises. What one should not do is take a drug designed to alter the structure of the human brain and be numb. I remember my aunt saying, as she faced a prefrontal lobotomy: "I know what they want. They want me to forget Dick. I don't want to forget Dick." Be careful out there.*

Rudolf Kempe, Berlin Philharmonic, 1955, Dietrich Fischer-Dieskau, Baritone.

http://www.overcomingdepressionwithoutdrugs.com/music

Some critics view this unsatisfactory conclusion as a mistake on Mahler's part (see Donald Mitchell). My point: Whether consciously or unconsciously the music Mahler wrote does not offer the satisfying religious consolation the words imply. The use of *Schoss* would be both consistent with the music and consistent with Mahler's view of ultimate reality. The principle message lies in the disembodied tenderness of the conclusion, where Mahler seems to find a new answer to the metaphysical questions that had always obsessed him—a belief in eternal renewal that flows from the union of human beings with nature, often manifest for him as "the Eternal Feminine."

"Ontologically, beauty is the secret sound of the deepest thereness of things," the late poet-priest John O'Donnohue was fond of saying. In 1904, Gustav Mahler, looking out of his Hütchen across the waters of the Wörthersee, heard that sound in the deepest recesses of his being, amid the laughter of his little children.

CHAPTER TEN

MAHLER, MUSIC AND THE ETERNAL FEMININE

"Music brings you back to the mystery of who you are and it surprises you by inadvertently resonating with depths inside your heart that you had forgotten or neglected."
—*John O'Donohue* (1)

"I can swim in existence, but for the mystical soaring I am too heavy."
—Kierkegaard (2)

THE MOST SIGNIFICANT MENTOR early in my psychotherapy training was Dr. Harry Stack Sullivan of the Washington School of Psychiatry. One of his favorite dictums (oft repeated) was that, "We are all more basically human than otherwise." It took me quite a while to understand what that line meant; but once I did, it fundamentally changed the way I related to my patients; indeed, it changed my life. In those days, most of my patients were said to be suffering from something we called schizophrenia and were distancing themselves from something we called reality. Sullivan said it was up to us to discover the pain that was behind this withdrawal, remembering that these troubled men and women were more like us than they were different (more basically human than otherwise). The official diagnostic labels were not much help. They stigmatized the patients, dehumanizing them, making it easier for us to distance ourselves protectively from their often frightening symptoms. At some level, we could identify with these people, and that connection disturbed us. We did not want to entertain the possibility that what had happened to them could happen to us as well—or entertain the even scarier possibility that what was called insanity was simply a human way of dealing with crazy relationships in a crazy world.

Pigeonholes are for the birds, not people. Because pigeonholes are good for corporate profits, however, they have increased rather than decreased over the years. Drug companies like them; insurance companies like them; harried doctors like them; even patients sometimes like them, if only because they give a local habitation and a name to suffering. As a result, the new DSM-V, scheduled to appear in 2013, will include over 800 diagnostic categories. Many of these pigeonholes are new, and troubling. For example, consider something called "psychosis risk syndrome."(3) It is designed to identify and treat (i.e. medicate) young people who aren't "mentally ill" but *might* become so in the future. "It's a bit like telling 10 people with a common cold that they are at risk for 'pneumonia syndrome," one skeptical British psychiatrist observed. The sheer number of diagnostic categories proposed raises the possibility that, in the near future, nobody will be "normal" any more:

> [The DSM V] is shrinking the pool of what is normal to a
> puddle . . . . with the classification of so many new disorders,
> we will all have disorders . . . This may lead to the belief that

many more of us 'need' drugs to treat our 'conditions'—(and) many of these drugs will have unpleasant or dangerous side effects. (4)

In short, the psychiatric community's view of insanity is itself insane!

Harry Stack Sullivan's sense of the human continuum has completely disappeared. Fragmented into an array of diagnostic codes (a 296.89 here, a 301.20 there), we are in danger of losing connection with each other; losing connection with our feelings; and, most of all, losing connection with the earth whose ancient rhythms drive our body-minded brains. Our frenetic virtual networking appeals to our primordial yearnings for community; but in practice, it generally moves us away from emotional intimacy toward agitated depression. (Anybody who has 500 friends on Facebook doesn't know what friendship means.) We live in a world buzzing with data noise. True connection requires stillness and silence. Without it, we cannot hear ourselves feel.

For Mahler, silence was the source of all music. He lived a frantically busy life most of the year, arranging, designing, conducting, controlling. He coped. But only when he stopped coping, only when he was still by the still water, could he access and express the flow within him. Mahler did not live in a world of words, but he befriended them upon occasion, trying to describe the nature of his artistic process and how he experienced the music he produced. Let's listen in on a conversation Mahler had with his friend Natalie while he was working on the first movement of his Third Symphony:

> M: Whereas I could clarify and to a certain extent 'describe' in words what happens in the other movements, that is no longer possible here; you would yourself have to plunge with me into the very depths of Nature, whose roots are grasped by music at a depth that neither art nor science can otherwise reach. And I believe that no artist suffers so much from Nature's mystic power as does the musician when he is seized by her.

> N: It must be terrifying, like the Earth Spirit appearing before Faust.

> M: Not only the Earth Spirit, but the Universe itself, into whose infinite depths you sink, through whose eternal spaces you soar, so that earth and human destiny shrink behind you into an indiscernibly tiny point and disappear. The greatest human questions, which I posed and attempted to answer in my Second [Symphony]: 'Why do we exist?' and 'Will we continue to exist in an after-life?'—these questions can no longer concern me here. For what can they signify in the totality of things, in which everything lives; will and must live? (5)

The Third Symphony, in which a woman despairs over having broken the commandments but is rescued by a loving chorus of her sisters, clearly reflects Mahler's belief in a loving universal presence he sometimes referred to as the Eternal Feminine (the Divine Mother), an idealization that looks back to the Romanticism of Wolfgang von Goethe (1749-1832) and forward to the dualisms of Carl Jung (1875-1961). For Mahler, the Eternal Feminine was the creative presence out of which we come and to which we return ("I am of God and will go back to God."). He told Alma that it was correct to see this abiding presence as love:

> That which attracts us with mystical power, which every creature, and perhaps even the stones, feels with absolute certainty to be the very centre of its being, which Goethe at this point—again in the form of an image—calls the eternal feminine—namely, that which is at rest, the goal—in contrast to the eternal longing, striving, and movement towards the goal—that is the eternal masculine!—You are quite right to describe it as the power of love. (6)

Like Goethe, whom he revered, Mahler intuitively moved away from Judeo-Christian religious tradition, with its legalisms and patriarchal concept of divinity, toward an all-embracing pantheism, a notion of the cosmos as at once sensual and embodied (Mother Earth) and Sublime—an incommensurate, incomprehensible power to which one must surrender oneself in order to find oneself. In Goethe's work, the Eternal Feminine remains a somewhat blurry construct. In his letter to Alma (above) Mahler is clearer in his focus: the

"Eternal Feminine" is "that which is at rest"—what the Taoists call "stillness." The opposite of this stillness is "striving," akin to the notion of agitated depression that I described earlier in this book, an empty busyness that estranges us from ourselves and from the universe. For Mahler, as for Lao-tzu and the Taoists, everything that exists *flows* . . . like water, like music. The Song of the Earth is a waveform. The Eternal Masculine is everything that tries (in vain) to go against the flow—resisting, objecting, damming up—the Army Corp of Engineers within our psyches that arm us against the flood, lest we be overwhelmed. For Mahler, the whole point of life was to be overwhelmed, to surrender, to take flood into oneself and become one with it. In other words, for Mahler, passivity was powerful.

> With wings that I have won for myself
> In the hot striving of love
> I will soar away
> To the light to which no eye has penetrated.

Commenting on this section of the fifth movement of Mahler's Second Symphony, philosopher Martha Nussbaum writes:

> The violins and violas leap up, bursting into a realm of brightness, where the harp celebrates their arrival. The contralto voice now follows—the dark voice that has sung of the terrible neediness of human life—celebrating, in her free

springing movement, release from "all penetrating pain." With a sensuous soaring movement the two female voices spiral around one another, like serpents made of light, coiling through the sky with the strings and harp, winged by their own passionate energy. (7)

Dr. Nussbaum adds that the significance of assigning this music to two female voices coiling around one other should be understood in the light of Mahler's many images of the feminine and the passive. The wings of ascent belong to the receptive, to those who feminize themselves in the sense of allowing themselves to be "played on by the Spirit of the world"—a world of bliss which must be a world of continued receptivity and vulnerability—a world in which general compassion for human suffering yields a love as fully universal as music itself.

This extraordinary receptivity marked Mahler as strange even in the context of 19th century Romanticism. Today the notion that passivity can be powerful seems even stranger. For both men and women, "power" is defined almost solely in terms of "striving"—goal-oriented "agency" (taking an active stance to get things done and constantly striving to achieve something). We spend 24/6.5 of our lives "putting out" and 0.5 of our lives "taking in" . . . less than that if we own a Blackberry or I-Phone.

The gender binary system Mahler and Goethe inherited divided the human psyche into complementary opposites, attributing inherent passive-receptivity to women and inherent agency to men. Women *feel*; men *DO*. Goethe and Mahler did not reject this either-or structure; they simply inverted its valence—elevating fem-feeling. (Hence Goethe's phrase, "The Eternal Feminine leads us upward.") Mainstream US culture today ostensibly rejects the idea that women are hard-wired for passivity, but it does not reject the hierarchical opposition of *ACTIVITY* and *passivity* (*DOING* and *feeling*) that values the former and denigrates the later. *Activity* = *agency* = *power* is the mantra for both men and women. The Eternal Feminine has very few spokespersons these days. All of which means that we are really much less liberated than we think we are. The movement toward greater androgyny over the last 40 years has largely been a movement of women toward what Mahler thought of as the Eternal Masculine. Men have pretty much stayed on the dime. (A lot of women wear pants; very few guys wear skirts.)

Carl Jung, writing shortly after Mahler's death, at once expresses and challenges the sexist formulations of his time, and of ours.

> What about masculinity? Do you know how much femininity man lacks for completeness? Do you know how much masculinity woman lacks for completeness? You seek the feminine in women and the masculine in men. And thus there are always only men and women. But where are people? You, man, should not seek the feminine in women, but seek and recognize it in yourself, as you possess it from the beginning. It pleases you, however, to play at manliness,

because it travels on a well-worn track. You, woman, should not seek the masculine in men, but assume the masculine in yourself, since you possess it from the beginning. But it amuses you and it is easy to play at femininity, consequently man despises you because he despises his femininity. But humankind is masculine and feminine, not just man and woman. You can hardly say of your soul what sex it is. But if you pay close attention, you will see that the most masculine man has a feminine soul, and the most feminine woman has a masculine soul. The more manly you are, the more remote from you is what woman really is, since the feminine in yourself is alien and contemptuous. (8)

This passage is a bit difficult to follow, as is much of Jung's writing; so it is easy to misread his emphasis on "completeness" as merely an updating of traditional notions of gender complimentarity (two opposites make a whole). His view is much more radical, however, first because he implicitly distinguishes between *sex* (whether or not we possess XX or XY chromosomes) and *gender* (masculinity and femininity); secondly, because he suggests that gender binaries are illusory ("You can hardly say of your soul what sex it is"); and finally, because he recognizes that men habitually define their masculinity by disowning and despising the "femininity" within them.

Many decades later, feminist theorists will make a similar point from a less essentialist point of view. Sociolinguist Cheris Kramarae argues that,

Men are *men* because of their insistence upon the subordinate category *women*; much of their understanding of their behaviors . . . comes from their consistent reiterated *otherness* from women. (9)

Psychoanalyst Nancy Chodorow, sees this "reiterated otherness" as fundamental to male identity: although a "boy's sense of *self* begins in union with the feminine, his sense of *masculinity* arises against it," (10) especially in rigidly binary cultures where women are subordinated. In such cultures, men have to spend a great deal of time proving to other men that they are real men by purging themselves of anything and everything that might be interpreted as girly or effeminate. Unfortunately, it is impossible to prove a negative, and thus the effort to demonstrate one's manhood tends to become an exhausting life-long project that never achieves its goal.

What does all of this have to do with depression? Plenty! Today, as in the era of Mahler and Jung, the fluid expression of emotion is coded as feminine, especially the expression of fear, hurt, or vulnerability. Passivity, receptivity, surrender are defined as female postures—quintessentially "queer" in a man. Boys [still] Don't Cry. In the current vernacular, they "nut up or shut up!" All this is bad news for women, suggesting that the more things change, the more they stay the same; but it is also bad news for men. The only open expression of feeling licensed for men—anger—is not really a feeling at all. It is a protective reaction that disowns fears and hurts, pushing fem feelings down out of sight. In short, the oppositional terms in which masculinity is still constructed and performed tend to encourage men to depress themselves. Women who seek a fair share of social power by "manning up" in this manner can easily move toward depression as well.

Before we go on, a footnote on the much misunderstood subject of anger:

Most people think of anger as an emotion, but it isn't. Anger is a *reaction*, designed to protect us from feeling hurt, rejected, disappointed, helpless, frustrated, impotent, vulnerable, frightened, and anxious. In a life-or-death situation, this reactive state helps us defend ourselves from harm, but as a habitual stance toward life, it is dysfunctional. Speaking from an evolutionary perspective, Antonio Damasio observes, "sure enough well-targeted anger can discourage abuse of many sorts and act as a defensive weapon as it still does in the wild. In many social situations, however, anger is a good example of an emotion whose homeostatic value is in decline." (11) As with depression, moving toward feelings makes the anger disappear.

I first saw Mike over 30 years ago. He probably came because his wife demanded that he schedule an appointment. A big bruiser of a guy, former football player, he had a problem with anger. Any experience of frustration could easily erupt into an episode of uncontrolled rage. The presenting problem was, I believe, that he had thrown a sofa out of a window. His marriage was in trouble, and so was his career. I remember that it was a difficult process trying to get Mike to entertain the possibility that there could be a more effective way of relating than punching his fist through a wall. When I told him he would need to identify and express the feelings behind his angry reactions—the frustration, the helplessness, the vulnerability, the hurt—his objections were ferocious at first. There was a lot at stake for him, however, and bit-by-bit he began to let go of the macho protectiveness that was estranging him from himself. Today, Mike has fundamentally transformed his life. Being sensitive to the feelings of others and believing that his own feelings matter has enabled him to establish relationships of trust. That trust, in turn, has allowed Mike to achieve great success in the business world. Far from a weakness, he believes his emotional receptivity is his greatest strength as an entrepreneur.

Mike and I re-engaged recently, this time about issues involving his teenage son, an all-star lacrosse player who had been having the same problems with anger with which his father had struggled. With a little support, Mike was able to do a great job modeling for his son a more healthy way of dealing with feelings of frustration and vulnerability. Mike firmly believes that if he had not been able to use the insight he had gained in therapy, his son would have trashed a promising career in lacrosse and might have come a delinquent. In addition to providing help for his son, Mike has become a sought-after life coach for midshipmen from the Naval Academy who flock to his house on weekend leave. They see Mike as a safe place to expose feelings they never would dare reveal at the Academy and even cry on occasion.

Looking back on his therapy, Mike insists that the turning point came when I told him that he had to stop being such a "prick" and learn to be more of a "pussy." I don't remember using exactly those words, but maybe I did, if only to shock him out of his protective stance. It worked not because of my rhetorical brilliance but because in his heart Mike knew that his aggressive behavior was not really making him happy or more secure in his masculinity. Eventually, he was able to recognize the difference between "manning up" and being a mensch and to integrate his ability to "put out" with a capacity to "take in," in this sense, "to feminize himself," a capacity we all must develop to be whole.

Like Mike, many men still have trouble tolerating vulnerability, being sensitive to their own feelings and the feelings of others, and developing a capacity for intimacy, qualities that have been traditionally marked as girly. In classic era Hollywood, relationships and tears were relegated to a genre known as Women's Pictures; the studios made Action Pictures for guys. Today, women are in on the action, too, however. "Action Chicks" such as Angelina Jolie and Uma Thurman routinely punch, kick, slash, and burn their way across the screen. This market trend both reflects and reinforces the fact that many women today have as much difficulty as their male peers with vulnerability and "taking in." In a society where virtually all rewards flow from doing, managing, and achieving, this stance is understandable; but machismo is no more fulfilling in women than it is in men.

In my practice, I often encounter strong, young, capable women for whom any expression of vulnerability is equated with being the victim in an abusive relationship. They are very aware of how women in the past were often compelled to accommodate to a life-long pattern of unfair treatment and are determined to protect themselves from that fate. In the process, however, they often protect themselves from their own feelings, much as Mike did, despising tears and expressions of hurt as signs of weakness, lack of ego strength, or a loss of personal integrity. Unfortunately, this stance makes intimacy impossible. Intimacy requires full emotional access—and emotional risk-taking as well. We have to be brave enough to express all of our feelings to our partner, especially the scary feelings (hurt, frustration, longing) with the expectation our partner cares what we are feeling. (If your partner *doesn't* care what you feel, then walk out the door! There is no intimacy.) We have to make ourselves anxious over and over and over again. Selectively withholding feelings in a close relationship invariably creates estrangement. People move away from each other and the relationship ends; or, worse, people stay together, pushing down their true feelings in order to maintain a facade of intimacy. In such situations, depression is inevitable. The pharmacological fix—antidepressants—fixes nothing; it merely numbs us to our emptiness and pain.

In this context, the emotional integration that Mike achieved is a model, not merely for macho men, but for us all. The first move is to apply Harry Stack Sullivan's dictum—"we are all more basically human than otherwise"—to the gender fictions that divide us from ourselves even as they divide us from each other. As long as we believe that *masculinity* and *femininity* are warring tribes (men from Mars and women from Venus) and that we must choose sides, we will end up trying to disguise or excise the parts of our humanity that don't fit with the role we think we have to play. In the process, we become less than we are, strangers in our own psychic house. When stresses and tragedies arrive and we need access to all of our human resources and all of our human feelings, our habitual self-estrangement can set us up for depression.

The second move is easier to explain but even harder to achieve. If we want joy in our lives, we need to *do* less and *feel* more. "Feeling more" is not really the problem. The ebb and flow of strong emotions is as natural to us as breathing; feeling flows through our bodies with every heart beat. It is our lifeblood. We can't live without it; we can't even think properly without it. We know this intuitively every time we see our young children and grandchildren, their smiling faces still wet with the tears they cried only a moment before. Feelings move through them like wind across the water, wave after wave. We never really lose that capacity (unless we take antidepressants!) but we become frightened of its existential implications: that, despite our Power Grids and PowerBooks, we have very little real power in the cosmos. We *are*. "What we *do* is like wind blowing on the grass." (12)

Listening to feelings requires stillness. I learned this years ago from Mr. H, the stillest person I have ever met, and the best listener. In another culture, Mr. H might have been regarded as a Seer, possessed of special gifts; in ours, he was abject, locked away for most of his life. And appropriately so. He couldn't *do* anything. He couldn't function in the outside world full of noise and busyness. In a sense, neither can we, unfortunately. Modern life is so noisy that we can't hear ourselves feel. Agitated depression is hardwired into every gadget we own. If we leave home without our cell phone, we feel naked and rush back in a panic to retrieve it. We check our email dozens of times a day, maybe a hundreds, our thumbs busy busy on the little keys. Like the proles in Fritz Lang's silent film *Metropolis*, we are chained to our clocks. We orient our entire lives around time: there is so much to get done, accomplish, measure and calculate. We move ceaselessly, as if we were afraid to stop, as if we were afraid to be alone with ourselves. And we *are* afraid.

"What is the feeling you are trying so hard not to feel?" I ask my clients, encouraging them to move toward the very thing they fear most. We need to ask that same question to ourselves as a culture. We need to inaugurate a global Day of Temporal Absence on which we stop all the clocks and relearn how to experience the world through our senses, taking a timeout to see, hear, smell, taste, and touch, as we did when we were little children. Experiencing a day when the only text available on Google is: "Wherever you go, there you are." We need to take time to *be*.

Since this cultural revolution is unlikely to happen any time soon, however, we need to find ways to take timeouts in our own lives, to create sensory spaces from which we can *take in* the world, integrating the figure and ground of our being. In this task, as in many others, Gustav Mahler shows us the way. In his music and in his life, he embodies a rich integration of human capabilities. Both *anima* and *animus,* adult and eternal child, Mahler achieves inner balance not by leveling out his emotions and senses (the depressing/antidepressant way) but by *moving through* the full cycle of ups and downs, riding the wave to shore.

For conductor/composer Leonard Bernstein, whose passionate devotion to Mahler sparked renewed 20th century interest in his work, Mahler's artistic power was inseparable from his childlike openness to emotional ebb and flow. In a 1960 Young People's Concert, Bernstein has the orchestra play several different passages from the Fourth Symphony. Then he asks,

> Is that heartbroken-sounding music the real Mahler? Or is it the other happy sleigh-bell music? No—they're both Mahler . . . But then, of course, you'll say, "Doesn't every composer go from happy to sad and back again? I mean, it's true of Mozart, isn't it, and Bach and everyone?" Yes, but no composer goes quite so far in each direction, so happy and so sad. When Mahler is sad, it is a complete sadness;

nothing can comfort him, it's like a weeping child. And when he's happy, he's happy the way a child is—all the way. And that's one of the keys to the Mahler puzzle: He is like a child; his feelings are extreme, exaggerated, like young people's feelings. That's another reason why it's so especially right to have you come to his birthday celebration; I think young people can understand Mahler's feelings even better than older ones. Once you understand that secret of his music—the voice of the child—you can really love his music.

So that's the main secret about him. He was struggling all his life to recapture those pure, unmixed, overflowing emotions of childhood. I'm sure you've all had emotions like that, that filled-up feeling that nature sometimes makes you have, especially in the spring, when you almost want to cry because everything is so beautiful. Well, Mahler's music is full of those feelings and full of the sounds of nature, like bird calls and hunting horns and forest murmurs—which are all part of his idea of beauty, childlike beauty. (13)

The beauty of the green world was central to Mahler, as it was for most romantics; he was not naive about nature, however. He knew in his flesh that bad things could happen to us at any moment. The soothing minuet in the second movement of the Second Symphony has a stormy, foreboding middle section. Sudden blows of fate occur frequently in Mahler's music, as in his life. "Most people shun sorrow," writes Norman Lebrecht. "Mahler embraces it. Sorrow is his retreat, the place he calls home when he is Lost to the World. Rather than avoid pain, he seeks it as a creative incubus." (14) Mahler was much more aware than most of us of the fragility of our human existence. (How could he not have been?) He was equally sensitive to the transitory nature of feeling. Bliss could not be maintained by will, and periods of despair never last except in our refusal to feel them.

Storms of murk are an inevitable feature of the emotional weather through which all of us travel. As I observed earlier, when a pilot is tossed about in a storm, it is easy to panic and forget that trying to *control* the plane is a fatal mistake. Being in an emotional storm is similar. The temptation is to reach for a controlled substance, an antidepressant that promises to stop our downward spiral. But that promise is false. The thing to do is to *do* nothing and to *feel* everything—to ride out the storm. All storms are transitory; all feelings are transitory. We *will* emerge on the other side of the cloud, into a place of beautiful tranquility where we can celebrate our survival, for a while.

Mahler seems to have internalized this truth by instinctively moving away from the empty busyness that was the way of his world, even as it is the way of ours. Sometimes this necessitated isolating himself physically: in the summer in his sylvan composing huts, he deliberately walled out the noise of human civilization in order to open his senses to the natural world and to the world of his heart. His composing huts were tiny rooms (barely 13 feet square) but the stillness they provided created immense emotional space for Mahler. During the winter, when Mahler was caught up in the busy-ness of conducting, this space shrunk, but he never let it disappear entirely. Walking along the street in the midst of conversation, Mahler could suddenly vanish like Alice down the rabbit hole, finding creative stillness within him in the midst of social noise. The herky-jerky rhythms of his gait were not a symptom of mental illness (obsessive compulsive disorder); they were the sign of a man who was taking little temporal timeouts throughout his day, surrendering to the emotional moment. Ultimately, wherever he was going was less important than where he was inside himself, the joyful *and* the painful places.

Is there a way we can find stillness and feeling space within our own busy lives? I think so. And music can help. In her essay "Music and the Resonating Body," Professor Hallgjerd Aksnes demonstrates that we experience music in the totality of our being, not simply in our minds. A wave of emotion evoked by music correlates with vital life processes such as breathing, coming and going, coming and going. Music is about balance, melodic, contrapuntal, harmonic, rhythmic, and many more features, which are both instinctually and culturally determined.

Aksnes says that Mahler's exceptionally harmonious music puts her in a harmonious mood—that it attunes her soul. Does that mean that everybody should throw away their antidepressants and buy a boxed set of Mahler's symphonies instead? This isn't a bad idea in principle; but, of course, Mahler doesn't work for everybody. His music relaxes Aksnes; and it moves me immensely, returning me to myself when I have wandered away from my feelings; but you may need to find different music that does the same thing for you. One of my favorite clients, a sophisticated visual artist with an interest in classical music (Bach can bring tears to his eyes), has used music very effectively to cope with depression over the years—but not Mahler. Whenever he realizes that he is pushing down painful feelings, he goes on a country music binge. "I'm So Lonesome I Could Cry" (Hank Williams) does a lot better job than "Das Lied von Der Erde" in helping him access the sadness, loneliness, and frustration he needs to feel.

As we listen to music—any music—our projections go well beyond the bounds of kinesthetic experience and enter into the realm of feelings, characterized by an interplay between somatosensory information—information about the state of the body—and the cognitive evaluations of this information and of the particular circumstances in which we find ourselves. In other words, music involves us totally, body, mind and soul.

Aksnes' studies suggest that music can help us overcome depression, restoring normal emotional flow, precisely because it is balanced. Music rises above the line in joy and below the line in sadness, a chromatic melodic line balanced with a *basso ostinato*. The main driving force of harmony in Western music is the tension between the dominant and the tonic as epitomized by the dominant chord's leading tone being pulled towards the tonic. In our culture, we both *hear* and feel this pull as a major source of musical tensions and releases: it is like breathing and can "take our breath away."

Music Selection Eight: *Mahler's Fifth Symphony, Movement Four. David Hurwitz says: "This adagietto, for strings and harps, is perhaps the most famous single movement in all of Mahler, not only due to its use in the film Death in Venice, but because it inhabits a special world of romantic tenderness." The long unresolved chord of this movement creates an unusual longing, a longing for love and life. The music was written in the summer following what Mahler viewed as a near-death experience from bleeding hemorrhoids. Mahler felt lucky to be alive and would have been inclined to meditate on a life that had nearly ended. Consequently, the association of Eros and Thanatos in Visconti's film is not unwarranted. Mahler on many occasions associated the longing for Beauty, Love and Life with the awareness of Death striding below. In this movement that poignancy is palpable.*

Bruno Walter, NY Philharmonic, 1947.
http://www.overcomingdepressionwithoutdrugs.com/music

Antonio Damasio agrees. He says there is an intimate and telling connection between certain kinds of music and feelings of either great sorrow or great joy and body sensations that include a host of skin responses such as 'chills' or 'shivers' or 'making the hair stand on end. To illustrate this point, Aksnes uses the famous "Adagietto" from Mahler's Fifth Symphony, a movement of exceptional beauty and sensuality.

> The slow, floating sensation of the piece can be felt as an expression of unspeakable sadness and unspeakable happiness; what is certain, is that the music immerses us in feelings of overwhelming power. The deep yearning of this movement is, I believe, due largely to the combined forces of its extremely slow tempo, delicate instrumentation, and harmonic suction created by the dominant pedal point which seems never to reach the longed-for tonic. The powerful feeling sense of tension is felt in our whole being. It is as if the music will simply not let us go. There is no complete feeling of resolution until we reach the very end of the movement. We have traversed a feeling landscape of indescribable happiness and sadness. (15)

Although I know my friends in the visual arts will disagree, I believe that music is more expressive of the entire range of human emotion than other creative form. Dr. Martha Nussbaum writes:

> Music seems to be profoundly connected to our emotional life, indeed perhaps more urgently and deeply connected to that life than any of the other arts. It digs into our depths and expresses hidden movements of love and fear and joy that are inside us. It speaks to us and about us in mysterious ways, going "to the bottom of things," as Mahler put it, exposing

hidden vulnerabilities . . . Emotions shape the landscape of our mental and social lives. Like geological upheavals in a landscape, they mark our lives as uneven, uncertain and prone to reversal. Are they simply, as some have claimed animal energies or impulses with no connection to our thoughts? Or are they rather suffused with intelligence and discernment, and thus a source of deep awareness and understanding? (16)

We can use this emotional power to avoid depression. Listening to music can often help us identify and release unwanted feelings. Going back to retrieve those feelings (in a *reculer pour mieux sauter*) we emerge more whole, more complete. It helps to have a good traveling companion on this journey, of course. It could be a psychiatrist. (But no pills, please.) It could be a psychologist. It could be a clinical social worker. Empathy and interpersonal skills matter more than specific training. The point is to find someone you can connect with in a special way, someone who can help you risk expressing feelings you are afraid to feel, feelings that increase your sense of vulnerability and make you anxious.

And, most of all, make time to be alone and quiet and still. Find a Japanese garden, perhaps designed by Kim Sorvig who says, "sit there until you stop behaving and begin to *be*: Relaxed yet alert, until all explanations are forgotten, you and your environment become not two, yet not one. Then you will know what I really should have said." (17)

CODA

Janet is back. This time she is dying. She has lung cancer; it has metastasized; no viable treatment is left, and she has chosen no heroics. Instead, she has enlisted a hospice to manage the pain. "I'm back here to work on the depression," she says. Obviously there are many feelings that Janet would rather not feel—not the least of which is the utter helplessness and unbearable sadness she experiences knowing that her life will soon end. Sometimes she says she would rather not feel anything at all, and she depresses herself, but then she becomes so lifeless that she might as well be dead already. "I want to feel," says she, "even all those bad dark feelings, and I need your help."

The next week Janet sees her pulmonologist. He has only bad news to give her. Because she reacts with great disappointment and sadness, he starts writing a prescription for an antidepressant. She explains her sessions with me, but she is in such distress that he will not let her leave the office without taking the prescription in her hand. It's easy to understand the physician in this circumstance. He has a patient in front of him clearly suffering emotional distress, and he has a medication he is certain will help. And, of course, in addition to her distress, there is *his* distress. He does not want to feel his own helplessness, facing a patient with a terminal illness.

Janet isn't interested in drugs, however. Her course is more direct: to wail and bemoan her fate. On about the fourth week, she came in very alive and excited and said: "I've decided what I am going to do. I talked with the kids. We're all going to Costa del Sol Mexico for two weeks. We're going to be by the ocean, watch some sunsets, and listen to the waves at night. We're going to laugh and play and talk about how good it is to be alive. And with your help I've trained them well. They know it will be OK if sometimes I want to cry a little."

I saw Janet when she returned from her trip. She looked good but a little troubled as well. On the trip she had discovered that a new grandchild was on the way—a child she would not live to see. She coped with this new blow by not coping: she allowed herself to feel overwhelmingly sad for a while, then reached a resolution. I've come to terms with death," she told me not long after. "You know, when you put it all together, it's been a great ride! Just make sure they manage the pain," she said, asking for my help. "What I dread most is not being able to breathe."

Over the next few weeks, we cried a lot together. But we also laughed. Many times we shared poetry. The last poem I recited to her ends this way:

> . . . But that future is all that's left of you—
> And me, (and everyone),
> And it grows smaller every day.
> We must hold it in the palms of our hands
> And kindle it to flame with our precious breath,
> And make it live for each of us.
> And make it live for each of us. (18)

Afterward I held her, or she held me. Then she looked up and smiled and said, "Thank you for being here." Not long after, she was gone. "When sorrow nears, the soul's gardens wither, joy and song die." The line ran through my mind. And the ones that follow. ("The autumn in my heart is lasting too long. Sun of love, will you never shine again and softly dry my bitter tears.") And so I went into my study and searched through the CDs lying on my desk until I found it: Mahler's *Das Lied von der Erde*, "Der Abschied ("Farewell"). Absorbed in the music, as I heard that long unresolved chord that gradually fades to silence at the end, I thought of Janet with that mischievous twinkle in her eye. *Ewig. Ewig.* I took a deep breath.

NOTES

INTRODUCTION

(1)   Jaret. "Hope for Depression," *AARP Bulletin*. May 1, 2010.

(2)   Damásio. *Looking for Spinoza*. p. 155.

(3)   Cohen, Elizabeth. "CDC: Antidepressants Most Prescribed Drugs in U.S." July 9, 2007.

(4)   Fourier *et. al.* "Antidepressant Drug Effects and Depression Severity." JAMA, pp. 47-53.

(5)   Angell. *The Truth about the Drug Companies*. p. 35.

(6)   FDA 2007

(7)   Freud in a 1934 letter to psychoanalyst Theodor Reik.

(8)   Jamison. *Touched with Fire*. p. 269. A more interesting diagnosis is that Mahler suffered from Sydenham's chorea (also known as "Saint Vitus" Dance") as the result a bacterial infection associated with a childhood bout of acute rheumatic fever. This is especially plausible since Mahler was diagnosed with a valvulopathy in 1907 and died of subacute bacterial endocarditis in 1911. Sydenham's chorea would account for both Mahler's odd gait and his pinched face. See Cardoso 2006. Some believe it would also account for his obsessive compulsive disorder, but here I demur: what clinicians diagnose as OCD I perceive as artistic passion.

(9)   Kennedy. *Master Musicians* Series. pp. 74-5.

(10) Greenberg, Robert. *Great Masters: Mahler—His Life and Music*. pp. 2-3.

CHAPTER ONE
A SHORT HISTORY OF DEPRESSION:
HIPPOCRATES TO THE DSM

(1)   LaGrange. *Mahler*. Vol. 1, p. 55.

(2)   Hippocrates. *Aphorisms,* VI. p. 23. Unlike the other three humours (yellow bile, phlegm, and blood) each of which denotes an actual bodily substance, "black bile" is a construct created to make a cluster of observed symptoms fit the humour theory.

(3)   Finkelstein. *MELENCOLIA I: The Postmodern Art of Albrecht Durer.* p. 10.

(4)   Weeks. "Depression's Upside," *New York Magazine."* Feb. 25, 2010.

(5)   Burton. *The Anatomy of Melancholia,* p. 5.

(6)   Stern-Gillet. "On (Mis)interpreting Plato's Phronesis. Vol. 4., no. 2.

(7)   Aristotle. *Problem XXX.* I, [i]

(8)   Finkelstein, *op. cit*: Dürer's work is really an allegory—the pose shows contemplation.

(9)   Feder, Stuart. *Gustav Mahler: A Life in Crisis.* pp. 47-50.

(10) Kennedy, *op. cit.* p. 34-35. Kennedy assures us that Mahler was completely uninterested in the visual arts, but this is probably an overstatement. Mahler had little technical interest in painting and sculpture, but subject matter often triggered strong feelings. e.g. See Alma Mahler's comments about her husband's obsession with Arnold Bocklin's *Self-Portrait.*

(11) LaGrange. Vol. 3, pp. 167-8.

(12) Greenberg, Gary. *Manufacturing Depression*. p. 90.

(13) Maisel. "Bedlam 1946," *Life Magazine*. May 6, 1946. pp. 102-118.

(14) Code. *Classic Cases in Neuropsychology, Volume 1*. pp. 251-252.

(15) Noll. The Encyclopedia of Schizophrenia and Other Psychotic Disorders. p. 174.

(16) Kalat. Biological Psychology, Tenth Edition. p. 103.

(17) "Rosemary Kennedy," John F. Kennedy Library.

(18) Marti-Ibanez, *et. al*, *The Great Physiodynamic Therapies in Psychiatry*. pp. 13-75.

(19) Scott. *America Fooled*. p.252.

(20) Marti-Ibanez, *et. al*. *The Great Physiodynamic Therapies in Psychiatry*. pp. 91-120.

(21) Breggin. *The Anti-Depressant Fact Book*. p.162. See also Breggin, *Brain-Disabling Treatments in Psychiatry: Drugs, Electroshock, and the Psychopharmaceutical Complex*.

(22) Breggin. *Toxic Psychiatry*. p. 54.

(23) Sterling. "Psychiatry's Drug Addiction." *New Republic*. Mar. 3, 1979, p. 17.

(24) Hughes and Brewin. *The Tranquilizing of America*. p. 157.

CHAPTER TWO
"BAD" FEELINGS BECOME A DISEASE

(1) LaGrange. Vol. 1, p. 383.

(2) Angell. "The Illusions of Psychiatry," *New York Review of Books*. July 5, 2011.

(3) Lane, Christopher. *Shyness*. p. 37.

(4)   Breggin. *Medication Madness*. p. 52.

(5)   Angell. "Illusions."

(6)   I cannot say enough about how well Lane documents this power-grab and how much I have depended on him for the evidence.

(7)   Lane, *op. cit.* p. 41.

(8)   *Ibid.* p. 23.

(9)   *Ibid.*

(10) *Ibid.* p. 45.

(11) Good. "Samson Diagnosis," *New York Times. Feb. 20, 2001. (in Lane, pp. 15-17)*

(12) Lane, *op. cit.* p. 16.

(13) *Ibid.* p. 45.

(14) *Ibid.*

(15) *Ibid.* p. 84.

(16) *Ibid.* p. 47.

(17) *Ibid.* p. 75.

(18) *Ibid.* p. 77.

(19) US Dept. of Veterans Affairs 2010

CHAPTER THREE
OBJECTING TO FEELINGS: THE ANTIDEPRESSANT FIX

(1)   Ehrenreic. *The Progressive*. Dec. 2009.

(2)   Menand. "Head Case . . . Can Psychiatry Be a Science?" *New Yorker.* 3/1, 2010, p. 73.

(3)   Refusing to bow to drug-company pressures, FDA reviewer Dr. Frances Oldham Kelsey blocked approval of Thalidomide,

an act courage for which she was later honored by President John F. Kennedy.

In an online interview with *Salon,* Whitaker, comments: "There'd been an explosion in the number of counselors and psychologists offering other forms of non-drug therapy. Psychiatry saw itself in competition for patients with these other therapists, and in the late 1970s, the field realized that its advantage in the marketplace was its prescribing powers. Thus the field consciously sought to tell a public story that would support the use of its medications, and embraced the 'medical model' of psychiatric disorders. This took off with the publication of the Diagnostic and Statistical Manual of Mental Disorders III in 1980, which introduced many new classes of "treatable" disorders."

(4) Menand, *op. cit.* p. 62.

(5) Tone; Whitaker; Menand; Smith.

(6) See also Crews, 2007.

(7) Healy. "The Three Faces of the Antidepressants." *Nerv Ment Dis.* 3/99, pp. 174-180.

(8) Angellia. "The Epidemic of Mental Illness: Why?" *New York Review of Books.* June 23, 2011.

(9) Whitaker, *op. cit.* pp. 6-7.

(10) Horowitz et. al., *The Loss of Sadness: How Psychiatry Transformed Normal Sorrow into Depressive Disorder.* pp. 168-70.

(11) Begley. "The Depressing News About Antidepressants." *Newsweek.* Jan. 29, 2010.

(12) Whitaker, *op. cit.* p, 74.

(13) Breggin. *Brain Disabling Treatments in Psychiatry*. pp. 27ff.

(14) Angell. "Epidemic."

(15) Whitaker, *op. cit.* pp.74-75.

(16) Schildkraut. "The Catecholamine Hypothesis of Affective Disorders: a Review of Supporting Evidence." pp. 609-622.

(17) Crews. "Talking Back to Prozac."

http://www.nybooks.com/articles/archives/2007/dec/06/talking-back-to-prozac/

(18) Breggin. *Brain Disabling Treatments in Psychiatry*. p. 10.

(19) Breggin. *Your Drug May Be Your Problem*. p. 54.

(20) *Ibid*. p. 62.

(21) *Ibid*. p. 10.

(22) Whitaker, *op.* cit. pp. 321ff.

(23) Angell. "Drug Companies & Doctors: A Story of Corruption." *The New York Review of Books*. Jan. 15, 2009.

(24) Beckelman, *et. al.* "Scope and Impact of Financial Conflects of Interest in Biomedical Research." JAMA. Jan. 22, 2003. Angell, *op. cit.* adds: "A recent survey found that about two thirds of academic medical centers hold equity interest in companies that sponsor research within the same institution. A study of medical school department chairs found that two thirds received departmental income from drug companies and three fifths received personal income."

(25) Vedantam. "Against Depression, a Sugar Pill is Hard to Beat." *Washington Post*. May 7, 2002. See also Angell, *op. cit.*

(26) Lenzer. "Antidepressants Double Suicidaltiy in Children, says FDA." BMJ, Mar. 18, 2006, p. 206.

(27) Angell. *The Truth About Antidepressants*. pp. xxvi-xxvii.

(28) Peter Breggin, for years, has reported the same scientific data.

(29) Angell. "Epidemic."

(30) Kramer. "In Defense of Antidepressants." *N.Y. Times Sunday Review*. July 9, 2011.

(31) Kirsch, *et. al.* (July 2002). "The Emperor's New Drugs." p.1.

(32) Lenzer, *op. cit.*

(33) Ratey, *et. al. The Revolutionary New Science of Exercise and the Brain*. p.120.

(34) Bahrick. "Post SSRI Sexual Dysfunction." *American Society for the Advancement of Pharmacotherapy*. July, 2006, pp. 2-10.

(35) Mignot. "Why We Sleep." Plos Biol. 6(4): e106.

(36) Other studies report that ADs cause emotional blunting include: Hoehn-Saric et. al. 1990; Hoehn-Saric et. al. 1991; Barnhart et. al. 2004; Garland and Baerg 2001; Harris *et. al.* 1991; Reinblatt and Riddle 2006; Wongpakaran *et. al.* 2007; Oleshansky and Labbate 2006; Knutson. Wolkowitz, and Cole *et al.* 1998; Andersen, Vestergaard, and Riis 1993; Nahas *et. al.* 1998; Panzer and Mellow 1992; McCullagh and Feinstein 2000; Seliger *et. al.* 1992. Wongpakaran *et. al.* report that "selective serotonin reuptake inhibitor use associates with apathy among depressed elderly . . . . Frontal lobe dysfunction due to alteration of serotonin is considered to be one of the possibilities."

(37) Breggin. *Toxic Psychiatry*. p. 82. There are many drugs that can cause depression. A review in the 1990 Health Letter listed fourteen categories of drugs known to cause depression, including nonpsychiatric agents such as beta-blockers, blood pressure drugs, a variety of pain medications, and even some antibiotics. However, it is likely that the major physical cause

of depression in our nation today is antidepressant drugs. Breggin says, "We are in no position to safely tamper with the extraordinarily complex activities of the brain."

(38) Whitaker, op. cit. pp. 307ff.

(39) Breggin. *The Antidepressant Fact Book.* pp. 306-7.

(40) Tamam, *et. al.* "Selective Serotonin Reuptake Inhibitor Discontinuation Syndrome." *Advances in Therapy,* Jan. 2002.

(41) Menand. "Head Case . . . Can Psychiatry be a Science?" http://www.newyorker.com/arts/critics/atlarge/2010/03/01/100301crat_atlarge_menand

(42) Whitaker, *op. cit.* p. 163.

(43) Price and Goodwin. "Emotional Blunting or Reduced Reactivity Following Remission of Major Depression." pp. 152-156.

(44) Hollis. *The Swamplands of the Soul.* 1996.

CHAPTER FOUR
OBJECTING TO FEELINGS: AGITATED DEPRESSION

(1) Burton. *The Anatomy of Melancholy.* p18.

(2) Lane, *op. cit.* p. 82.

(3) The human brain consists of two lobes, right and left, connected by a bridge of nerve fibers called the corpus callosum. In adults, each hemisphere is somewhat specialized, i.e., in right-handed people the left hemisphere tends to process language. Left-handed people are wired somewhat differently, however.

(4) Damásio. *Looking for Spinoza.* p. 3.

(5) Damasio and Damasio. "Minding the Body." *Dedalus.* Summer, 2006.

(6)   Lane, *op. cit.* p. 16.

(7)   Baltimore Symphony Off-the-Cuff Concert: "Analyze This: Mahler and Freud." Nov. 5 & 6, 2010. (John Snyder, *consultant).*

(8)   LaGrange. Vol. 4, p. 920.

CHAPTER FIVE
LISTENING TO FEELINGS, LISTENING TO MAHLER

(1)   Damásio. *Looking for Spinoza.* p. 138.

(2)   Meyer and Damásio. "Convergence…" *Trends in Neuroscience.* July, 2009. p. 376.

(3)   Damasio, op. cit. pp. 177-8.

(4)   Damasio and Damasio. "Minding the Body."

(5)   Damasio, op. cit, pp. 55-7.

(6)   "O red rose!" Mahler: 2nd Symphony, 3rd movement.

(7)   Breggin, *op. cit.* p. 25.

(8)   LaGrange. Vol. 3, p. 685.

(9)   Boisen. *The Exploration of the Inner World.* p. 52.

CHAPTER SIX
INTROVERSION AND THE FEELING LIFE

(1)   O'Donohue. *Divine Beauty.* pp. 38-39.

(2)   The symptoms of schizoid personality disorder include: "An enduring pattern of inner experience that deviates markedly from the expectations of the individual's culture," individuals who seem "to prefer spending time by themselves rather than

with other people," and who "may be oblivious to normal subtleties of social interaction" and "seem socially inept and self-absorbed." (Fairbairn, 1952). Jennifer Kahnweiler (2009), writing in *Forbes*, suggests introverts may in fact make the best leaders because they draw on strengths extroverts may not possess. She reports that at least 40% of executives would describe themselves as introverts, including Bill Gates and Warren Buffett, and adds that odds are, so is Barack Obama. She describes that these leaders are good listeners and invite suggestions. She mentions their preference for authentic relating: "They are drawn to meaningful conversations, not superficial chitchat, and they know how to ask great questions and really listen to the answers." She also describes that one most defining characteristic of those with the slight "schizoid" tendency; they are energized by spending time alone. "They suffer from people exhaustion and need to retreat to recharge their batteries frequently. These regular timeouts actually fuel their thinking, creativity and decision-making and, when the pressure is on, help them be responsive, not reactive. When introverts honor that inner pull, they can do their best work."

(3)   Bauer-Lechner. *Recollections of Gustav Mahler*. p. 69.

(4)   LaGrange. Vol.1, pp. 6-8.

(5)   *Ibid.* p. 14.

(6)   *Ibid.* p. 16.

(7)   Bauer-Lechner, *op. cit.* p. 69.

(8)   Kennedy, *op. cit.* p. 8.

(9)   Mahler, Alma. *And the Bridge is Love*. p. 7.

(10) Kennedy, *op. cit.* p. 6.

(11) Sikov. "On Sunset Boulevard: the Life and Times of Billy Wilder." p. 9.

(12) LaGrange, Vol.1, p. 17.

(13) Feder, *op. cit.* p. 4.

(14) Kennedy, *op. cit.* p. 23.

(15) Lawton, Mary. *Mme. Schumann-Heink—The Last of the Titans,* p. 360.

(16) Kennedy, *op. cit.* p. 51.

(17) Walter. *Gustav Mahler.* pp. 4-9.

(18) Kennedy, *op. cit.* p. 40.

(19) Sadie and Sadie. *Calling on the Composer.* p. 245.

(20) Mahler, Alma. *Gustav Mahler: Memories and Letters.* p.13

(21) LaGrange. Vol. 4, p. 216.

(22) Mahler, Alma *op. cit.* p. 134.

(23) LaGrange. Vol. 1, pp. 684-90.

(24) Lebrecht. *Why Mahler. p.* 135. Lebrecht offers a new perspective, demonstrating that Alma's account is augmented by invented quotes.

(25) LaGrange. Vol. 3, p. 458.

(26) LaGrange. Vol. 3, p. 86; LaGrange. Vol.1, pp. 383-84; LaGrange. Vol. 3, p. 86.

CHAPTER SEVEN
JOY AND ANGST

(1) Max Graf, a composer and a critic contemporary to Mahler.

(2) Becker. *The Denial of Death.* p. 26.

(3) *Ibid.* p. 89.

(4)   Walter. *Guatav Mahler*. p. 32.

(5)   Becker. *op. cit.* p. 88

(6)   Breggin. *Toxic Psychiatry*. p. 249.

(7)   Kierkegaard. *Fear and Trembling*. p. 167.

CHAPTER EIGHT
REGRESSION IN THE SERVICE OF THE EGO

(1)   Mahler: Annotation, Tenth Symphony.

(2)   Mahler, Alma. *Gustav Mahler: Memories and Letters*. p. 151.

(3)   *Ibid.* p. 172.

(4)   *Ibid.*

(5)   LaGrange, Vol. 4, p. 838.

(6)   Mahler, *op. cit.* p. 152.

(7)   *Ibid.* p. 174.

(8)   *Ibid.*

(9)   LaGrange, Vol. 4, p. 872.

(10) Feder, *op. cit.* p. 193.

(11) LaGrange, Vol. 4, p. 844.

(12) Mahler, *op. cit.* p. 12.

(13) LaGrange, Vol. 4, p. 848.

(14) *Ibid.*

(15) *Ibid.* p. 850.

(16) Boisen, *op. cit.*

(17) Feder, *op. cit.* p. 225.

(18) Mahler, *op. cit.* p. 335.

(19) LaGrange. Vol. 4, pp. 937-8.

CHAPTER NINE
DEATH AND THE PRECIOUSNESS OF LIFE

(1)   LaGrange. Vol. 1, p. 784.

(2)   Mahler, Alma. *Gustav Mahler: Memories and Letters.* pp. 156-160

(3)   *Ibid.* p. 190.

(4)   LaGrange. Vol. 1, p. 26.

(5)   Feder, *op. cit.* pp. 55-6.

(6)   LaGrange. Vol. 2, p. 434.

(7)   Bauer-Lechner. *Recollections.* p. 73.

(8)   Feder, *op. cit.* p. 320.

(9)   Bauer-Lechner, *op. cit.* p. 31.

(10) *Ibid.* p. 173.

CHAPTER TEN
MAHLER, MUSIC AND THE ETERNAL FEMININE

(1)   O'Donohue, *op. cit.,* p. 62.

(2)   Kierkegaard, *op. cit.* p. 60.

(3)   Kelland. "Mental Health Experts Ask: Will Anyone Be Normal." *Reuters* July 27, 1910.

(4)   *Ibid.*

(5)   Bauer-Lechner, *op. cit.* p. 62.

(6)   LaGrange. Vol. 4, pp. 46-7.

(7)   Nussbaum. *Upheavals of Thought: The Intelligence of Emotions.* pp. 614-44.

(8)   Jung, *Liber Novus,* p. 263.

(9)   Kramarae, Cheris. "Changing the Complexion of Gender in Language Research." p. 350.

(10) See Kahn, "Man's Estate . . ." pp. 9-10.

(11) Damasio. *Looking for Spinoza: Joy, Sorrow, and the Feeling Brain*. p. 139.

(12) LeGuin. *The Lathe of Heaven*. p. 82.

(13) Bernstein. "Young People's Concert: Who is Gustav Mahler? Feb. 7, 1960.

(14) Lebrecht, *op. cit.* pp. 17-18.

      Lebrecht reiterates what I believe to be essential in understanding Mahler: "Mahler's attitude to life is clinically sane." Lebrecht sees as I do that Mahler came through the most dramatic crisis of his life, the betrayal of Alma, never again considering suicide, but taking great strength from that adversity as he did from the other personal tragedy, the death of a beloved child. With heart-rending grief he extracted from that darkness a Song of the Earth that affirms the essence of human connection. "He loves life, no matter how badly it treats him." (p. 5)

(15) Asknes. "Music and its Resonating Body." pp. 97-8.

(16) Nussbaum, *op. cit.* p. 254.

(17) Kim Sorvig, Gardening Master of Zen Gardens (personal communication).

(18) (Source unknown)

(Note: All brief quotes, not listed above, by Mahler or about Mahler are referenced from the four volume biography by Henry—Louis de LaGrange.)

WORKS CONSULTED

Angell, Marcia. "Drug Companies & Doctors: A Story of Corruption." *The New York Review of Books* 56(1) 15 January 2009.

_____. *The Truth About the Drug Companies: How they Deceive Us and What to do About It.* New York: Random House, 2004.

Antonuccio, David O. and David D. Burns. "Antidepressants: A Triumph of Marketing Over Science?" *Prevention & Treatment.* Volume 5, Article 25, posted July 15, 2002.

Asknes, Hallgjerd. "Music and Its Resonating Body." *Dansk Årbog for Musikforskning* 2001. Vol. XXIX, 2002: 81-101.

Bachrach, L.L. "The state of the state mental hospital 1996." *Psychiatric Services* 47 (1996): 1071-1078.

Bahrick, A.S. "Post SSRI Sexual Dysfunction." *American Society for the Advancement of Pharmacotherapy*, 2006. 7:2-10.

Bauer-Lechner, Natalie. *Recollections of Gustav Mahler.* Cambridge: University Press, 1980.

Becker, Ernst. *The Denial of Death.* New York: Free Press, 1973.

Begley, Sharon. "The Depressing News About Antidepressants." *Newsweek*, 29 January 2010.

Bekelman, Justin E. *et. al.* "Scope and Impact of Financial Conflicts of Interest in Biomedical Research: A Systematic Review," *JAMA*. 22 January 2003.

Bernstein, Leonard. "Young People's Concert: Who is Gustav Mahler?" [hypertext script] 7 February 1960.
http://www.leonardbernstein.com/ypc_script_who_is_gustav_mahler.htm

Blaukopf, Kurt and Herta. *Mahler: His Life, Work & World.* New York: Thames & Hudson, 1991.

Boisen, Anton. *The Exploration of the Inner World.* Philadelphia: Univ. of Penn. Press, 1971.

Breggin, Peter R. *The Anti-Depressant Fact Book: What Your Doctor Won't Tell You About Prozac, Zoloft, Paxil, Celexa, and Luvox.* Cambridge: Perseus Books, 2001.

_____. *Toxic Psychiatry.* New York: St. Martin's Press, 1991.

_____. *The Conscience of Psychiatry: The Reform Work of Peter R. Breggin, MD.* Edited by the International Center for the Study of Psychiatry and Psychology. New York: Lake Edge Press, 2009.

_____. *Brain-Disabling Treatments in Psychiatry*, 2nd *ed.* New York: Springer Publishing Co., 2008.

_____. *Your Drug May Be Your Problem: How and Why to Stop Taking Psychiatric Medications.* Philadelphia: Da Capo Press, 1999.

_____. *Medication Madness: The Role of Psychiatric Drugs in Cases of Violence, Suicide and Crime.* New York: St. Martin's Griffin, 2008.

Brown, Walter A. "Are Antidepressants as Ineffective as They Look?" *Prevention & Treatment.* Volume 5, Article 25, posted July 15, 2002.

Burton, Robert. *The Anatomy of Melancholia.* New York: Wiley & Putnam, 1847. http://books.google.com/books?id=RXw4AAAAIAAJ&source=gbs_navlinks_s

Campbell, Eric *et al.* "Institutional Academic–Industry Relationships." *JAMA,* 17 October 2007.

Cardoso, F. and A.J. Lees. "Did Gustav Mahler have Sydenham's chorea?" *Movement Disorders.* 2006 March 21(3): 289-92. http://www.ncbi.nlm.nih.gov/pubmed/16437586

Christakis, N. and J. Fowler. *Connected: The Surprising Power of Our Social Networks and How They Shape Our Lives.* New York: Little, Brown & Company, 2009.

"Class Suicidality "Labeling Language for Antidepressants" FDA. 2005. http://www.accessdata.fda.gov/drugsatfda_docs/label/2005/20031s045,20936s020lbl.pdf

Code, Christopher. *Classic Cases in Neuropsychology, Volume I.* East Sussex: Psychology Press Ltd. 1996. http://books.google.com/books?id=d1dlq4ZrZZoC&printsec=frontcover&source=gbs_ge_summary_r&cad=0#v=onepage&q&f=false

Cohen, Elizabeth. "CDC: Antidepressants most prescribed drugs in U.S." *CNNHealth.com,* Mon July 9, 2007. http://www.cnn.com/2007/HEALTH/07/09/antidepressants/index.html

Cohen, Jacob. "The earth is round (p < .05)." *American Psychologist*, Vol 49 (12), Dec 1994, 997-1003.

Crews, Frederick. "Talking Back to Prozac." *The New York Review of Books*. 6 December 2007. http://www.nybooks.com/articles/archives/2007/dec/06/talking-back-to-prozac/

Damasio, Antonio. *Looking for Spinoza: Joy, Sorrow, and the Feeling Brain*. Orlando: Harcourt Inc., 2003.

_____ and Hanna Damasio. "Minding the body." *Dedalus*. Summer 2006.

Delate, Thomas *et. al.* "Trends in the use of Antidepressants." *Psychiatric Services*, 55 (April 2004): 387-391. http://psychservices.psychiatryonline.org/cgi/content/full/55/4/387

Dixon, T. *From Passions to Emotions: The Creation of a Secular Psychological Category*. Cambridge: Cambridge University Press, 2003.

Ehrenreich, Barbara. "Monthly Column" *The Progressive, December,* 2009.

Fagin, Leonard. "Deinstitutionalization in the USA." *Bulletin of the Royal College of Psychiatrists* 9 (June 1985): 112-114.

Fairbairn, W.R.D. *Psychoanalytic Studies of the Personality*. London: Tavistock/ Routledge, 1952 [Routledge Paperback, 1994].

Feder, Stuart. *Gustav Mahler: A Life in Crisis*. New Haven: Yale Univ. Press, 2004.

Finkelstein, David. "MELENCOLIA I: The postmodern art of Albrecht Durer." http://arxiv.org/abs/physics/0602185v2

Fournier, Jay C. *et al.* "Antidepressant Drug Effects and Depression Severity: A Patient-Level Meta-analysis." *JAMA,* 2010. 303(1): 47-53.

Frattaroli, Elio. *Healing the Soul in the Age of the Brain: Why Medication Isn't Enough*. London: Penguin Books, 2002.

Glenmullen, Joseph. *Prozac Backlash: Overcoming the Dangers of Prozac, Zoloft, Paxil, and Other Anti-depressants with Safe, Effective Alternatives.* Simon and Schuster, 2000.

Goethe, Johann Wolfgang. *Faust I & II.* Ed. & Trans. S. Atkins. Princeton: Princeton University Press Paperback, 1994.

Goethe, Johann Wolfgang. *The Eternal Feminine: Selected Poems of Goethe.* Ed. F. Ungar. New York: Frederick Ungar Publishing Co., 1980.

Goode, Erica. "Samson Diagnosis: Antisocial Personality Disorder, With Muscles." *New York Times.* February 20, 2001.
http://www.nytimes.com/2001/02/20/health/samson-diagnosis-antisocial-personality-disorder-with-muscles.html

Greenberg, Gary. *Manufacturing Depression: The Secret History of a Modern Disease.* New York: Simon & Schuster, 2010.

Greenberg, Robert. *Great Masters: Mahler –His Life and Music.* Cantilly, Va.: The Teaching Company. 2001.

Greenberg, Roger P. "Reflections On The Emperor's New Drugs." *Prevention & Treatment.* Volume 5, Article 27, posted July 15, 2002.

Hanganu-Bresch, Cristina. *Faces of depression: a study of antidepressant advertisements in the American and British Journals of Psychiatry, 1960-2004* [Dissertation]. University of Minnesota: 2008.

Healy, David. (2001). "The Antidepressant Drama" in Weissman MM. *The Treatment of Depression: Bridging the 21ˢᵗ Century. American Psychiatric Publication.* 10–11.

_____. (1996). The Psychopharmacologists: interviews. London: Chapman and Hall. p. 8.

_____. (1998). *The Psychopharmacologists: Volume 2.* A Hodder Arnold Publication. pp. 132–4.

_____. "The three faces of the antidepressants: a critical commentary on the clinical-economic context of diagnosis." *Nerv Ment Dis.* 1999 Mar;187 (3):174-80.

Hippocrates. *Aphorisms.* Francis Adams Trans. Dodo Press, 2009.

Hollis, James. *Swamplands of the Soul: New Life in Dismal Places.* Toronto: Inner City Books, 1996.

Horwitz, Allan V. and Jerome C. Wakefield. *The Loss of Sadness: How Psychiatry Transformed Normal Sorrow into Depressive disorder.* Oxford University Press, 2007.

Hughes, Richard and Robert Brewin. *The Tranquilizing of America: Pill Popping and the American Way of Life.* New York: Harcourt Brace Jovanovich, 1979.

Jackson, Grace E. *Rethinking Psychiatric Drugs: a Guide for Informed Consent.* Bloomington, Indiana: Author House, 2005.

Jamison, Kay. *Touched with Fire: Manic-Depressive Illness and the Artistic Temperament.* New York: Free Press Paperback, 1994.

Jaret, Peter. "Hope for Depression: Treatments that help older adults." *AARP Bulletin.* May 1, 2010.

Jung, Carl. *Liber Novus.* New York: W.W. Norton, 2009.

Kabat-Zinn, Jon. *Wherever You Go, There You Are: mindfulness meditation in everyday life.* New York: Hyperion, 1994.

Kahn, Coppelia. *Man's Estate: Masculine Identity in Shakespeare.* Berkeley: University of California Press, 1981.

Kahnweiler, Jennifer. "Why Introverts Can Make the Best Leaders." *Forbes*, Nov. 30, 2009.

Kalat, James W. *Biological Psychology. Tenth Edition.* Belmont, CA. Wadsworth. 2007.

Kelland, Kate. "Mental health experts ask: Will anyone be normal?" *Reuters*: July 27, 2010. http://www.reuters.com/article/idUSTRE66Q4BJ20100727

Kennedy, Michael. *Mahler.* Master Musicians Series, Stanley Sadie, ed. [1974] Second Edition. Oxford: Oxford UP, 1990.

Kierkegaard, Soren. *Fear and Trembling and the Sickness Unto Death*. [1849] Trans. W. Lowrie. Garden City, New York: Doubleday Anchor Books, 1954.

_____. *Purity of Heart is to Will One Thing*. [1847] Trans. D. Steere. New York: Harper Torchbooks, 1956.

Kirk, Stuart A. and Herb Kutchins. *The Selling of DSM: the Rhetoric of Science in Psychiatry*. Transaction Publishers. 1992.

Kirsch, I. *et. al.* (July 2002). "The emperor's new drugs: An analysis of antidepressant medication data submitted to the U.S. Food and Drug Administration." *Prevention and Treatment* (American Psychological Association) 5 (1).

_____. and Alan Scoboria. "Antidepressants and Placebos: Secrets, Revelations, and Unanswered Questions." *Prevention & Treatment*. Volume 5, Article 33, posted July 15, 2002.

Kirsch I, *et. al.* (2008) "Initial severity and antidepressant benefits: A metaanalysis of data submitted to the Food and Drug Administration." *PLoSMed* 5(2).
http://www.plosmedicine.org/article/info:doi/10.1371/journal.pmed.0050045

_____ and Guy Saperstein. "Listening to Prozac but Hearing Placebo: A Meta-Analysis of Antidepressant Medication." *Prevention and Treatment,* Volume 1, Article 0002a, posted June 26,1998.
http://psycnet.apa.org/index.cfm?fa=buy.optionToBuy&id=1999-11094-001

Kramarae, Chris. "Changing the Complexion of Gender in Language Research." In Howard Giles and W. Peter Robinson, (eds.). *Handbook of the Social Psychology of Language*. New York: Wiley & Sons, 1990.

Kutchins Herb and Stuart A. Kirk. *Making Us Crazy: DSM: The Psychiatric Bible and the Creation of Mental Disorders*. Free Press, 1997.

LaGrange, Henry-Louis. *Mahler. Volume 1*. Garden City, New York: Doubleday & Company, 1973.

_____. *Gustav Mahler. Volume 2: Vienna: The Years of Challenge (1897-1904)*. Oxford: University Press, 1995.

_____. *Gustav Mahler. Volume 3: Vienna: Triumph and Disillusion (1904-1907)*. Oxford: University Press, 1999.

_____. *Gustav Mahler. Volume 4: A New Life Cut Short (1907-1911)*. Oxford: University Press, 2008.

Laing, R.D. *The Divided Self*. New York: Pantheon Books, 1969.

Lane, Christopher. *Shyness: How Normal Behavior Became a Sickness*. New Haven: Yale University Press, 2007.

Lawton, Mary. *Mme. Schumann-Heink—The Last Of The Titans*. New York: The Macmillan Company, 1929.

Lebrecht, Norman. *Why Mahler? How One Man and Ten Symphonies Changed the World.* London: Faber & Faber, 2010.

LeGuin, Ursula. *The Lathe of Heaven.* New York: Avon, 1971.

Lenzer, Jeanne. "Antidepressants Double Suicidality in Children, says FDA." BMJ. 2006 March 18; 332(7542): 626.

_____. "Secret US Report Surfaces on Antidepressants in Children." BMJ. 2004 August 7; 329(7461): 307.

Lipinski, Jed. "Anatomy Of An Epidemic": The Hidden Damage Of Psychiatric Drugs" *Salon.* Apr 27, 2010.

Mahler, Alma. *And The Bridge Is Love.* New York: Harcourt, Brace, 1958.

_____. *Gustav Mahler, Memories and Letters* (4th ed.). Trans. B. Creighton. London: Sphere Books Ltd., 1990.

_____. *Diaries 1898-1902.* Selected and Trans. A. Beaumont. Ithaca New York: Cornell University Press, 1999.

Maisel, Albert Q. "Bedlam 1946: Most U.S. Mental Hospitals are a Shame and a Disgrace." *Life Magazine,* May 6, 1946: 102-118.

Manning, Martha. *Undercurrents: a therapist's reckoning with her own depression.* New York: HarperCollins, 1994.

Marti-Ibanez, F. *et al.* (eds.). *The Great Physiodynamic Therapies in Psychiatry.* New York: Hoeber-Harper, 1956.

Martin, Robert Scott. "Wilhelm Reich's War With Space." 19 August 1999. http://www.abovetopsecret.com/forum/thread273592/pg1

Menand, Louis. "Head Case . . . Can Psychiatry be a Science?" *The New Yorker.* 1 March 2010.
http://www.newyorker.com/arts/critics/atlarge/2010/03/01/100301crat_atlarge_menand

Mignot, E. (2008) "Why We Sleep: The Temporal Organization of Recovery." *PLoS Biol* 6(4): e106.

Mitchell, Donald. *Gustav Mahler: the Early Years.* University of California Press, Jul 1, 1980.

Moncrieff J., and S. Wessely and R. Hardy. "Active Placebos Versus Antidepressants for Depression." *Cochrane Database of Systematic Reviews* 2004, Issue 1. Art. No.: CD003012. DOI:10.1002/14651858. CD003012.pub2

Mula, Marco and Michael R. Trimble. "Music and Madness: Neuropsychiatric Aspects of Music." *Clinical Medicine* (9:1) February 2009: 83-86.

Meyer, K. and A. Damasio. "Convergence and Divergence in a Neural Architecture for Recognition and Memory." *Trends in Neuroscience.* 32(7)July 2009: 376-82.

http://www.ncbi.nlm.nih.gov/pubmed/19520438?dopt=abstract&otool=uscnmlib

"New Warnings Proposed for Antidepressants." FDA. May 2, 2007.
http://www.fda.gov/ForConsumers/ConsumerUpdates/ucm048950.htm

Nolan, S. *Electroshock Therapy*, TED Talks. Monterrey, CA 2001.

Noll, Richard, Ph.D. *The Encyclopedia of Schizophrenia and Other Psychotic Disorders*. New York: Facts on File. 2007.

Nussbaum, Martha. *Upheavals of Thought: The Intelligence of Emotions*. Cambridge, 2001.

O'Donohue, John. *Divine Beauty: the Invisible Embrace*. London: Random House, 2003.

Olfson, Mark and Steven C. Marcus. "National Patterns in Antidepressant Medication Treatment." *Arch. Gen. Psychiatry*, 2009; 66(8): 848-856.

Opbroek, Adam, Pedro L. Delgado, Cindi Laukes, Cindy McGahuey, Joanna Katsanis, Francisco A. Moreno and Rachel Manber. Emotional blunting associated with SSRI-induced sexual dysfunction. Do SSRIs inhibit emotional responses?*" International Journal of Neuropsychopharmacology*, 2002; 5:147-151.

Papoulias, Constantina and Felicity Callard. "Biology's Gift: Interrogating the Turn to Affect." *Body and Society*. 2010. 16: 29.

http://bod.sagepub.com/content/16/1/29.full.pdf

Price, J. and M. Goodwin. "Emotional Blunting or Reduced Reactivity Following Remission of Major Depression." *Medicographia,* 2009. 31(2):152-56.

Ratey, John and Eric Hagerman. *Spark: The Revolutionary New Science of Exercise and the Brain.* New York: Little, Brown, 2008.

Reik, Theodor. *The Haunting Melody: Psychoanalytic Experiences in Life and Music.* New York: Farrar, Straus & Young, 1953.

"Rosemary Kennedy." John F. Kennedy Presidential Library. http://www.jfklibrary.org/Historical+Resources/Biographies+and+Profiles/Biographies/Biography+of+Rosemary+Kennedy.htm

Schildkraut, J.J. "The Catecholamine Hypothesis of Affective Disorders: a Review of Supporting Evidence." *The American Journal of Psychiatry,* 1965. 122:609-22.

Sadie, Julie and Stanley Sadie. *Calling on the Composer.* New Haven: Yale UP, 2005.

Sawyer, Claire, ed. *Japanese Gardens.* New York: Brooklyn Botanic Garden, Inc., 1990.

Scott, Timothy. *America Fooled: The Truth About Antidepressants, Antipsychotics and How We've Been Deceived.* Victoria, Texas: Argo Publishing, LLC, 2006. http://www.americafooled.com

Sikov, Ed. *On Sunset Boulevard: The Life and Times of Billy Wilder.* New York: Hyperion, 1998.

Smith, Mickey. *A social history of the minor tranquilizers: the quest for small comfort in the age of anxiety.* Informa Health Care, 1991.

Snyder, John A. *Flying Lessons: the Psychology of Intimacy and Anxiety.* Bloomington, Indiana, 2005.

Solomon, Robert C. *Spirituality for the Skeptic: The Thoughtful Love of Life.* Oxford: Oxford University Press, 2002.

Stagnitti, Marie N. "Antidepressant Use in the U.S. Civilian Noninstitutionalized Population, 2002." Medical Expenditure Panel Survey. Agency for Health Research and Quality. US Department of Health and Human Services. May 2005.

Sterling, Peter. "Psychiatry's Drug Addiction", *New Republic*, March 3, 1979: 14-18.

Stern-Gillet. "On (Mis)interpreting Plato's "Ion" *Phronesis*, Vol. 4, No. 2, 2004.

Tamam, Lut and Nurgul Ozpoyraz. "Selective Serotonin Reuptake Inhibitor Discontinuation Syndrome: A review." *Advances in Therapy.* 19(1) January, 2002.

Tone, Andrea. *The Age of Anxiety: a History of America's Turbulent Affair with Tranquilizers.* Basic Books, 2008.

Trivedi, M.H. and A.J. Rush and S.R. Wisniewski. "Evaluation of Outcomes with Citalopram for Depression Using Measurement-based Care in STAR*D: Implications for Clinical Practice". *The American Journal of Psychiatry,* 2006. 163 (1): 28–40.

Turner, Erick H. and Robert Rosenthal. "Efficacy of antidepressants is not an absolute measure, and it depends on how clinical significance is defined." [Editorial] *BMJ,* 2008. 336:516-517(8 March 2008). http://www.bmj.com/cgi/content/full/336/7643/516

Turner E. H., *et. al.* "Selective Publication of Antidepressant Trials and its Influence on Apparent Efficacy." *N. Engl. J. Med,* January 2008. 358 (3): 252–60.

US Department of Veterans Affairs. "Clinician's Guide to PTSD." National Center for PTSD. June 15, 2010. http://www.ptsd.va.gov/professional/pages/clinicians-guide-to-medications-for-ptsd.asp

Valenstein, Elliot S. *Blaming the Brain: The Truth About Drugs and Mental Health.* Free Press, 1998.

Vedantam, Shankar. "Against Depression, a Sugar Pill Is Hard to Beat . . ." *Washington Post*, 7 May 2002; p. A01.
http://www.chelationtherapyonline.com/technical/p58.htm

Vertes, Robert P. and K.E. Eastman. "The Case Against Memory Consolidation in REM Sleep". *Behavioral and Brain Sciences,* 2000. 23 (6): 867–876.

Walter, Bruno. *Gustav Mahler.* New York: Knopf, 1958.

Weeks, Ben. "Depression's Upside." *New York Magazine.* February 25, 2010.

Weissman, Myrna. *Treatment of Depression: Bridging the 21st Century.* American Psychiatric Pub, 2001.

Welch, H. Gilbert, Lisa Schwartz and Steven Woloshin. "What's Making Us Sick Is an Epidemic of Diagnoses." *New York Times*, January 2, 2007.

Wessely, Simon. "How Shyness Became Social Phobia." *The Lancet,* March 2008. 371: 29.

Whitaker, Robert. *Anatomy of an Epidemic.* New York: Crown Publishers, 2010.

Wongpakaran, N. *et. al.* "Selective Serotonin Reuptake Inhibitor use Associates with Apathy Among Depressed Elderly: a Case-Control Study." *Annals of General Psychiatry*, 2007. 6:7.

Wright, Patrick. "On Melancholy and the Humour of the Night." 2003. An article derived from a lecture given for the Roche foundation before the premiere of Birtwistle's 'Night's Black Bird', Lucerne, Switzerland, 21 August, 2004. Creative Commons.
http://www.patrickwright.net/2001/08/21/on-melancholy-and-the-humour-of-the-night/

ABOUT THE AUTHORS

Dr. John A. Snyder

Dr. Snyder received his doctorate in 1967 from the University of Pennsylvania and was subsequently appointed an Instructor in Psychiatry in the School of Medicine to train psychiatric interns and residents in relational psychotherapy, using an approach developed under grants from the National Institute of Mental Health. For the last forty years, he has devoted his professional life to the independent practice of clinical psychology, helping hundreds of people to overcome depression and the pain of estrangement in relationships, and to live more exciting and rewarding lives. In the process, he has shaped the practice of many psychiatrists, psychologists, and family therapists as well. His innovative approach to relational dynamics is outlined in his 2005 book *Flying Lessons: The Psychology of Intimacy and Anxiety*. A licensed pilot and an avid sailor, Dr Snyder lives in the Chesapeake Bay town of St. Michaels with his life partner, Carolyn Mills. He has a pair of dancing shoes.

Dr. Nancy Steffen-Fluhr

Nancy Steffen-Fluhr is an associate professor in the Humanities Department at the New Jersey Institute of Technology and director of the institute's Murray Center for Women in Technology. She received her B.A. degree from Stanford University and her Ph.D. from Brandeis. She lives in a 100-year-old cottage in northern New Jersey with her husband Michael.